THE
UNREDEEMED

I have been a stranger in a strange land.

—Exodus, II, 22

THE

UNREDEEMED

Anti-Semitism

in the Soviet Union

EDITED WITH AN INTRODUCTION BY

Ronald I. Rubin

FOREWORD BY
Abraham J. Heschel

CHICAGO

Quadrangle Books

Published simultaneously in Canada by Burns and MacEachern Ltd.
Library of Congress Catalog Card Number: 68-26447

Designed by Vincent Torre

GRATEFUL acknowledgment is made to the following sources for permission to reprint copyrighted materials:

American Jewish Committee and Shelomo Ben-Israel for "The Power of a Song" from *Russian Sketches* by Shelomo Ben-Israel.

Anti-Defamation League of B'nai B'rith for "Sovyetish Heymland" from *Sovyetish Heymland: An Analysis* by Joseph and Abraham Brumberg.

B'nai B'rith International Council for "The Forgotten Martyrs of Babi Yar" by William Korey from *Babi Yar Fact Sheet*.

Christian Century for "Tishah B'ab in Moscow" by Ronald I. Rubin, copyright © 1966 by the Christian Century Foundation.

Congress Bi-Weekly for "Passover and Matzoh: A Case History of Soviet Policy" by Moshe Decter.

Foreign Affairs for "The Status of the Jews in the Soviet Union" by Moshe Decter, copyright © 1963 by the Council on Foreign Relations.

Hadassah magazine for "Student Struggle for Soviet Jewry" by Ronald I. Rubin.

Holt, Rinehart and Winston, Inc., for "The Rejoicing of the Law" from *The Jews of Silence* by Elie Wiesel, copyright © 1966 by Holt, Rinehart and Winston, Inc.

Jewish Community Relations Council of Greater Philadelphia for "Philadelphia Supports Soviet Jewry" from *A Summary Report of Three Projects on the Issue of Soviet Anti-Semitism*.

Jewish Life for "Visit to Babi Yar" from "Visit to Russia" by Michael Kaufman.

Jewish Publication Society of America for "The Old Bazaar of Samarkand" and "The Ships That Will Sail to Jerusalem" from *Between Hammer and Sickle* by Ben Ami.

Jewish Social Studies for "Soviet Jewry and the United Nations" by Ronald I. Rubin.

Jews in Eastern Europe for "Israel in the Soviet Mirror" and "Moshe Adolfovich Dayan."

Journal of the International Commission of Jurists for "Soviet Jews as Economic Criminals."

Isi Leibler for "Australian Communists and Soviet Jewry" from *Soviet Jewry and Human Rights* by Isi Leibler.

Midstream for "Soviet Law and the Jews" from "The Legal Position of the Jews in the Soviet Union" by William Korey.

National Community Relations Advisory Council for "Soviet Jewry and the Six-Day War" from *Implications for Soviet Jewry in the Middle East Crisis.*

New Politics for "Judaism Without Embellishment" by Moshe Decter.

Synagogue Council of America for "Jewish Institutions in the Soviet Union" from *A Partial Listing of Jewish Institutions in Eastern Europe.*

Washington Post for "The Death of Charles H. Jordan" from "Reds and Arabs Cast as Villains in Prague Death of an American" by Robert H. Estabrook.

Zionist Organization of America for "When the State of Israel Was Proclaimed" from *Zionism and Zionists in Soviet Russia: Greatness and Drama* by Joseph B. Schechtman.

For the Six Million
and Their Survivors in the Soviet Union

Preface

The Jew has always fared poorly in politically messianic societies. The anchored elitism of the right and the mobocracy of the left have more often enslaved rather than freed the Jew. His unique religious values, his minority status, his refusal to spout, unthinkingly, ephemeral political orthodoxies, his ties to foreign co-religionists, his sensitivity to injustices perpetrated on fellow citizens for the "greater good"—all these factors make the Jew both victim and outcast for political extremists. The democratic center, for all its hurly-burly, most assures Jewish survival.

That the Jew has taken a terrible beating from Soviet communism is an old story. What marks its anti-Semitism today, however, is the emergence of the Soviet Union as the chief single foe of the Jewish people. More than five million of the world's thirteen million Jews are endangered by Soviet policies. The Soviet Union poses a dual threat to Jewish survival: its spiritual strangulation of three million Soviet Jews; its support of Arab militants bent on destroying Israel's two million Jews.

This book deals with the first problem, the human-rights tragedy of Soviet Jews. In one sense, it is a sad account: the suffering, fear, and isolation of the remnant of Nazi extermination drives. In another, the refusal of Soviet Jews to succumb, their burning desire to hold the link

9

in the chain of Jewish continuity represents an inspiring rebuff to modern complacency.

Included here are essays from many sources that lay bare the fraudulent humanitarian guise of Soviet communism. Ideologically, the oppression cited in this book is meant to attack the "convergence" theory of relations between the United States and the Soviet Union—that both nations are becoming increasingly similar and over the years will converge from different poles. As long as the Jew, the historic whipping-boy of the racist, is so ruthlessly discriminated against, enlightened opinion must shudder at the claim that Soviet tyranny is easing. Too many well-intentioned people of the free world are mistaken in believing that the evils of communism will go away simply by wishing it so.

More specifically, these articles are meant to insure action. Soviet Jews may well be nearing the end; their fate rests, in large measure, on the protests of free men. To remain silent, to neglect the cries of Soviet Jewry, is to hasten its disappearance. Our courage to protest must match the courage of Soviet Jews to continue living.

Acknowledgments

I would like to thank the following individuals for their advice, both as to the selection of material for this book and as to their judgments on Soviet anti-Semitism: Jacob Birnbaum, honorary vice president, Center for Russian Jewry; Albert D. Chernin, executive director, Jewish Community Relations Council of Greater Philadelphia; Moshe Decter, director, Jewish Minorities Research; Rabbi Irving Greenberg, Riverdale Jewish Center; William Korey, director, United Nations Office of B'nai B'rith; G. Andrew Pinsky, director, Co-ordinating Center for Democratic Opinion; Glen Richter, New York co-ordinator, Student Struggle for Soviet Jewry.

Alex Littmann, a graduate student in the Department of History, New York University, helped to prepare the Suggested Reading list. Rosalyn Grubart, my aunt, brought me closer to the drama of Jewish survival. Evelyn Cappell of Barnard College provided valuable secretarial aid.

Among those students in my classes in "Political Process and Decision-Making" whose concern with this tragedy has been of much personal encouragement in my own research are: Anthony Bole, Mitchell Benveniste, Seymour Feder, Morris Hettena, Peter Lemmo, Wayne Jones, Leonard Pearlman, Michael Schachter, Robert Sherman, George Strum, Toby Weider, and Melvin Weinstein.

The Memorial Foundation for Jewish Culture provided a research grant toward this work.

Foreword

We are perplexed and even stunned by the official policies of the U.S.S.R. toward the religious and cultural rights of her Jewish citizens. These policies deprive the large masses of the Jewish population of their rights as guaranteed by the Russian constitution and in fact contradict statements made in public by Soviet leaders. They have caused so much agony to so many Jewish citizens in Russia, and so much indignation in the hearts of many millions of people outside the U.S.S.R., that the issue has become one of the most widely discussed topics of concern all over the world.

The Jewish people, who have only recently witnessed the physical extermination of six million of their numbers, cannot afford to remain indifferent to a systematic spiritual extermination of nearly three million Jews in the Soviet Union. The question must be raised: Does the U.S.S.R., which is committed to the principle of giving cultural rights to the numerous minorities in her vast country as well as religious rights to the Christian churches, insist upon a special policy in regard to the Jews, namely, to liquidate Jewish religion and culture? Or is the actual liquidation and cultural persecution of the Jews a process on which the highest authorities have taken no stand, but which is being carried out by subordinate officials, and is due to sadism and the stupidity of bureaucracy? Is it not likely that the Soviet leaders are misinformed and have been misguided about the mind of the Jews in Russia by dishonest and self-hating Jews?

Some evils are ephemeral, other evils have a dreadful permanence and the tendency to increase, particularly when they are senseless, devoid of social meaning, evil for the sake of evil. The present policy of the Soviet government, forcing millions of human beings to keep their identity a *secret,* to forget what they cherish, to cast their inwardness into oblivion, is a kind of sadism which goes back to Stalin and is in effect the survival of Stalinism, the great curse, the enormous and innermost perversion, the blind hatred for which no means are too venomous, too underhanded, too underground, and too petty.

The situation is hard to fathom. The attitude that certain Soviet officials display toward the Jews is more appropriate to tsarist Russia than it is to a socialist society. Capitalist and Communist alike are confused, completely at a loss to understand why Soviet power is so bent on destroying Jewish culture and religion. Why should the Jews be singled out for spiritual and national extinction? Why can every other minority group enjoy the right to maintain its own culture—but not the Jews? Why are the values of Jewish culture chosen for derision and contempt? Why foster hatred for a people who only recently suffered untold disaster and have not recovered from the nightmare of Nazi persecution? Is it because of their great contributions to social justice and the advancement of science and music? Is Moscow resolved to remain loyal to Stalin's mad hatred of the Jews and his extermination schemes? Is Moscow influenced by elements of Hitler's demonic theory that the Jewish people and Jewish culture must be destroyed?

We are gripped with horror. Is this the Utopian plan of Russian policy, for Russia to be a graveyard for our people?

Is this the will, the vision, and the design of the Russian government, to complete the work started by the Nazis—the liquidation of the Jewish people?

Do houses of worship or courses for the study of Hebrew and Yiddish represent a menace to the security of that mighty land? Is the misery and resentment of three million citizens an asset to her power?

A person is effective when he is allowed to be what he wants to be. Inner turbulence and bitterness in the hearts of so many human beings, though not capable of being reported in surveys and statistics, are a malignant disease in the body politic. What will Russia gain if that senseless oppression is victorious and the Jewish minority loses its identity and eventually perishes?

Many Jews may, indeed, succumb in the spiritual suffocation and surrender their integrity. Yet suffering passes; having suffered never passes. The memories of contempt will live on in souls for generations to come as incessant gall, corroding every thought, blasting inner peace, a thorn in the flesh of integrity.

Three million souls will not be blackmailed into suicide. They may pretend to be silent, but they will not betray their dignity. Communist Russia would then repeat the example of Spain: a country full of Marranos, living in the shadow of the Inquisition.

Soviet Russia's treatment of its Jewish citizens represents the outstanding example of cultural persecution today. The systematic effort to deprive a people of the knowledge of its legacy and ideals is like forcing a person to get rid of his soul, of his spirit, of his identity. It is difficult to see why granting cultural freedom to the Jewish minority should be incompatible with the social order.

The first necessity of civilization is the rule of law, of a law based on tacit recognition of what is by nature right. To be what one is, the claim to identity, is man's first natural right.

The systematic campaign to deprive the Jews of their cultural identity, the ruthless repression, elimination, and extirpation, bringing pain and distress to nearly three million people, is both senseless and cruel. It is an atrocity that poisons those who are responsible for it. As an official and consistent policy, it is bound to sap the country's moral foundations.

Mankind's most precious weapon is care, concern for harms done to our fellow men. Our concern for the cultural persecution of our fellow Jews in Russia is growing.

At a time of world-shaking events and stunning anticipations of things to come—astronauts within the reach of the moon, the production of nuclear bombs within the power of more and more nations, Telstar and supersonic bombs—one is inclined to be surprised by the fact that so many men of wisdom and sensitivity pay so much attention to the problem of Russian Jews. The issue of human rights, the issue of human dignity, seems to be trivial and light in terms of megatons and intercontinental missiles. Yet it is the heart of all national and international problems.

If the elementary rights and the dignity of so many human beings can be consistently trampled in the open view of all humanity, then such cruelty and such indifference to cruelty indicate a sickness that may forecast doom and disaster for all of us.

An old proverb says: If you wish to imagine or to attain a conception of infinitude, think of human stupidity.

The stupidity of the persecution of the Jewish minority, which stands in such tremendous contrast to the grandeur and intelligence of the Russian nation, remains a puzzle to all sensitive citizens living in Russia and a source of bewilderment to decent men all over the world.

We abhor any form of cold war. In any act of aggression, in any utterance of hatred, we are the first to suffer. We do not attack, we only plead, addressing ourselves to the conscience of the Russian people.

I speak as one who ardently desires friendship between our two countries. Yet how can we cultivate friendship for Russia, knowing that our fellow Jews are being kept in agony, jailed for teaching the language of the prophets?

ABRAHAM JOSHUA HESCHEL

July 1968

Contents

PREFACE   9
ACKNOWLEDGMENTS   11

FOREWORD BY *Abraham J. Heschel*   13

Introduction   23

ONE
The Plight of Soviet Jewry: An Overview

The Old Bazaar of Samarkand   37
    BY *Ben Ami*
The Status of the Jews in the Soviet Union   42
    BY *Moshe Decter*

TWO
Religious and Cultural Deprivations

Soviet Law and the Jews   61
    BY *William Korey*

Sovyetish Heymland   83
    BY *Joseph Brumberg*

Passover and *Matzoh:* A Case History of Soviet Policy   97
    BY *Moshe Decter*

THREE
Popular Anti-Semitism

Soviet Jews as Economic Criminals   115
    FROM THE *Journal of the International Commission of Jurists*

The Forgotten Martyrs of Babi Yar   127
    BY *William Korey*

Judaism Without Embellishment   135
    BY *Moshe Decter*

FOUR
Soviet Jewry and Israel

When the State of Israel Was Proclaimed   149
    BY *Joseph B. Schechtman*

Israel in the Soviet Mirror   158
    FROM *Jews in Eastern Europe*

FIVE
The Aftermath of the Six-Day War

Soviet Jewry and the Six-Day War   179
    BY *Abraham Brumberg*

Moshe Adolfovich Dayan   193
    FROM *Krokodil*

The Death of Charles H. Jordan   196
    BY *Robert H. Estabrook*

SIX
At the United Nations

The Need for a Jewish State   207
BY *Andrei A. Gromyko*

The "Two Masters" Charge   210
BY *Morris B. Abram*

Soviet Jewry and the United Nations: The Politics of
Non-Governmental Organizations   213
BY *Ronald I. Rubin*

SEVEN
Eyewitness Accounts

The Rejoicing of the Law   235
BY *Elie Wiesel*

Tishah B'ab in Moscow   250
BY *Ronald I. Rubin*

The Power of a Song   254
BY *Shelomo Ben-Israel*

The Ships That Will Sail to Jerusalem   260
BY *Ben Ami*

Visit to Babi Yar   264
BY *Michael Kaufman*

EIGHT
Response and Protest

Student Struggle for Soviet Jewry   271
BY *Ronald I. Rubin*

The State Department's Position   276

Australian Communists and Soviet Jewry   279
BY *Isi Leibler*

Philadelphia Supports Soviet Jewry   289
FROM THE Jewish Community Relations Council of
Greater Philadelphia

19

APPENDIX

Eighteen Points: The Rights of Soviet Jewry   305
Jewish Institutions in the Soviet Union   308
Suggested Reading   313

THE
UNREDEEMED

Introduction

In this tragedy-shadowed age, the Jews of Russia merit a special martyrdom. Having survived the pogroms of the czars, the purges of the 1930's,
Hitler's death hunts, and Stalin's mad extermination schemes, they face
slow spiritual strangulation by the technocrats who today govern the
Kremlin. If successful, the Soviets will have wiped out the second largest
Jewish community in the world, some one fourth of today's Jews. What
makes this prospect more horrendous is the awareness that these are the
survivors of the 2.5 million Jews murdered by the Nazis in the Soviet
Union in World War II. This spiritual genocide campaign is without
precedent in the ordeals of the Jewish people; it is unparalleled in modern
history.

Not a Jew in the Soviet Union is remote from this threat; not a Jew
who is not affected when Israel is linked with Nazi racism by Soviet
propaganda; not a Jew immune to accusations that he belongs to a bloodthirsty, primitive religion, an antisocial and unpatriotic culture, and a
crafty and vindictive people. In this setting, the refusal of Soviet Jewry
to be hounded into oblivion is in itself something of a mystery, defying
standard social-science tenets of assimilation and group endurance.

To some circles, charges that the Soviet Union is bent on crushing the

Introduction

Jewish soul seem tendentious and exaggerated, attributable to the hyper-emotionality of Jews, anti-Soviet interests, or the sensationalism of the press. Others deny the singular oppression of Judaism in the Soviet Union: in a nation of materialistic atheism, they argue, all religions survive precariously. Some "peace" advocates fear that too loud an outcry for Soviet Jewry endangers prospects for a détente between the Soviet Union and the United States. Finally, faceless victims are always hard to sympathize with, especially in a generation that has seen the cheapness of Jewish blood.

In counseling silence, these arguments bear ominous parallels to the world's inaction as the Nazi disaster engulfed Europe. To fail to recognize the problem for what it is—the final disappearance of Jewish life in the Soviet Union—is to echo the oft-cited excuse for silence in the face of Hitler—"We never knew." Surely those who would pay lip service to Jewish martyrdom twice in a generation are to be pitied even more than the Jews of Moscow and Dachau.

The nature of the problem rests in the fact that the Soviet Jew belongs to what can best be described as a "shadow people"—despite his having lived in the Soviet Union for more than a thousand years. His past is denied, his present existence as Jew *qua* Jew is unrecognized, and, as for his future, the Soviets destine his soul for extinction. Investigation of official Soviet domestic statements and publications invariably fails to turn up any favorable references to things Jewish—whether it be the vast contributions of Russia's Jews to every important current of world Jewish life today; their heroism in World War II; their sacrifice at Babi Yar. Among the diverse nationalities in the Soviet Union, no one group has been so callously denied self-perpetuation or portrayed in such an unremittingly hostile light.

With the notable exception of the early 1960's, when they were set up as scapegoats in a drive to stamp out "capitalist" illegalities, Soviet Jews do not have to fear for their lives. They have, however, to contend with the assault that is being subtly, insidiously waged against the Jewish soul itself.

In theory, three courses are open to Soviet Jews—affirmation, assimilation, emigration—all amounting to dead ends.

Ideally, affirmation would find expression either through their nationality or religion or both, since Judaism is recognized as both a nationality

24

and a religion under Soviet Law—a dual status unknown in the West. From the religious standpoint, however, Soviet Jews lack any of the national or regional organizations of the other recognized sects. Only sixty synagogues remain, with five aged rabbis to minister to three million Jews (since no rabbinical training is permitted today). Unlike other faiths, Judaism is denied the freedom to publish prayer books and bibles, print devotional articles, or engage in religious contacts with Jews abroad.

And, as a nationality, Jews suffer from similar restrictions. The only major group to lack a territorial Soviet republic, they are dispersed instead throughout the country and are therefore vulnerable to the passing repressions of the indigenous nationalities. In addition, publications, classes, and theaters in Yiddish, the language of Jewish nationals, have been virtually eliminated, while nationality groups far smaller in size are provided by the government with educational and cultural facilities in their native languages.

As for the Jew who seeks to cast off his heritage (and the stock Soviet claim is that many *do*), assimilation is no simple matter. At the age of sixteen, all Soviet citizens acquire an internal passport, on which they must state their nationality. Now, if both parents are registered as Jewish nationals, the youth is legally bound to do likewise; only if he is the child of a mixed marriage can he choose either nationality.

Mixed marriages, however, are rare among Soviet Jews (particularly as compared with figures in the 1930's),[1] and for two reasons: First, the family unit, the last bastion of Jewish identity in the Soviet Union, remains solid. As Eric Goldhagen, of Brandeis University, writes:

The Jewish family in the Soviet Union is an island unto itself, bearing the pricks and stings of the outer world in solitude. Strong ties of common feeling, the awareness of a common fate, united the Jewish family with thousands of other islands of its kind into a fraternity, self-conscious, invisible, and mute.[2]

Second, Jews remember all too well the shock of what happened in the Soviet territories held by the Nazis in World War II. The Jewish partner of an intermarriage, if not turned in by his spouse, was just as likely

1. See Zvi Gitelman, "Nationalities and Nationalism in the USSR: The Jews," *Problems of Communism* (September–October, 1967), p. 99.
2. "Do Not Remain Silent," *Jewish Life* (Spring 1965), p. 38.

to be exposed by his children. And what happened once in one situation could happen again in another.

Even if the Soviet Union changed this registration procedure in order to promote assimilation, other barriers work against it. There are few Soviet Jews who can turn their backs on their spiritual origins only a quarter-century after World War II; for, unlike the situation in certain unscathed Western nations, there is hardly a Soviet Jewish family that does not now mourn a killed, maimed, or missing relative.

Even young intellectual Jews sympathetic with the "liberalizing" trends operating in Soviet society find assimilation uninviting. Dissident intellectuals associate anti-Semitism with the bitter Stalinist heritage, and the Jewish struggle for survival symbolizes to them their own yearning for self-expression and the removal of all shackles of the creative spirit.

Then there is the reverse reaction. The intensification of anti-Semitism has galvanized a pride and a defensiveness in the Soviet Jew, much as it had in the Marranos who braved the Spanish Inquisition and in the Warsaw Ghetto partisans. The tightening quotas on Jewish university admissions, the thrust of so many press references to Jews as "security risks," the cartoons vilifying Israel in the wake of the Six-Day War—cruder than any Soviet portrayals of the United States role in Vietnam, by comparison—and the full-blown domestic propaganda attacks on the Israelis, said to be Hitler's heirs, for the aggression and atrocities perpetrated against the "peace-loving" Arabs—all of these have not been without meaning for the Soviet Jews. However much they may have sought to assimilate earlier, Soviet hostility has drawn the Jews closer to their people.

Finally, Soviet Jews will not assimilate because—strange as this seems—the Soviet authorities do not want it. The Kremlin's rulers continue to believe in the "international Jewish conspiracy" and other similar fictions harking back to *The Protocols of the Elders of Zion*. Better, they feel, to keep the Jews readily identifiable; once assimilated, they would undoubtedly succeed in undermining the national security.

In view of the restrictions on Jewish affirmation and the ambiguities of and resistance to assimilation, the third and final option, emigration, appears all the more attractive. More than any other Soviet nationality during World War II, Jews saw their family life torn apart by the Nazi invaders. Many escaped or found themselves in the West in the aftermath of the war, leaving relatives behind in the Soviet Union. Over the years, Soviet rulers have at least acknowledged the reality of this tragedy. In the mid-sixties, Premier Kosygin issued a statement in Paris promising that the Soviet Government would do "all possible for us" to enable families to reunite, and in fact a few thousand Jews were permitted annually to rejoin relatives abroad. However, the inflammation of anti-Semitism after the Six-Day War brought this exodus largely to a halt.

If given the choice, most Jews wanting to emigrate would undoubtedly head for Israel: many youths, the ones who learn Hebrew in secret, translate *Exodus* into Russian, and defiantly wear the Star of David at their necks; the old—the synagogue Jews—who have prayed all their lives for the "rebuilding of Jerusalem in mercy" and longed to kiss the Western (Wailing) Wall before they died; the Jew abused once too often for his religion; the Oriental Jews who have painstakingly carried down the religious tradition; the Jews in the lands annexed after the Holocaust (Latvia, Lithuania, Estonia, and parts of Rumania), still eager, after many years of Soviet rule, to pick up where they left off in the East European *yeshivas*, continuing their chain of scholarship. Probably one million of the Soviet Union's three million Jews would leave, for these and other reasons.

The refusal of the Soviet Union to permit Jewish emigration must be seen in the light of Soviet political policy. Soviet ideology maintains that the U.S.S.R. is a country of friendship and equality marked by the "drawing together" of diverse national groups. Such harmony, it is claimed, sharply contrasts with the ongoing ethnic and racial frictions in the capitalist world. In fact, this formula, at least from the Soviet standpoint, is grossly overstated. The cultural imperialism of the Russian Republic over the smaller Soviet republics is a basic source of divisiveness in the U.S.S.R. today.

Nonetheless, Soviet domestic and foreign propaganda triumphantly boasts of this alleged pluralism. Easy to see, then, that the granting of emigration rights to a sizable minority—especially one highly Western in its ties and traditions—would not only be incongruous with professed policy; it would also provide embarrassing evidence of Soviet suppression. Thus, the Soviets place higher priority on retaining the myth of nationality heterogeneity than on assuaging Jewish discontent.

Nor is the U.S.S.R. anxious to lose the valuable brain power now being employed toward its economic well-being. Although Jews, by now, are generally barred from certain political decision-making areas, they occupy many scientific and technical positions, and the U.S.S.R. could ill afford the industrial reverses their departure would bring about.

Jewish emigration also runs counter to Soviet objectives in the Middle East, the chief one being the strengthening of U.S.S.R. influence with the Arabs. An influx of scientists, engineers, and artisans into the Jewish State would surely destroy any possibility of gaining that objective, and the Soviet Union is not likely to sacrifice its interests in this area so that its oppressed Jews will find happiness in Israel.

Thus, we have the total predicament of the Soviet Jew: forbidden to join with others of his people in the U.S.S.R.; cut off from the greater community of Israel in the West; he is atomized, defenseless, and desperately alone. He is trapped in a vise that threatens to stifle his very life spirit.

There are various factors that account for the Jewish plight, one of which may be seen in the context of modern totalitarianism. Consider, for example, Nazism and communism, both movements of isolated individuals; both, in their demands for total loyalty, bent on destroying ties to family, friends, and comrades, so that the individual, as Hannah Arendt (in *The Origins of Totalitarianism*) puts it, "derives his sense of having a place in the world only from his belonging to a movement, his membership in the party." In this system, any form of individuality is intolerable, for, "as long as all men have not been made equally superfluous . . . the ideal of totalitarian domination has not been achieved."

A substantially coherent Soviet ideology has also determined present Jewish misfortunes. Much as Nietzsche blamed the "slave morality" of Christianity on its Jewish antecedents, Soviet ideologists conceive of Judaism—the mother of monotheistic faith—as the first threat to be stamped out in their fight to eliminate Christianity and Islam in the U.S.S.R.

Furthermore, the paranoid, materialistic Soviet world political outlook cannot treat indifferently a religion espousing a "Return to Zion"—which it resents as condescending and disloyal to the Soviet motherland. Tell the Soviets that this yearning refers to the *spiritual* Zion, and, to boot, that New York City counts more Jews than Israel despite these prayers and the absence of American emigration curbs, and one will likely be attacked for "Talmudist sophistry." Take away the Jewish religion and retain the Jewish people or nationality, and the conspiratorial-minded Soviets would go on suspecting their Jews because of their many relatives in the West, especially the United States, and in Israel.

Take away both the Jewish religion and the Jewish nationality and you have the pogrom-ridden history of the czarist Pale of Settlement. "Popular" anti-Semitism stems from this climate, designating the Jew for convenient scapegoating. Take away the three foregoing features, and there remains, finally, a Jewish individualism, idealism, and legacy of freedom in direct opposition to the deadening uniformity of communism.

In the half-century of Soviet rule, the extent of Jewish suffering has not been uniform, although each wave of repressions has gradually withered away the vitality of Jewish life under the czars. To his credit, Lenin denounced anti-Semitism; but, at the same time, he denied Jews the status of a nationality because they lacked the prerequisites—a territory, language, and rooted peasantry—and dismissed their claims of such as "manifestly reactionary."

Under the Stalin regime, all Jewish cultural institutions in the U.S.S.R. were destroyed and Jews removed from key political posts. To appreciate the enormity of Stalin's efforts to eliminate Jewish life, one need only consider the "Black Years" (1948–53), when every Yiddish theater and school was shut and not a single Yiddish book appeared (compared with thousands previously published). While some Yiddish works saw publication under Khrushchev and Kosygin, no Yiddish theaters or schools have yet reopened their doors as of this writing.

To what was Stalin's anti-Semitism attributable? As a theological seminary drop-out, he probably absorbed some of the more blatant anti-Semitic fabrications of the Russian Orthodox Church. Leon Trotsky, his early political rival, seemed to him to bear all the discredited earmarks of the universal Jew (despite the fact that Trotsky never affirmed his Jewishness or took any measures in assisting beleaguered Jews).

The World War II experience strengthened Stalin's hostilities to the Jews. (In her memoirs, Svetlana Alliluyeva reports that Stalin had his son Yakov's Jewish wife, Yulia, arrested for allegedly "tricking" her husband into being taken a prisoner by the Germans in 1943.) He believed that the encounters between many Jewish troops in the Red Army and Jews of other Allied nations, particularly in the German campaign, enhanced

29

pro-Western sentiments of Soviet Jewish soldiers and might well materialize into an increased world Jewish fraternity ("All of Israel are brethren"). The emotional response of Soviet Jewry to Israel's creation represented, for Stalin, sentiments that should have long since perished. As with all modern anti-Semites, Stalin was haunted by the spectre of "world rule for the Zionists." There is clear evidence today that at his death, he was planning the deportation of all Soviet Jews to Siberia.

Under Khrushchev, every Soviet group benefited from the new "liberal" atmosphere except the Jews. The best that can be said in Khrushchev's defense is that he substituted more sophisticated means for Stalin's terror and violence in inexorably tightening the noose around the Jewish spirit. In his famous speech to the Twentieth Congress of the Communist Party of the Soviet Union in February, 1956, while he roundly denounced Stalin for the people he had murdered and betrayed, and stated the grievances of the many nationalities that had been persecuted, not one word of solace or reassurance did he speak in behalf of the group that had suffered most—the Jews.

This was the period in which the ban on the baking of *matzoh* was imposed; in which the remaining synagogues in the U.S.S.R. fell under vicious attacks as being dens of drunken brawls over money. In the early 1960's, the Jew was designated a new scapegoat status—an economic criminal perpetrating illegal capitalist deals. Judging by the high proportion of death sentences meted out to Jews for these alleged crimes, one might be led to conclude that Jews were chiefly responsible for continuing capitalism in the Soviet Union!

The mushrooming of the Jew-Judaism-Zionism-Israel syndrome also took place at this time. Propagating an absurd and destructive image of Israel became the central propaganda vehicle for fostering dislike and fear of Jews among the Soviet citizenry. In assessing this unmitigated attack on Israel, *Jews in Eastern Europe* noted:

No other country is depicted with quite the same degree of malevolence by the Soviet press. It is a picture of unrelieved social and political squalor, except for an occasional reference to the Israel Communist Party. The amount of newspaper space allocated to this small nation of 2¼ million population is inexplicable in rational terms. The Soviet reader could easily get the impression that Israel was a powerful country; that she played a key role in the aggressive policies of imperialists, conducting far-reaching subversion in Africa,

Introduction

Asia, and even in the Soviet Union itself; also, that Zionism was one of the major hostile ideologies of the world closely connected with neo-Nazism and American economic colonialism.[3]

Whatever gains for Soviet Jewry did emerge with Stalin's passing, then, must be seen from the broader perspective of changing Soviet diplomatic strategy. Foreign opinion, favorable or unfavorable, mattered little to Stalin in his policies of Soviet imperialism, whereas it is a factor to be considered in current Soviet foreign policy. A bimonthly magazine (now a monthly), *Sovyetish Heymland*, appeared in 1961, with an altogether insufficient press run of 25,000 copies—many copies being sent abroad for propaganda purposes. Some Yiddish books were published, also in far too limited quantities for culture-starved Soviet Jews. Published references to Jewish economic crimes ended, *matzoh* became available in large cities, emigration restrictions for families disjointed by World War II eased slightly, and promises were made for the reopening of a rabbinic seminary and the production of religious articles.

These shifts represented at best only token departures from the attrition campaign; but even these scattered concessions were vitiated by the virulent anti-Jewish phobia in the wake of the Six-Day War. To the Soviet public, the Israeli victory resulted in a loss of billions of dollars in Soviet-supplied military equipment—resources that should have been spent instead in boosting production of consumer goods. The Arab defeat also heightened public skepticism as to the infallibility of Soviet diplomatic machinery. To remove the onus for Soviet complicity in this ill-fated Middle East venture, the Jew once again became the scapegoat—with the new twist that the Israeli "aggressors" were as brutal as their Nazi persecutors had been.

What of the future? Will Soviet Jewry live on? The answers to these questions will depend on three factors: (1) Soviet Jews themselves; (2) internal Soviet politics; (3) worldwide exposure of the Jewish plight.

(1) Soviet Jews: We are witnessing a new man in Jewish history: the Jew without Judaism. On the one hand, Soviet prejudice forces Jews to remain Jews, but, on the other, bars the transmission of what this Jewishness means. With the passing of the older generation, there will be few Jews able to perform the tangible rites of religious continuity: circum-

3. *Jews in Eastern Europe*, December, 1965, p. 4.

cision, marriage, and burial. As synagogues continue to disappear, Judaism will be restructured from a communal into a monastic faith. The prohibitions on Yiddish culture will be reflected in marginal familiarity with its prodigious literature and drama; and Yiddish will be transformed from a written to a spoken language.

Nevertheless, lacking all else, Soviet Jewry will survive by faith. The knowledge that the State of Israel endures, that Jewish existence flowers elsewhere, that the children of Abraham affirm the covenant as in the past, plays no small part in the refusal of Soviet Jewry to submit.

(2) Internal Soviet Politics: Policy on the Jews can go one of three ways: a) continue at the same pace of oppression, selectively scapegoating Jews, now as the Middle East situation dictates; b) tighten the noose to the extent of deporting all Jews to Siberia; c) evolve along more democratic lines, tolerating increased individualism and free expression. As Soviet society becomes more committed to materialistic comforts rather than revolutionary ardor, there will be more room for the Jew. Of course, in a country lacking the Western political heritage, the degree of liberty—particularly religious liberty—in the foreseeable future will remain restricted. Still, this must be the hope of Soviet Jewry—a liberalized climate in which his identity will be upheld rather than trampled down.

(3) Worldwide Exposure: In an era of international political communication, violations of human rights are no longer uniquely national crimes. They demean all men. Mass media have brought the "man in the street" (supplementing official envoys) into the foreign-policy-making process. Placards and leather soles are his universally understood means for voicing opinions on domestic and diplomatic issues.

In this light, public focusing on Soviet persecution is a formidable weapon in helping Jews. Within limits the Soviet Union is responsive to world opinion, evidenced by its readiness to treat seriously the protests from "our friends" in the West. By contrast, "quiet diplomacy," the intercession of influential persons to plead privately with Soviet officials for more Jewish rights, is weak in this age of political activism.

Effective public protests have any number of avenues from which to choose: demonstrations, classes, periodicals; the communications media, letter-writing campaigns to Soviet and United States politicians, and ongoing community workshops. The Soviet Union is keenly embarrassed by petitions of intellectuals, educators, Western Communists, fellow travelers, and pacifists on this issue. Soviet intelligence knows that human rights rather than Cold War considerations motivate the opposition of these sources toward its mistreatment of Jews. And it is likely that the louder the protests from such "progressives," the greater the willingness of the U.S.S.R. to grant Jews more freedoms.

Soviet Jews learned in the law realize that to Jews there is no holier undertaking than the Redemption of Captives (*Pidyon Shevuyim*). The *Code of Laws (Shulchan Aruch)* states: Every moment one postpones the redemption of captives it is as though one commits murder. Even the Torah, if necessary, must be ransomed on their behalf.

Accordingly, protests prove to Soviet Jews, in addition to their Communist rulers, that they have not been abandoned. The half-century of communism has conditioned them to survive the terror and withstand the anguish, but what they fear most is that either through self-interest, indifference, or cowardice, they will be forgotten by the humane community of man.

A quarter-century after the ovens of Auschwitz have been cooled, the hunting out of the guilty—whether by action or inaction—goes on. What better way for free men to honor the dead than to guarantee that the Jews of Russia, the principal survivors of the Holocaust, endure. Arthur D. Morse, in *While Six Million Died,* frames the warning starkly:

The six million lie in nameless graves. But what of the future? Is genocide now unthinkable, or are potential victims in the world going about their business, devoted to their children, aspiring to a better life, unaware of a gathering storm?

ONE

The Plight of Soviet Jewry: An Overview

The Old Bazaar of Samarkand

BY *Ben Ami*

The ancient bazaar of Samarkand is one of the most colorful and noisy spots in Uzbekistan, even on an ordinary weekday. But imagine the excitement that takes place on the eve of the First of May, the great national and spring festival of the Soviet peoples. The year I was there the parade attracted thousands from the furthest reaches of the Republic of Uzbekistan, and the market places were filled with a multicolored throng.

The bazaar itself is a unique medley of Bukharan and Persian architecture: arched domes and minarets dotted with mosaics in blue, turquoise, and green dominate the markets and squares of the town. A riot of red flags, posters, and slogans added a new touch to the ancient scheme. Pictures of Marx, Engels, and particularly Lenin covered entire walls; alongside them were photographs of the Soviet leaders of the day, all grouped in a prearranged hierarchic order that suggested an unbroken continuity.

I loved walking through this tumultuous crowd. Heavy-footed Uzbek peasants wandered between the stalls, their wives dressed in yellow, speckled, artificial silks that fluttered in the breeze. Slanty-eyed, bushy-bearded Tajiks walked about in groups, talking loudly in a strange idiom. Thickset Bukharans engaged in smiling conversations with tall, slim, stern-looking Turkmen. Russian and Ukrainian *kolkhoz* members moved through the crowd, tall, broad, blue-eyed, and yellow-hatted, their thick-set Slavic wives wearing colored kerchiefs on their heads. The sound of Turkish, Persian, and Mongolian dialects, mingled with Russian and Ukrainian, echoed through the market place. At sunset, as the blue mosaics and the glass covering the red pictures reflected the sun's yellow rays, the bazaar and its throng looked as though it had been cut out of the colored frescoes which adorn the palaces of the Persian princes or the emirs of Bukhara.

I was certain that many of the people selling rugs, cloth, and colored cotton material were Bukharan Jews, descendants of that remarkable and ancient Jewish group who had handed down the profession to their descendants. Now, under the Soviet regime, their private enterprise had become a nationalized trade; but nothing else about it had changed. For all the uniformity imposed by official policy, this place, far away from Moscow, had retained intact much of the special flavor of the bazaars: the loud bargaining and the give-and-take that made commerce a rite and an art.

Walking through the alleyways of the market, I suddenly came across a Jew who seemed to have dropped from another world. He stood facing me on the narrow sidewalk, an old man of seventy or more, above aver-age height but bent with age, his beard white and short, his face fur-rowed with wrinkles, his eyes deep blue. He wore a long black coat, old and faded, and shabby half-length boots. He stood behind a little valise-like table which rested on a tripod and was attached to a wide leather belt which hung loosely over his shoulders. The table was filled with an assortment of little things—all sorts of haberdashery.

I felt sure that this was no native Bukharan Jew, but an Ashkenazi Jew from Europe. My curiosity changed to eager excitement as I came close to the peddler. The man suddenly reminded me of my late father. The build, the beard, the features, and, above all, the wonderful blue eyes were all the same. He seemed so out of place in this Oriental Samarkand bazaar that his very presence there aroused pity. Nobody stopped to buy his wares. He stood there, lonely, sad, and foreign, amidst the noise and tumult around him.

I came closer and greeted him in Yiddish: "*Sholem aleichem, Reb Yid.*"

So absorbed was the old man, that he started when I spoke; and when he saw before him a man much younger than himself, dressed as a foreign tourist, he seemed utterly amazed. He peered at me with suspicious eyes and answered in a whisper: "*Sholem aleichem.*" I asked him: "*Reb Yid*, what have you got to sell?" He showed me his wares: shoelaces, hairpins, cheap bottles of perfume, combs, matches, tacks, and the like. I picked up a pair of shoelaces and, while examining them at length, asked: "Well, and how is my fellow Jew?" He countered with a quick question. "Please tell me, sir, where do you come from, and what are you doing here?" I answered slowly: "I come from Israel and I am here on a pleasure trip."

Beside himself with surprise, the Jew leaned on his tripod and breathed a long "*Oy!*" I bought the black laces as the old Jew held my hand and looked deep into my eyes. Then he suddenly started speaking quickly: "Please buy something else so that you do not seem conspicuous. You are the first Israeli, probably the last, I'll ever see. I must speak to you." I examined the things on the little stand and bought a brown comb, all the while listening to the man's life story, which he told in short, broken, breathless sentences.

He was born in a little town near Vilna in Lithuania, and attended a *heder* and a *yeshiva*. When he reached adolescence, he joined a religious Zionist movement in his town; then he moved to Vilna, the big city. He made good in the textile trade, married, prospered, and raised a Jewish family; he had sons and daughters, was an active Zionist, contributed to all the drives for the pioneers in the Land of Israel. He did not emigrate to the Land of Israel because he did not want to leave his thriving business. Then came the war. . . .

I bought another comb and two more pairs of laces. . . . "Yes, war broke out." Two of his sons died at the Red Army front. He, his wife, and his little son wandered to Siberia. There he was accused of being a "former great merchant and active Zionist." He was arrested and deported to a prison camp in the far north.

I bought some buttons and safety pins. "The camps, yes . . . They are in the land of the white bear, as the saying goes. I lived there thirteen years, working like a slave, chopping trees, mining coal, and laying railway ties. Look at me, I'll be sixty-four next year."

I looked closely at him.

"Yes, yes, I know. I look like an old man of eighty. This is the price I paid for what I learned in those camps. After that barbarian died, I was liberated. My wife and I were given permission to live only in Samarkand. And this is how I make my living."

I picked up some boxes of matches and two packets of candles and added them to my stock of purchases. "I have relatives and friends in Israel, but it is many years since I wrote to them. My heart is with them, and, do you know, my son works as an electronics engineer in some large plants in northern Siberia. He came to see me once in Samarkand and told me how easily he can pick up Israeli broadcasts and get the news. Don't be so surprised. I educated him myself and taught him to love the Land of Israel and the Jewish people. He also told me that someone with the same name as mine was appointed to an important position in the Israeli Government. I worked out my family tree and told my son: 'Do you know, son, I am sure this is my cousin who emigrated to Palestine and was one of the first pioneers forty years ago.' What do you think, sir, could that be true?"

I bought a little bottle of scent and some more haberdashery, then learned the full name of the peddler. I told him: "Yes, my friend, I do believe that your cousin is now something like a minister in Israel." The Jew looked at me with his beautiful sad eyes and as his tears fell slowly, he murmured: "*Nu* . . . that He has kept us alive and preserved us and enabled us to see this day."

He wiped away his tears with a tattered handkerchief and added: "When you return to Israel, greet him for me. As for me, if I perish, I perish! I am afraid to write to him, not for my own sake, but for that of my son. He has such a responsible job and his position is so delicate— I may hurt him."

I asked whether he had a specific message.

"Yes," he answered. "When you get back, please tell my cousin and all other Jews . . . *Nu* . . . this is what you'll tell them." And here the peddler began to hum the opening bars of the "*Hatikvah*," the anthem of the Zionist movement and, now, of the State of Israel. But he could not go on, for tears choked him.

I gathered up all the things I had bought, paid him, doubling and trebling the sum, swung his emaciated hand, and told him: "I shall bring your cousin and all the people of Israel your greetings and those of your wife and of your son the engineer in northern Siberia."

That night, after watching the fine performance of the national Uz-bekistan folk-dance ensemble, and then the fireworks display, I returned wearily to the Intourist hotel. I could not sleep. I was obsessed by the face and the story of the old peddler—the more so because of his amaz-ing resemblance to my father. A strange thought haunted me: It is mere chance that brings me, a foreign tourist, to the market places of Central Asia, wandering without a care in the footsteps of Marco Polo. Had my father not been a Zionist, had he not decided to leave Russia forty years ago and travel to Israel, I would now be another resident of the Soviet Union, provided, of course, I had survived all that had befallen my gen-eration, the hunger, the liquidations, prison, war, and—worse than all—the Holocaust. Who knows but that I might also be working now as an electronics engineer in northern Siberia.

The Status of the Jews
in the Soviet Union

BY *Moshe Decter*

During the past quarter-century, enlightened public opinion throughout the world has become keenly sensitive to the treatment of minorities as a barometer of moral decency and social sanity. The awesome experiences of this period have drawn particular attention to the symbolic and actual position of the Jewish minority. In this light, the status of the Jews in the Soviet Union warrants special concern.

The situation of Soviet Jews can be comprehended primarily within the framework of Soviet nationalities policy. That policy, as reflected in Communist Party directives, the Soviet Constitution, and public law, is based on the ideological acceptance of the concept of national self-determination and on the legal recognition of the right of all nationalities within Soviet borders to cultural freedom. Actual Soviet policy toward the Jews clearly violates these principles. It is tantamount to a policy of discrimination, for it denies to the Jews such ethnic-cultural rights as are generally accorded all other Soviet nationalities.

The Soviet Union officially recognizes Jews as a nationality. In the personal identification papers which all Soviet citizens carry (the internal "passport"), Jews must list their nationality as "Jewish" (*Yevrei*) just as other nationalities—such as Russians, Ukrainians, Georgians, and others—must list theirs. Thus, in the official Soviet census returns of 1959, published in *Pravda* on February 4, 1960, Jews are listed among the official nationalities. In all previous censuses, citizens were required to provide proof, in the form of their internal passport, of their claim to belong to one or another nationality. In 1959, for the first time, they were allowed to volunteer, without proof, the nationality with which they chose to be identified. Despite the possibility thus provided for Jews to "pass," 2,268,000 people specified their nationality as Jewish (there are reasons to believe that the total number more closely approximates three million).

Soviet Jews constitute 1.09 percent of the population, but they occupy a far more significant place than this figure suggests. Of the considerably more than 100 diverse Soviet nationalities, the Jews are eleventh numerically. The great majority of them live in the three most populous Union republics: 38 percent in the Russian Republic, 37 percent in the Ukraine, 7 percent in White Russia; but there is no republic of the U.S.S.R. where Jewish communities may not be found. And an important reflection of their sense of identification after several decades of direct and indirect forcible assimilation is that 472,000 (20.8 percent) gave Yiddish, which is the traditional language of speech and literature of East European Jews, as their mother-tongue.

The Jews are also regarded, secondarily, as a religious group. This complicates their status and makes it even more precarious. For though their unique dual character is a natural outgrowth of Jewish history and tradition, it creates unusual difficulties for them under Soviet conditions. An assault upon the Jewish religion, for example, will inevitably be taken, by Jews and non-Jews alike, as an attack upon the Jewish nationality as a whole—upon Jews as such. And they have come increasingly to be considered an alien group in a land where they have resided for more than a thousand years.

Their vulnerability is increased by the fact that, unlike most other

43

Soviet nationalities, which have their own geographic territories, the Jews are widely dispersed throughout the country. They are also the only Soviet nationality a majority of whose total world population lives outside the U.S.S.R. Because the Soviet Jewish minority has historic and traditional ties of culture, religion and family with Jewish communities throughout the world outside the Communist bloc, it is subject to even greater suspicion.

Soviet Jews are especially sensitive to their vulnerable condition because their memory of what they themselves call the "Black Years"—the last five years of Stalin's rule, when his terror assumed a viciously and openly anti-Semitic form—has not been erased. One reason they have not forgotten is that Soviet policy toward Jews and Judaism has remained essentially the same since 1948—with the vitally important exception, of course, that the terror is gone. And they are not less keenly cognizant of the fact that, of all the crimes of Stalin catalogued by Premier Khrushchev and his colleagues at the Twentieth and Twenty-second Congresses of the CPSU, his crimes against the Jews were passed over in utter silence.

The significance of Soviet policy toward the Jews was dramatically highlighted in September, 1961, by the publication of a poem, "Babi Yar," in the *Literary Gazette*, organ of the Soviet Writers' Union. This poem by a loyal Communist, Yevgeny Yevtushenko—one of the most popular young Soviet poets—caused a sensation. It is a searing indictment of anti-Semitism both historically and as a facet of contemporary Soviet society. In his opening line, the poet protests that there is still no monument to the scores of thousands of Jewish martyrs slaughtered by the Nazis in 1941 at Babi Yar, a vale on the outskirts of Kiev. This is a pointed reflection of the fact that Soviet authorities have been consistently silent about the nature, dimensions and even the very existence of the unique Jewish tragedy during the Second World War. Though not himself a Jew, Yevtushenko identifies himself in his poem with persecuted Jewry throughout history. He thus points up the existence of a historic Jewish people, which Soviet doctrine denies—and of Jewish history, which Soviet policy prevents Jews from learning.

Yevtushenko is not alone in mirroring the mood and sensibility of the literate younger Soviet generation. There is a whole "underground" literature that passes from hand to hand among the university and literary youth, and one of its frequent leitmotifs is isolated, disadvantaged Soviet Jewry. In this, as in their general quest for a purified idealism, Yevtushenko and his confrères are in the main stream of the honorable tradition of the liberal Russian intelligentsia from Pushkin to Tolstoy and Gorky.

The Jews are the only nationality which is deprived of the basic cultural rights accorded to all others in the U.S.S.R. These rights have recently been reaffirmed by no less an authoritative source than the new Party program adopted by the Twenty-second Congress in October, 1961: "The Communist Party guarantees the complete freedom of each citizen of the U.S.S.R. to speak and to rear and educate his children in any language—ruling out all privileges, restrictions or compulsion in the use of this or that language."

Until 1948 the Jews were permitted a cultural life in their own language, Yiddish (though Hebrew was forbidden), on a large scale: newspapers, publishing houses, thousands of books, a variety of literary journals, professional repertory theaters and dramatic schools, literary and cultural research institutes, a network of schools, and other means of perpetuating Jewish cultural values, albeit in a Communist form. In 1948 (and in some cases during the purges of 1937–39), the whole vast array of institutions was forcibly closed.

No basic change in this policy of cultural deprivation occurred, despite Stalin's death and the gradual easing of the tyranny, until 1959. Since then, a grand total of 6 Yiddish books has been published—by writers long dead. (None has been published in 1962 as of November.)[1] They were put out in editions of 30,000 each, mostly for foreign consumption, but those copies that were available to Jews inside the U.S.S.R. were eagerly and quickly snapped up.

This total of six books is to be compared with the facilities made available to many ethnic groups far smaller than that of the Soviet Jews, and which do not possess as ancient, continuous and rich a culture. Two

1. Since 1964, seven Yiddish books appeared. Increasingly, the works are authored by living Soviet Jews, a new development since 1948.—Ed.

striking examples are in order. The Maris and Yakuts are two tiny primitive Asian groups which number 504,000 and 236,000 respectively. In 1961 alone, Soviet printing presses produced 62 books for the Maris and 144 for the Yakuts, in their own languages.

The Soviet Yiddish theater was once considered one of the prides of Soviet artistic achievement. Today there is only a handful of amateur theatrical groups, made up of Jewish workers banded together after working hours, existing on a marginal basis; there is not even such a group in Moscow or Leningrad, the two major centers of Soviet Jewry, together totaling nearly one million.

In the autumn of 1961, for the first time since 1948, a Yiddish literary journal, *Sovyetish Heymland*, began publication as a bimonthly.[2] Welcome though this is, it is no more than the exception proving the rule. But it does represent, along with the meager half-dozen Yiddish books (and the "concerts" of Yiddish dramatic readings and folk songs which have been permitted and which have been attended by millions of Jews in recent years), a tacit repudiation of the oft-repeated Soviet assertion that Soviet Jews have lost interest in their culture. This state of affairs is again to be contrasted with the press available to the Maris and Yakuts. The former have 17 newspapers, the latter 28.

A frequent Soviet rationalization for the absence of cultural institutions for the Jews is that the Jews are so widely dispersed. This is invalidated, however, by the fact that tiny minorities like the Chechens (418,000), Ossetians (410,000), and Komis (431,000), which do not have their own territories, yet have their own newspapers and literatures in their own languages, and schools where their languages are taught. The Tajik minority in Uzbekistan (312,000 out of a total republic population of 8,106,000) has similar rights and institutions, as have the Poles in White Russia (539,000 out of 8,055,000).

It is not just schools that are forbidden to the Jews.[3] They are not even allowed classes in Yiddish or Hebrew in the general schools; nor, for that matter, classes in the Russian language (comparable to Sunday School education in the United States) on Jewish history and culture. Nor are

2. This journal today is published on a monthly basis. For analysis of *Sovyetish Heymland*, see the selection by Joseph Brumberg below, pp. 83–96.—Ed.

3. Though Soviet law permits any ten parents who request it to organize instruction for their children in their own language, Jewish parents have been understandably loath to take advantage of this provision.

Soviet Jews permitted to have contact on purely Jewish cultural matters with Jewish institutions abroad.

All religions in the U.S.S.R. exist very precariously within a context of official anti-religious ideology and propaganda. In a variety of fundamental respects, however, Judaism is subjected to unique discrimination. Jewish congregations are permitted no variant of the right enjoyed by the others to maintain nationwide federations or other central organizations through which religious functions are governed, religious needs serviced, religious belief bolstered, and communication between congregations strengthened. Rabbis and synagogue leaders have nothing at all comparable to the Holy Synod of the Russian Orthodox Church, the All-Union Council of Evangelical Christians-Baptists, the National Ecclesiastical Assembly of the Armenian Church, the Lutheran Churches of Latvia and Estonia or the Moslem Board for Central Asia and Kazakhstan.

These churches are permitted a wide range of religious publishing facilities, publishing houses, and paper supplies. Thus, the Russian Orthodox version of the Bible was reprinted in 1957 in an edition of 50,000. In 1958, 10,000 copies of a Russian-language Protestant Bible were published by the Baptists. The same year the Moslem Directorates in Ufa and Tashkent produced editions of 4,000 and 5,000 copies, respectively, of the Koran. And in May, 1962, the Moslem Board for Central Asia issued still another new edition. It should be noted that these editions of the Koran are in Arabic, a language not spoken by Soviet Moslems, but used for religious study and other religious functions. This is comparable to what the status of Hebrew might be there.

Judaism is permitted no publication facilities and no publications. No Hebrew Bible has been published for Jews since 1917. (Nor has a Russian translation of the Jewish version of the Old Testament been allowed.) The study of Hebrew has been outlawed, even for religious purposes. Not a single Jewish religious book of any other kind has appeared in print since the early 1920's. In contrast, prayer books are available to the other denominations in relatively ample supply: the Baptists were authorized in 1956 to publish 25,000 hymnals; the Lutheran Church of Latvia has produced 1,500 copies of a psalter and is now preparing a new edition of its 1954 hymnal. Religious calendars, indispensable guides for religious holidays and observances, are freely available. Other types of religious publications are also permitted. The Russian Orthodox Church publishes the *Journal of the Moscow Patriarchate*, its official monthly organ. It has also published collections of sermons and several annuals. The All-Union Council of Baptists puts out a bimonthly, the *Fraternal Review*.

No such prerogatives have been vouchsafed to the Jews. Until 1958, no *siddur* (Sabbath prayer book in Hebrew) was printed. In that year, an edition of 3,000 copies of a pre-Revolutionary *siddur* was provided by photo-offset—a ridiculously small figure for the hundreds of thousands of religious Jews whose prayer books are tattered and torn. No edition at all has been allowed of special prayer books which Jews use on their high holidays and major festivals. As for calendars, the Jews have had to depend on photographed copies of handwritten ones, surreptitiously circulated from hand to hand.

A subtler but harsher form of discrimination has resulted from the ban on Hebrew. The Russian Orthodox, Baptist, Lutheran, Georgian, or Armenian believer is not handicapped in his participation in religious services, for they are conducted in his native spoken tongue. But the half-century-old ban on Hebrew has made it impossible for Jews educated under the Soviet regime to make sense of their synagogue services. Thousands come—and must stand mute and dumb.

The other major ecclesiastical bodies are authorized to produce a variety of religious articles—ritual objects such as church vessels, vestments, candles, beads, crucifixes, and icons. The mass sale of such articles, especially candles, is an important source of church income. But the production of such indispensable religious objects as the *tallith* (prayer shawl) and *tefillin* (phylacteries) is prohibited to Jews.

A brief statistical examination illuminates the extent to which the faithful are served by churches and priests, synagogues and rabbis. For the 40 million Russian Orthodox there are some 20,000 churches and 35,000 priests (quite apart from those in the 69 monasteries and convents). This comes to one place of worship for each 2,000 believers and one priest for each 1,100 believers. For the 3 million Baptists (including women and children who are affiliated through family membership) there are roughly 6,000 parishes and pastors, which amounts to one place of worship and one minister for each 500 believers. The Lutheran Churches of Latvia and Estonia have 100 churches and 150 pastors for about 350,000 communicants—approximately one church for each 3,500 believers and one minister for each 2,300. By contrast, there are some 60 or 70 synagogues and rabbis for the nearly 1 million Jewish believers—which amounts to one synagogue and one rabbi for each 15,000 to 16,000 Jewish believers.[4]

Most religious groups also maintain educational institutions to prepare men for the priesthood. The Russian Orthodox have 2 academies and 5 seminaries; the Moslems have a *madrassa* where their mullahs are trained. In addition, quite a few Moslem clerical students have been permitted to advance their studies at the theological seminary in Cairo. Young Baptist seminarians have attended theological schools in Great Britain and Canada. Such programs serve the twofold function of maintaining spiritual contacts with co-religionists abroad and of enhancing the quality of religious education at home.

Until 1957, religious Jews had no institution to train rabbis. In that year, a *yeshiva* (rabbinical academy) was established as an adjunct of the Great Synagogue in Moscow. Since then, precisely 2 men have been ordained as rabbis, neither of whom has functioned as a synagogue leader. Of the 13 students at the *yeshiva* until April, 1962, 11 were over 40— which means that very little provision was made for replacing the rabbis now serving in the U.S.S.R., all of whom are in their seventies and eighties. This is to be contrasted with the "accent on youth" for Russian Orthodox seminarians. The Jewish community is thus being deprived of needed religious leadership.

A most serious restriction was imposed on the *yeshiva* in April, 1962, when a majority of the students, who came from the oriental Jewish communities of Georgia and Daghestan, were forbidden to resume their studies in Moscow, on the ground that they lacked the necessary residence permits for the capital city, which is suffering from a housing shortage. This left just four students in an institution that has been transformed into a virtually empty shell.[5] Nor has any Jewish seminarian in the last five years been allowed to advance his studies at institutions of Jewish learning abroad.

In addition to their prerogatives at home, other Soviet ecclesiastical bodies have enjoyed the privilege of regular and permanent ties with co-

---

4. In 1968, there were an estimated five remaining rabbis, most of them seventy and older, for all the Jews in the U.S.S.R.—Ed.

5. This one *yeshiva* has since been shut completely by the government.—Ed.

religionists abroad, an incalculably important boost to their morale. Since 1956 there have been innumerable exchange visits of religious delegations —Russian Orthodox, Baptists, and Moslems—between the U.S.S.R. and Western Europe, the United States and the Middle East. The Soviet Moslems have for years been associated with a World Congress of Moslems. At the end of October, 1962, a national conference of Moslem leaders, meeting in Tashkent, was authorized to establish a permanent department for international relations, with headquarters in Moscow, which would speak for all Moslem boards in the country. And within the past year, the World Council of Churches (Protestant) accepted the full-fledged membership of the Russian Orthodox Church and of five other major Soviet ecclesiastical bodies: the Georgian and Armenian Churches, the Baptists, and the Lutheran Churches of Latvia and Estonia.

No Jewish religious delegation from the U.S.S.R. has ever been permitted to visit religious institutions abroad.[6] Nor are synagogues in the Soviet Union allowed to have any kind of official contact, permanent ties, or institutional relations with Jewish religious, congregational, or rabbinic bodies outside their country.

The process of attrition and pressure against Judaism and Jewish religious institutions and practitioners has been systematically stepped up since the middle of 1961. In June and July of that year, the synagogue presidents in six major provincial cities were deposed. In the same period, six lay religious leaders in Moscow and Leningrad were secretly arrested. In September, 1961, on the occasion of the Jewish High Holy Days, the authorities ordered the construction of a special loge in the Moscow Great Synagogue to seat the Israeli Embassy officials who came to attend services—the better to cut off the thousands of Jews who came to the synagogue from their fellow Jews from abroad. In October, 1961, the Moscow and Leningrad leaders were secretly tried and convicted of alleged espionage, and sentenced to lengthy prison terms. In January, 1962, *Trud*, the central Trade Union paper, published a notorious article that portrayed these devout religious Jews as agents of Israeli spies who, in turn, were described as tools of American intelligence.

6. In June, 1968, Rabbi Judah Leib Levin of the Moscow Synagogue, accompanied by Cantor David Stiskin of the Leningrad Synagogue, visited the United States under the sponsorship of the anti-Zionist American Council for Judaism. That the Soviet government permitted this two-week trip shows a growing awareness of foreign criticism of its anti-Semitic policy.—Ed.

On March 17, 1962, Rabbi Judah Leib Levin, of the Moscow Synagogue, announced that the public baking and sale of *matzoth* (the unleavened bread indispensable to the observance of the Passover) would be forbidden. This was the first time in Soviet history that a total ban on *matzoth* was enforced throughout the country. The ban was actually part of the larger official attempt to destroy the bonds between Soviet Jewry and the traditional roots of Judaism that have a national historical significance. Since Passover is the ancient feast that commemorates the liberation of the Hebrews from Egyptian slavery and their establishment as a religious people, this holiday is subjected to especially virulent assault in the Soviet press. It is linked with "Zionist ideology," the State of Israel, chauvinism, and so forth. The propaganda goes so far as to brand Jewish religious holidays, and Passover in particular, as subversive. "Judaism kills love for the Soviet motherland"—this is a slogan from a typical press article.

All this adds up to a systematic policy of attrition against religious Jews and their religious practices. The synagogues are the only remaining institutions in the U.S.S.R. which still embody the residues of traditional Jewish values and where Jews may still forgather formally as Jews. The objective of this policy is clearly to intimidate and atomize Soviet Jewry, to isolate it both from its past and from its brethren in other parts of the world, to destroy its specifically Jewish spirit.

This policy of cultural and religious repression is conducted within the charged atmosphere of a virulent press campaign against Judaism. From it the image of the Jew emerges in traditional anti-Semitic stereotypes. The majority of the articles appear in the provincial press—in the larger cities, frequently the capitals, of the various republics, primarily the Russian Republic, the Ukraine, and White Russia. These are the regions where the bulk of Soviet Jewry lives and where "popular" anti-Semitism is still widespread and endemic.

A study of a dozen such publications reveals that the following themes recur repeatedly:

1. The stereotype that emerges most blatantly is that of Jews as money worshipers. Rabbis and lay leaders of the synagogues are consistently portrayed as extorting money from the faithful for ostensibly religious

purposes, their object in fact being to feather their own nests. Thus, whether it is the religious service itself or some ancient rite, it is all presided over by religious figures who are "in reality" money-grubbing thieves.

2. Judaism is constantly denigrated. All its rites are mocked in a manner which contrasts harshly with the Soviet Union's boasts of religious toleration. Circumcision, for example, is denounced in the crudest terms as a barbarous and unhealthful ritual: "The priests of the synagogue offer the regular sacrifice to their God Jehovah."

3. Drunkenness in the synagogue is another favorite theme. The scandalous rogues who pocket the money innocently contributed by the believers are shown as devoted to drink—guzzlers who confuse their prayers under the influence of alcohol. The leader of a synagogue burial society is quoted as saying: "In booze—I believe; in God—I don't."

4. Brawling is alleged to occur frequently in the synagogue, invariably over the division of the ill-gotten profits from religious "speculation." The newspapers "name the names" of the religious "mis-leaders" allegedly involved and frequently give their addresses and public positions, if any.

5. In these articles Jews are often used to inform on fellow Jews and to denounce Judaism. Many articles are signed by Jews; some contain recantations, usually by elderly men, of their religious faith.

6. A favorite device is for the writer to single out for special attention the adult children of elderly religious Jews. They are usually named and their public positions (teacher, engineer, nurse, etc.) noted, as well as their places of work and, where relevant, their party membership. Thus not only the parents but the presumably loyal, non-religious Communist children are held up to public obloquy, in a not very subtle effort to exert social blackmail on them.

7. Propaganda assaults on private prayer meetings are also frequent. Since many synagogues throughout the country are closed, Jews have taken to forgathering in each other's homes for prayers. Such gatherings are frowned upon, indeed unauthorized, and have regularly been dispersed, and their members warned and even punished. Articles list those who organize and attend such prayer meetings.

8. Perhaps the most ominous of all the themes is the consistent portrayal of the tenets and practitioners of traditional Judaism as potentially

or actually subversive. The following references are typical: "The Jewish clericals and bourgeois nationalists provide grist for the mills of our class enemies, distract workers from their class and Communist interests, and weaken their consciousness with chauvinist poison." "The traditions bolstered by the synagogue are doubly harmful. First of all, they contribute to the perpetuation of the false religious world outlook. Secondly, they serve as an instrument for the propagation of bourgeois political views which are alien to us."

This must be contrasted with the resolution of the Central Committee of the Communist Party, signed by Premier Khrushchev on November 10, 1954, and re-echoed in *Pravda* on August 21, 1959: "It must not be forgotten that there are citizens who, though actively participating in the country's life and faithfully fulfilling their civic duty, still remain under the influence of various religious beliefs. Towards these the Party has already demanded, and will always demand, a tactful, considerate attitude. It is especially stupid to put these under political suspicion because of their religious convictions."

These standards have been clearly violated where Jews and Judaism are concerned. In the Soviet Union, official atheism affects all religious groups; but it is only with regard to Jews and Judaism that the theme of lack of patriotism, disloyalty and subversion is injected into the propaganda. When the religion of the Russian Orthodox, the Armenian Orthodox, the Georgian Orthodox, the Baptist, or the Moslem is attacked in the press he does not thereby come under political suspicion, nor does he feel his loyalty impugned either as a member of a given nationality or as a Soviet citizen. By the same token, the mass of non-believing Russians, Armenians, Georgians, or Uzbeks do not feel that they are involved when the religious members of their nationality see their religion attacked in the official propaganda.

But with the Jews it is different. Because of the persistence of "popular" anti-Semitism, subtly encouraged from above, an attack upon the religious Jew and the portrayal of the Jewish image in traditional anti-Semitic stereotypes is felt even by the non-religious Jew as somehow involving him too. And he is not far wrong in feeling that many of his non-Jewish neighbors understand it in the same way. Small wonder, then, that—in the absence of a consistent educational campaign against anti-

Semitism, such as was conducted in Lenin's time—an assault upon the Jewish religion will be sensed, by Jews and non-Jews alike, as an assault upon the entire Jewish group.

In such an atmosphere, it is hardly surprising that Jews should be subject to a subtle policy of discrimination in employment, education and other sectors of public life. That policy may be summarized in the phrase attributed, perhaps apocryphally but none the less aptly, to a top-level Soviet leader: "Don't hire, don't fire, don't promote."

A few especially gifted or brilliant Jewish individuals can still be found within the Soviet leadership. Many occupy positions in the middle ranks of professional, cultural, and economic life. But virtually all face potent discriminatory measures in key "security-sensitive" areas of public life. The instrumentality for this exclusion, carried out quietly and informally, is the nationality listing on the internal passport. Thus, Jews have virtually disappeared from positions of major responsibility in the diplomatic service and, with rare exceptions, in the armed forces. This contrasts sharply with the situation that prevailed from 1917 to the late 1930's. The proportion in higher education, science, the professions, and political life has also been declining for many years. The key to the decrease is the system of nationality quotas in university admissions. A considerable body of evidence points to the existence of a *numerus clausus* for Jews in the universities and, in some cases, of a *numerus nullus*. This explains the decline of Jewish representation in important activities.

The extent of the decline in higher education is reflected in the fact that Jews today represent 3.1 percent of all students in higher education, as contrasted with 13.5 percent in 1935. During this twenty-seven-year period, the Jewish proportion of the population decreased merely from 1.6 to 1.1 percent. There is no way of accounting for this drastic decline in a country with an expanding economy and growing opportunities—except by discrimination.

Even the present 3.1 percent is a skewed figure, for it fails to take account of two decisive factors. In the first place, the category "higher education," as given in Soviet statistics, lumps together both universities and many other types of specialized academies such as teacher training schools, music conservatories and journalism institutes. Jews have a strong position in the latter types, and this fact artificially raises the total by balancing out the much lower proportion of Jews in the universities as such. Secondly, it is estimated that 90 percent of Soviet Jews are urbanized. Most universities are located in the larger cities and recruit their student bodies from the children of the urban intelligentsia, in which the Jews have traditionally occupied a leading position. To get a more accurate measure of Jewish representation in higher education in proportion to the population, the Jewish proportion would have to be compared not with the percentage of Jews in the total population of a given republic, but with the percentage of Jews in an urban university area.

As for the professions, the declining proportion of Jews has been as much as admitted by Premier Khrushchev and Culture Minister Furtseva themselves as a matter of policy. (In making such admissions, they have referred to the necessity of making room for "our own intelligentsia"— clearly giving away their feeling that the Jews are not truly indigenous.) In general, the proportion of non-Jewish nationalities among professionals has been rising at a very rapid rate, but that of the Jews at a much slower rate. For example, since 1955 the number of Russians and Ukrainians in science has increased by 40 percent, that of the Jews by 25 percent. In 1955, Jews constituted 11 percent of Soviet scientists; the figure was 10.2 percent by 1958 and 9.8 percent by 1960. Even this figure is deceptively high, for it includes a substantial number of an older generation who had far freer access to the universities and the professions in the '20's and '30's. It is obviously the Jewish youth who are hardest hit by the declining rate; they have to be very good indeed even to get into the universities, and they find it increasingly difficult to enter the professions.

The disappearance of Jews from leadership positions in political life has been striking and dramatic. Soviet spokesmen have tried to counter this fact by noting recently that 7,623 Jews were elected to local soviets all over the country. This seems impressive until it is realized that, as of 1960, more than 1,800,000 such local deputies were elected. The "large" number of Jews thus comes to less than one-half of 1 percent. Moreover, in all but one of the Supreme Soviets of the 15 republics, the number of Jews is far below their proportion of the population.

When this pattern of discrimination is linked to other facets of Soviet policy toward the Jews, it becomes clear that they are considered a security-risk group—suspected of actual or potential disloyalty, of essential alienness.

Many nuances of the same pattern of hostility have been revealed in the massive campaign waged with increasing severity in the past few years against the widespread economic abuses that characterize so much of Soviet life. A series of decrees, beginning in May, 1961, called for capital punishment for such offenses as embezzlement of state property, currency speculation, and bribery. The authorities have made no attempt to conceal their concern over these activities or the fact that vast numbers of the population engage in them. Major pronouncements by leading officials have, indeed, given a picture of a country shot through with corruption —ironically, of a "capitalist" sort. All organs of the Party, the Komsomol, the State, the press, and other major institutions have been pressed into service in the campaign against it. The secret police, one of the last strongholds of Stalinism, plays a key role. And the public at large has been strenuously urged on to be vigilant, with all the overtones of vigilantism.

Though the campaign's objective may not be anti-Jewish, there is little doubt that it has had anti-Jewish implications and consequences, of which the authorities—and the secret police—cannot but be aware.

Thus the Soviet press has especially featured those trials that have resulted in death sentences (frequently accompanied by the denial of the right of appeal). To date, 36 such trials have been reported in 26 different cities.[7] In these trials, death sentences have been meted out to 70 individuals—of whom 42 (and possibly 45) are Jews. In a number of cases, the Jewish religious affiliation of some of the culprits was made explicit: the synagogue was portrayed as the locus of illegal transactions, religious Jews were mockingly described as money worshipers, the rabbi was shown as their accomplice, their family connections in Israel and the United States were pointed up. In general, the Jews are presented as people "whose only God is Gold," who flit through the interstices of the economy, cun-

7. Between 1961 and 1964, at least 250 persons were executed for economic crimes, more than half of them Jews. For elaboration of this point, see "Soviet Jews as Economic Criminals" below, pp. 115–126.—Ed.

ningly manipulate naïve non-Jewish officials, prey upon honest Soviet workers and cheat them of their patrimony. They are portrayed as the initiators and masterminds of the criminal plots; the non-Jews are depicted primarily as the recipients of bribes and as accomplices.

The ominous significance of this publicity is clear. It informs the conditioned Soviet reader that the government thinks the tiny community of Jews, which constitutes little more than 1 percent of the population, is responsible for nearly two-thirds—and in some areas 100 percent—of the economic crimes that warrant capital punishment. Anti-Semitic feelings are exacerbated. From many cities come reports of grumbling on the food queues: "The Jews are responsible for the shortages." Western travelers who were in Vilna during and immediately after a major economic trial in February, 1962—where all 8 accused were Jews, 4 of them receiving capital punishment and 4 lengthy prison terms—reported that the authorities mobilized the entire population to attend what was universally called the "Jewish show trial." The atmosphere of fright in the Jewish communities may be imagined.

In sum, Soviet policy places the Jews in an inextricable vise. They are allowed neither to assimilate, nor live a full Jewish life, nor to emigrate (as many would wish) to Israel or any other place where they might live freely as Jews. The policy stems, in turn, from doctrinal contradictions abetted by traditional anti-Jewish sentiments. On the one hand, the authorities want the Jews to assimilate; on the other hand, they irrationally fear the full penetration of Soviet life which assimilation implies. So the Jews are formally recognized as a nationality, as a religious group, as equal citizens—but are at the same time deprived of their national and religious rights as a group, and of full equality as individuals.

Though the Jews are considered a *Soviet* nationality, official doctrine has consistently denied the existence of a historic Jewish people as an entity, and official practice has always sought to discourage Soviet Jews from feeling themselves members of that entity throughout the world.

Soviet policy as a whole, then, amounts to spiritual strangulation—the deprivation of Soviet Jewry's natural right to know the Jewish past and to participate in the Jewish present. And without a past and a present, the future is precarious indeed.

TWO

Religious and Cultural Deprivations

Soviet Law and the Jews

BY *William Korey*

Since the inception of the Soviet State, the Jewish community has been accorded the legal status of a nationality. Even those Bolshevik ideologists, prior to the October Revolution, who denied that the Jewish community possessed the specific characteristics which they considered essential for nationhood, most notably a "closed territory of settlement" and a "large and stable stratum associated with the soil," nonetheless recognized in Jews a "common 'national character.'"

As early as March, 1914, V. I. Lenin drafted a thesis on nationality which clearly defined the future legal status of the Jewish community. This was to provide for "the repeal of all restrictions upon the rights of Jews, and, in general, of all restrictions based on a person's national descent." Significantly, a Communist Party resolution, adopted at its Tenth Congress in 1921, after referring to the "equality of nationalities" and to "the right of national minorities to free national development," specifically mentioned the Jews among a very small list of examples.

Formal political expression to the acknowledged legal status of a Jewish nationality was given in January, 1918, when a Commissariat for Jewish National Affairs was established as a special section of the People's Commissariat for National Affairs. Its principal task became the establishment of "the dictatorship of the proletariat" in the Jewish community—broadcasting the message of the Bolshevik Revolution to the Jewish masses.

Alongside the Jewish Commissariat (and its provincial sub-bodies) the Communist Party, in 1918, created "Jewish Sections" (*Yevsektsii*) whose task it was to carry out Communist Party policy and propaganda among Jewish workers in the Yiddish language and "to see to it that the Jewish masses have a chance to satisfy all their intellectual needs in that language . . ." While the Jewish Commissariat passed out of existence early in 1924 (along with the People's Commissariat itself), the Jewish Sections continued to maintain a checkered existence until January, 1930, when they, too, were liquidated. The legal classification of a Jewish nationality, however, was retained; the term is to be found in all official publications dealing with nationalities or indicating national categories.

In the specified functions of the Jewish Sections, the Yiddish language was formally recognized as integral to the legal identity of the Jewish nationality. Indeed, the Byelorussian Republic—which had the largest number of compact Jewish communities and where 90.7 percent of the Jews expressly stated, in the 1926 census, that Yiddish was their mother-tongue—made Yiddish one of its four official languages. In contrast, the teaching of Hebrew, after being barely tolerated for a few years, was finally proscribed by the authorities as "reactionary" and an instrument of Zionism. (In July, 1963, the Soviet Government finally allowed the publication of a massive Hebrew-Russian Dictionary, prepared by the late F. Shapiro, but it is clearly intended for students only.)

The Jewish community as such thus has a fixed legal status as a nationality; so too do individuals born of Jewish parents. Jewish legal identity in the U.S.S.R. is not a matter of personal choice but of strict juridical procedure: a Jew is ineluctably a member of the Jewish nationality. The determining legal factor here is not the distinctive attributes, supposed or real, of the ethnic group, but rather the simple biological fact of having been born of Jewish parents.

The legal classification permanently fixing the national identity of a person descended from Jewish parents was not established until late 1932, and, ironically, under circumstances which bore no direct relation to the question of nationality. On December 27, 1932, a decree was adopted by the Central Executive Committee and the Council of People's Commissars calling for the creation of a "single passport system" for the U.S.S.R.—a system which still exists. The decree stipulated that all passports (which were first issued in 1933) were to indicate the "nationality" of the bearer. Urban residents sixteen years of age and over were obliged to acquire passports.

The nationality of a passport bearer is listed virtually automatically. The registrant is required to produce papers specifying the nationality of each of his parents. If both are of the same nationality—which has typically been the case—then that nationality is inserted in "Point 5" of the passport. No voluntary choice is permitted: If both parents are Jewish, the youngster is listed as *Yevrei*—Jewish. The only option is in the case of parents of different nationalities. Then the sixteen-year-old may select either of the two nationalities as his own.

Since the passport is the principal means of identification in the U.S.S.R., not only in obtaining housing, but in applying for jobs and, indeed, in dealing with all government institutions, it has become a powerful means for discrimination on grounds of nationality. The possibilities for "passing" as a member of another nationality are severely limited.

This legal categorization has particular significance for the Jews, since, unlike most other nationalities, they lack a distinct geographic national base. There is, of course, the so-called Jewish Autonomous Region of Birobidzhan, established by decree of the Central Executive Committee of the U.S.S.R. on May 7, 1934. But despite government pronouncements in the mid-thirties recommending Birobidzhan as a "homeland" for Soviet Jews, the area, lacking in historical sentiment, attracted relatively few Jews as permanent residents; today only 8.8 percent of the region's population—14,270 persons—are Jews.

According to the census of 1959, Russia's 2,268,000 Jews are dispersed throughout all of the 15 Union republics: 38 percent in the Russian Republic; 37 percent in the Ukraine; 7 percent in Byelorussia; another 15 percent in Uzbekistan, Georgia, Lithuania, Moldavia, Latvia, and Estonia; and the balance of 95,000 in the remaining 6 republics. In all places they constitute a small minority, attaining their highest percentage of the population in Moldavia (3.3 percent) and in the Ukraine (2 percent). On the national level, Jews comprise but 1.09 percent of the total population.

These figures do not, however, reflect the relative numerical strength of the Jews in the U.S.S.R. nationality pattern. Actually, among the 108 nationalities that inhabit Soviet territory, Jews rank eleventh in numbers —and the numerical spread from seventh to eleventh place is less than three-quarters of a million. Nevertheless, the Jews are more vulnerable than most to abuses of the passport system.

Jewish dispersal, together with the fact that they are one of the most highly urbanized nationalities in the U.S.S.R. (95 percent live in urban areas), has no doubt accelerated the normal trend to linguistic assimilation. This is reflected in the 1959 census figures reporting the use of "mother-tongue" or "native language." In contrast to the census figures of 1926, when over 70 percent of Soviet Jews indicated Yiddish as their native language, the 1959 census reported only about 18 percent, or a little over 400,000 Jews, claiming Yiddish. (The figure of 20.8 percent, or 472,000 persons, often cited by both Western or Soviet analysts, is an error resulting from a misreading of the data, which was broken down to indicate whether respondents declared their native language to be that of their nationality, or Russian, or yet another language other than that of their nationality. 20.8 percent of the Jews were indeed reported as saying that their native language was that of their nationality, but in fact the "native language" or "mother-tongue"—*rodnoi yazik*—of the Jews of Georgia, Bukhara, and Daghestan is *not* Yiddish. The figures on the language declarations of these Jews were erroneously added to those of the other Soviet Jews, to arrive at a mistaken total.)

Census figures showed that Jews ranked lowest among Soviet nationalities in declaring that the official language of their nationality, namely Yiddish, was the one which they used. The overwhelming majority of most Soviet nationalities indicated that they used the "mother-tongue" of their respective nationalities. Other dispersed nationalities did show considerable linguistic assimilation, but by no means so great as that of the Jews: 45 percent of the Poles reported using their "mother-tongue"; 59 percent of the Gypsies; and 75 percent of the Germans.

Yakov Kantor, however, a Moscow sociologist specializing in Jewish culture, has stated that the structuring of the census questionnaire distorted and exaggerated the extent of this linguistic assimilation. In an analysis published by the Warsaw Jewish Historical Institute, Kantor noted that since the census instructions did not define what was meant by "native language" many Jews took it to mean "language spoken." Consequently, "many people who speak and read Yiddish, enjoy Yiddish books, and appreciate Yiddish plays, nevertheless indicated Russian as their langauge because they speak Russian at work, in the street, and even to an extent at home."

The distinctiveness of the Jewish community as a dispersed nationality is further complicated by the legal status accorded to the Jewish *religious* community. A government decree of June, 1944, which formally established the Council for the Affairs of Religious Cults, specifically mentioned the Jewish religious community among the approximately dozen faiths, other than the Russian Orthodox, which were granted formal status. (A Council for the Affairs of the Russian Orthodox Church had been established in 1943.)

Unlike the category of Jewish nationality, participation in the Jewish religious community is, from a legal viewpoint, exclusively a voluntary act on the part of the Jew (or any citizen), since everyone has the right "freely to choose his religion" or "to profess no religion at all . . ." An official government report to the United Nations states that "the laws in force in the Soviet Union on religious matters bar any state registration of citizens of the Soviet Union according to religion . . ."

Notwithstanding the voluntary character of membership in the Jewish religious community, the fact that the same root term—"Jew" or "Jewish" —is used for both the nationality and the religion makes the complete separation of the two in the public mind difficult. This is particularly apparent in the atheist propaganda campaign directed by the Communist Party. The Jewish religion is frequently attacked on grounds that it stimulates *nationalist* feelings, or that it expresses "national exclusiveness." In the mind of the reader of such propaganda, the Jew takes on the character of an objective category in which both nationality and religion are conjoined.

Nonetheless, despite the peculiarities of actual Jewish identification, the laws on Jewish status are clear. A Jew is entitled by law to a set of constitutionally prescribed rights embracing the areas of nationality, religion, and civil law. Lenin once said: "A constitution is a fiction when law and reality part, not when they meet." What follows is an inquiry into the laws governing the rights of Jews in the Soviet Union and the reality of their implementation.

As a distinctive nationality in the U.S.S.R., the Jewish community is formally entitled to a host of national rights, inscribed in law, that stretch back to the early days of the Soviet regime. Only a week after the seizure of power, on November 15, 1917, the government issued a formal Declaration of Rights of Peoples which proclaimed the "free development of national minorities and ethnic groups inhabiting Russian territory."

In keeping with this principle, the first Soviet Constitution of 1918 stipulated, in Article 22, that "to oppress national minorities or impose any limitations whatsoever on their rights" is "contrary to the fundamental laws" of the regime. Following the formation of the U.S.S.R. in 1922 and the enactment of the new Federal Constitution in 1924, the principle of equality of rights for nationalities was restated in the constitutions of the individual republics. Thus, the constitution of the RSFSR (1925), in Article 13, declared that "oppression of national minorities in whatever form, [or] any restriction of rights . . . is wholly incompatible with the fundamental laws of the Republic." The same Article stipulated that RSFSR citizens "have the right to use their native language freely in meetings, in the courts, in administrative bodies, and in public affairs." It further specified that national minorities "have the right to receive education in their native tongue." In both the Ukraine and Byelorussia, where sizable Jewish communities existed, statutes were passed safeguarding linguistic rights.

The decrees in the Ukraine and Byelorussia led in the twenties to the establishment of a complex of Jewish administrative and judicial institutions. With the stepped-up industrialization campaign of the thirties, however, which broke up old Jewish communities and dispersed their population to new industrial areas, the institutional complex—with the exception of the school system—disintegrated. By the end of 1940, according to Jacob Lestchinsky, there were still some 85,000 to 90,000 Jewish children

—about 20 percent of the Jewish student population—studying in schools where Yiddish was the language of instruction.

The 1936 Constitution of the U.S.S.R. no longer made reference to the right to use the native language in meetings, courts, and administrative bodies. However, it reaffirmed, in Article 121, the right to "instruction in schools . . . in the native language." Similar provisions existed in the constitutions of the Union republics and of the autonomous republics.

In August, 1962, the U.S.S.R. ratified the UNESCO Convention against Discrimination in Education, which obligated it, according to Article 5 (1c), "to recognize the right of members of national minorities to carry on their own educational activities, including the maintenance of schools . . . and the use or the teaching of their own language . . ."

Ratification of the UNESCO Convention was reflected earlier in a law adopted on April 16, 1959, in the Russian Republic "Concerning the Strengthening of the Connection of the Schools with Life and the Furthest Development of the System of People's Education in the RSFSR." The law, in Article 15, declared:

. . . education in schools will be conducted in the native language of the students. The right is given to parents to decide the language in which their children will be registered in schools.

A 1956 letter from the Deputy Minister of Education in the Russian Republic, A. Arsenyev, stated that Soviet law requires that in the event ten parents request an education for their children in their native tongue, "the organization of such a class in any school" will be arranged.

These numerous laws and decrees notwithstanding, there is today in the entire length and breadth of the U.S.S.R. not a single Yiddish school or a single Yiddish class. The Jewish schools in the Ukraine and Byelorussia that were destroyed by the Nazis were never reopened. Afterward, efforts to re-establish a Yiddish school system in Lithuania came to nought. And by 1946, the few Jewish schools in Birobidzhan were closed.

Two types of arguments have been advanced by Soviet authorities to explain the absence of Jewish schools. One argument invokes the burdensome costs involved in establishing schools for a widely dispersed nationality. The validity of this argument becomes suspect in the light of recent school developments involving the Germans, another dispersed minority in the Soviet Union.

Numbering over 1,600,000 persons (according to the 1959 census) and, since a decree of August 28, 1941, dispersed over a wide area embracing eastern parts of the RSFSR and almost a dozen other Union republics, the former German inhabitants of the Volga were fully restored to their national rights by a 1964 decree of the Presidium of the U.S.S.R. Supreme Soviet. This decree provides that "districts in a number of provinces, territories and republics containing a German population have secondary and elementary schools where teaching is conducted in German or German is taught to children of school age . . ."

The second argument offered to explain the absence of a Jewish school system is the extent of Jewish assimilation. A parliamentary delegation of French socialists was told by Khrushchev in 1956 that assimilation is so advanced that "even if Jewish schools were established, very few would attend them voluntarily." This type of argument raises more questions than it answers. For assuming there are insufficient numbers to build a Jewish school, why are there no special Yiddish classes? If all that is required is the request of ten parents to provide such classes, is it conceivable that in areas of large Yiddish-speaking populations (as in Vilna, Kovno, Riga, and elsewhere in the Western Ukraine, Western Byelorussia, and Moldavia), no such request would be forthcoming?

Simply to ask these questions is to suggest that school administrators are determined to discourage such requests, or to avoid informing parents of their right to make them. A recent article in the Soviet German weekly, *Neues Leben*, criticized a village high school principal for his failure to inform the sizable German community of its legal rights to request teaching in the "native language." Might this failure be deliberate with regard to the Jews?

Perhaps we should ask a more fundamental question: Does not Jewish assimilation at least in part *result* from this lack of specific Jewish institutions for perpetuating Jewish language and culture, rather than the converse? In 1964, Yakov Kantor observed:

Such things as schools of all kinds, museums, theatres, libraries, even sections of academies, and so on, all work toward the consolidation, the support, and the strengthening of minority cults.

Unhappily the Jews belong to that group of national minorities where such supporting and strengthening factors for their cultures do not exist. They have not existed for a number of years, since the time of the reinforced cult of personality.

For Kantor, as the word "unhappily" implies, the absence of schools and other cultural institutions is the decisive factor in causing assimilation. It is significant that Kantor's analysis was published in Warsaw, and not in the Soviet Union, where he lived until his death in September, 1964.

The complete destruction of the complex of Jewish cultural institutions followed, by just a few years, the elimination of the last Jewish schools in the U.S.S.R. By 1946–47, a large part of what remained from the extensive prewar publishing structure had been dismantled. Then in November, 1948, *Der Emes*, the Moscow publishers of the thrice-weekly *Eynikayt* and a total of 110 publications during the three postwar years, was shut down. Early in 1949 the famed Jewish State Theater in Moscow was closed, a year after its leading actor, Solomon Mikhoels, was murdered by the secret police. (The Jewish Anti-Fascist Committee, of which he was a leading official, was dissolved in November, 1948. Most of its other officials were also liquidated.)

For eleven years the Jewish national scene in the U.S.S.R. was a cultural desert—no theater, no books, no publications (except for the *Birobidzhaner Shtern*, a small triweekly with a circulation of 1,000, published in Birobidzhan). The only linguistic sustenance was provided by popular Yiddish concerts performed by troupes of traveling singers. Then, beginning in 1959, a small trickle of publications began to appear: a total of nine books and a literary monthly, *Sovyetish Heymland*, begun in 1961 as a bimonthly, have since come on the scene. The most recent of the published novels, E. Schechtman's *Erev*, as well as a number of articles that appeared in *Sovyetish Heymland* during 1965, reveal a deep Jewish awareness and suggest the possibility of future development.

In contrast to the legal situation with regard to schools, there are no laws or statutes in the U.S.S.R. providing for the cultural rights of minorities. These rights, however, have been implicit in Party policy since the twenties. As early as March, 1921, the Tenth Party Congress resolved to assist nationalities in setting up "a press, schools, theaters, community centers, and cultural and educational institutions generally, using the native language." In a famous speech at the Communist University of the Toilers of the East in May, 1925, Stalin provided an elaborate dialectical rationale for Party support of "national cultures." They must, he said, "be given an opportunity to develop, expand, and reveal all their potentialities in order to establish conditions for their fusion into a single common culture with a single common language."

The early years of the postwar period were marked by a decisive reversal of this policy so far as the Jewish national culture was concerned, and the new line was implemented by arbitrary administrative actions. This new policy has been continued by Stalin's successors, with the exception of the minor changes introduced since 1959 and noted above. Future developments involving the Jews can properly be understood in the context of Party decisions taken at the Congress in 1961. The ultimate objective of a "single common culture" as expressed by Stalin has become even more urgent. In its new program, the Party calls for "the effacement of national distinctions . . . including language distinctions."

However, it was also noted at the Party Congress that quite apart from the expressed goal of "drawing together" nationalities, a contrary development of "tempestuous all-round [national] development" was now taking place. For a number of nationalities this is clearly the case. Professor Richard Pipes has shown that a number of major Soviet national groups, in those areas in which they enjoy a numerical and administrative preponderance, are acquiring a "linguistic hegemony" of their own, counterposed to the all-Russian hegemony in the country as a whole. Such hegemonies, he observes, indicate the continued "viability" of the nationalities. Yakov Kantor has also taken note of these two opposing tendencies— assimilation on the one hand and the strengthening of minority cultures and languages on the other—but he underscores the fact that the decisive factor lies in the presence or absence of vital institutions. In the case of the Jews it is precisely because such institutions have been systematically dismantled, in violation of rights inscribed in Soviet law and expressed in Party policy, that the victory of the first tendency has been facilitated.

Dedicated to scientific materialism and to the conviction that religion is the opiate of the masses, the Soviet Communist Party conducts an unceasing, vigorous campaign against all religions. At the same time, however, the Soviet State distinguishes the Party's attitude toward religion from its own:

There are fundamental differences between the two [State and Party]. In its legislation on religion, the Soviet State . . . accords completely unrestricted freedom of worship to citizens of the Soviet Union who are believers.

The rights guaranteed to recognized religions are spelled out in the still valid Decree of the Council of People's Commissars of January 23, 1918, in the Order of the All-Union Central Executive Committee and the Council of People's Commissars of the RSFSR of April 8, 1929, and in the various criminal codes. The Soviet Government has provided the United Nations with a detailed listing of these rights, together with a commentary, in two major documents, available as *Study of Discrimination in the Matter of Religious Rights and Practices*, Conference Room Paper No. 35, and *Manifestations of Racial Prejudice and Religious Intolerance*, Doc. A/5473/Add.1.

At the very heart of the January, 1918, decree is a statement on the equality of all religions. In Article 2, the decree abolished the position of dominance formerly enjoyed by the Russian Orthodox Church, by prohibiting governmental actions that would "establish any kind of privileges or advantages on the grounds of the religious affiliations of citizens." The Soviet Government, in commenting upon this provision, stressed that the legislation was designed to respect "scrupulously" the "equality of faiths"; the State, therefore, "accords no special privileges to any one religion over any other."

In a number of vital respects, where Judaism is concerned, the principle of equality of religious rights is observed only in the breach. This became particularly apparent in the immediate postwar period when, according to one authority, "favorable treatment" by the State was given to Russian Orthodoxy, Islam, and other religions, while Judaism was held in "disfavor."

One crucial area is the right to organize a central or federative body. The order of April 8, 1929, entitles:

. . . religious communities of the same denomination . . . [to] form religious associations which may or may not coincide geographically with the administrative subdivisions of the Union of Soviet Socialist Republics . . . and to

71

set up *religious centers*. . . . These *religious centers*, which are governed by their own rules and regulations, may hold republic or All-Union congresses, church councils, and other conferences on matters related to the administration of church affairs. . . . (Emphasis added)

The order further notes that the "religious centers" may publish "periodicals and the necessary devotional literature."

Unlike other recognized religious bodies, Judaism has lacked any semblance of a central co-ordinating structure since 1926. In August, 1919, the Soviet Government banned the Central Board of Jewish Communities, and no central body has been allowed to replace it. A Conference of Rabbis of the Soviet Union met for the last time in 1926. The meeting took place in Korosten with twenty-five rabbis—principally from the local and nearby areas—as delegates and ninety more rabbis as invited guests.

The absence of a central or federative Jewish structure results in the fragmentation of religious life and limits effective resistance to the anti-religious campaign. It also makes the enjoyment of specified (and unspecified) rights difficult, if not impossible. Thus, while the "religious centers" of other faiths are in a position to publish periodicals and devotional literature, Judaism finds this task virtually impossible. It publishes no periodical, and what is more pertinent, it has not published a Hebrew Bible since the late twenties. In contrast, the Russian Orthodox Church printed 50,000 copies of a 1926 edition of their Bible in 1957; the Baptists, in 1958, printed 10,000 copies of the Bible; the Moslems in 1958 printed 9,000 copies of the Koran and brought out still another edition in 1962.

Jewish prayer books are scarce. The State has assured those faiths having no "religious centers" a supply of the "necessary paper and the use of printing plants," yet this privilege has been only rarely extended to Judaism. In 1957, for the first time since the twenties, a printing of the *siddur* (prayer book) was permitted in an edition of a mere 3,000 copies. Recently, the Chief Rabbi of Moscow announced that the State would soon allow the publication of an additional 10,000 copies. It is apparent, however, that even so the supply will hardly meet the demand.

Without a "religious center," Judaism has also been deprived of the opportunity to produce such essential devotional articles as the *tallith* (prayer shawl) and *tefillin* (phylacteries). The Soviet Government points out that it permits "religious organizations to set up installations such as candle factories and icon printing studios for the manufacture of the requisite articles for religious worship." This right becomes meaningless without the presence of a "religious center."

Of even greater significance is the fact that the existence of "religious centers" enables the religions of the U.S.S.R. to enjoy formal contacts with their co-religionists abroad. A lengthy U.N. report on this subject by the Soviet Government in 1963 shows, indirectly, how Judaism is harmfully affected. Every major religion except Judaism is mentioned as having formal affiliations with co-religionists abroad.

This situation was tacitly acknowledged and explained at a U.N. seminar in Yugoslavia in the summer of 1965. The Soviet representative insisted that since individuals have no status in international law, citizens of an ethnic or religious group cannot be accorded the right to associate with international bodies composed of the same ethnic or religious affiliation. Such status, he argued, can only be conferred on duly recognized organizations. The fact that Judaism has no "religious center" in the U.S.S.R. precludes its right to associate with co-religionists abroad. Only at the very end of the seminar did the Soviet representative agree to accept the principle of an individual's right of association. Whether or not it will be put into practice is still uncertain.

Besides permitting formal contacts between religious organizations, the Soviet Government allows many theological students to journey abroad and study at foreign seminaries or religious educational institutions. Once again, as the 1963 report from the Soviet Government to the U.N. indicates, Judaism is an exception.

Nor, for the most part, are Jews permitted to leave Russia to be reunited with their families in Israel—despite the fact that in July, 1960, Premier Khrushchev officially sanctioned the principle of voluntary family reunion and certain ethnic groups have been expressly allowed to enjoy that right. Between 1956 and 1960, the Soviet Government, for example, allowed some 2,000 Spaniards living in the U.S.S.R. to travel to Spain "to live with their own people, to share its destiny," as an article in *Literaturnaya Gazeta* expressed it. Tens of thousands of Armenians from a number of countries have been vigorously encouraged since 1946 to rejoin their people in Soviet Armenia. In 1956, Khrushchev told Professor Jerome Davis: "I am sure that the time will come when all [Soviet] Jews . . . who want to go to Israel will be able to do so." Clearly, the "time" has not yet arrived.

The anti-religious propaganda campaign directed against Judaism displays certain distinctive features that have ramifications beyond the Party-supervised anti-religious effort itself. A 1954 policy resolution of the Central Committee of the Party, which provides guidelines for the anti-religious propaganda effort, warns against "offensive attacks of any sort against believers and the clergy," and calls for a "tactful" and "considerate" approach toward those who "still remain under the influence of various religious beliefs." The resolution specifically deplores the placing of "Soviet citizens under political suspicion because of their religious convictions."

Despite the warning against the use of offensive language, however, anti-Judaism propaganda has frequently been characterized by the kind of vulgarity that stimulates and reinforces anti-Semitic stereotypes. Synagogue leaders have often been depicted as money-worshipers who use the religious service, kosher slaughtering, religious burial, *matzoth* baking, and other ritual practices to exploit a duped congregation. A typical example is an article which appeared in a Minsk newspaper in 1961: "Money! That is the God of the Minsk Jewish religious community and its aides." Or from the notorious *Judaism without Embellishment:* "What is the secular God [of the Jews]? Money. Money—that is the jealous God of Israel." And even after the Party's Ideological Commission acknowledged that this book carried anti-Semitic overtones, it recommended as a "useful publication" another book, by A. Osipov, which contained such crudities as: "Where Jews are concerned, the principal blood-sucker turns out to be God himself," and "The first thing we come across is the preaching of intolerance, the bloody extermination of people of other faiths . . . God recommends real racial discrimination to the Jews."

Another distinctive characteristic of the anti-Judaism campaign has been to attribute to religious practitioners potential or actual disloyalty to the regime—this despite the 1954 resolution prohibiting such attacks. Judaism has been depicted as an instrument of the State of Israel, which, in turn, is linked with American imperialism. One typical article summarized it as follows: "Judaism kills love for the Soviet motherland." A more recent article, written in February, 1965, charges Judaism with conducting "ideological subversion . . . of the working Jews in our country . . ."

Current Soviet law against incitement to hatred is limited to national and racial agitation. The earlier criminal code had provided prison sentences for those engaging in "propaganda and agitation" aimed at arousing "religious enmities" as well. The new code deleted the reference to religion—as Soviet commentators have argued—because there have been no prosecutions on religious grounds for a number of years. But other Soviet legal specialists have observed that religious intolerance may be a veiled form of national hostility and hence, punishable under the current criminal code. It remains to be seen whether this interpretation will receive support. But it is of interest to note that the crudities which characterized the treatment of Judaism have considerably declined in recent months. "Extreme caution" has been urged in dealing with religious believers, to avoid offering "offense to religious feelings." Nonetheless, the religious rights of Jews cannot be said to equal those enjoyed by other major religions in the U.S.S.R.

In response to charges of discrimination against the Jewish community as such, on either national or religious grounds, Soviet authorities and spokesmen usually shift the basis of discussion by pointing to statistics showing the extent to which Jews participate in numerous occupations and various aspects of public life. Stress is thus placed upon the rights of Jews *as individuals*, and the question is arbitrarily changed from one of *communal* rights to one of *civil* rights. What, then, we must ask, is the state of Jewish civil rights?

Under the czars, severe limitations were put on the civil rights of Jews, with regard to place of residence, military service, participation in the government or in elections, schooling, etc. The very first decree of the Provisional Government that took power following the overthrow of the czar, in March, 1917, abolished all ethnic, religious, and social discrimination.

The Bolshevik seizure of power in November, 1917, was accompanied almost immediately by assurances concerning hard-won civil rights. On November 15, 1917, the new regime issued a Declaration of Rights, signed jointly by Lenin as Head of Government and by Stalin as Commissar of Nationalities, which formally abolished "all national and national-religious privileges and restrictions." The first Soviet Constitution reaffirmed the declaration at least so far as non-discrimination on ethnic grounds was concerned. And, following the formation of the U.S.S.R. in 1922, the new Republic Constitution repeated, with slight variations, the earlier formulations on civil rights.

The 1936 Constitution of the U.S.S.R. places historic emphasis upon the civil rights of all Soviet citizens:

Any direct or indirect restriction of the rights of, or conversely, the establishment of any direct or indirect privileges for citizens on account of their race or nationality . . . is punishable by law.

Constitutional provisions on civil rights are supported by articles in the new criminal codes. Article 74 of the recently adopted criminal code of the RSFSR (January 1, 1961), which is entitled "Infringement of National and Racial Equal Rights," specifies that "any direct or indirect privileges" on grounds of race or nationality will be punished by deprivation of freedom for a period of from six months to three years or by exile from two to five years.

In a number of areas, Jews do in fact enjoy the civil rights guaranteed them by law. Residential restrictions are non-existent, nor are there any barriers to participation in various aspects of social life—the Party, trade unions, army, the social services, clubs. Employment opportunities in a number of fields—particularly in science, medicine, law, and the arts—are wide-spread, as available data indicate.

However, there is considerable evidence that, despite the numerous constitutional provisions and criminal statutes, discrimination against Jews in a number of vital and decision-making fields does exist. Indeed, in some instances, unpublished governmental regulations have been issued, in written or oral form, calling for quotas to limit the number of Jews in certain specified areas. And there is no evidence that the criminal codes have been used to punish anyone for discriminating against Jews on racial or national grounds.

It is clear that opportunities for employment in administration and in various governmental bureaus have been subject to discriminatory quota regulations. Certainly this was not the case in the twenties. But the thirties and forties were characterized by a sharp drop in the percentages of Jews employed in these areas. Three interviews in 1956 with top Soviet officials revealed that the central government had consciously established quota systems to restrict Jewish employment, and that even sharper quota devices were installed in the governments of various Union republics.

The first interview was conducted with Khrushchev and other officials by a visiting parliamentary delegation of the French Socialist Party. At the third meeting, held on May 12, Khrushchev said:

At the outset of the Revolution, we had many Jews in the leadership of the Party and State. They were more educated, maybe more revolutionary than the average Russian. In due course we have created new cadres. . . .

Should the Jews want to occupy the foremost positions in our republics now, it would naturally be taken amiss by the indigenous inhabitants. The latter would ill receive these pretensions, especially as they do not consider themselves less intelligent or less capable than the Jews. . . .

In a second interview, the following month, the Minister of Culture, Yekaterina Furtseva, told a correspondent of the *National Guardian:*

The government has found in some of its departments a heavy concentration of Jewish people, upward of 50 percent of the staff. Steps were taken to transfer them to other enterprises, giving them equally good positions and without jeopardizing their rights.

The third interview was conducted in August by J. B. Salsberg, a former Canadian Communist leader, with a number of key Soviet officials. One of them corroborated Furtseva's statement. Six years later, Khrushchev was to return to the same theme in an unpublished speech delivered at a meeting of Soviet artists held on December 17, 1962. He told the audience that if Jews were to occupy too many top positions it would tend to create anti-Semitism.

Although these interviews and the Khrushchev speech were withheld from the Russian public and appeared only in the Western press, the facts about restrictions and the use of quotas were nonetheless known to many in the Soviet population. In March, 1962, at a meeting of the Central Committee, the academician Konstantin Skriabin, speaking on the importance of appointing competent cadres in the scientific field, critically commented, in an indirect manner, upon the misuse of the passport.

From my point of view, a scientist should not be evaluated by his passport but by his head, from the point of view of his ability and social usefulness.

An article in the Party theoretical journal, *Kommunist*, in June, 1963, further confirmed that quotas had been widely used in the training and placement of cadres in various Union republics. (The use of quotas in deciding admission to Soviet universities, and its impact upon Jews, has been extensively documented by Professor N. DeWitt, formerly of the Harvard Russian Research Center.)

An editorial that appeared in *Pravda* on September 5, 1965, suggests that the discriminatory employment devices used against Jews may harmfully affect the current efforts to maximize production. After stating that Lenin had "wrathfully assailed any manifestations of nationalism whatsoever, and, in particular, demanded an unceasing 'struggle against anti-Semitism, that malicious exaggeration of racial separateness and national enmity,'" the editorial declared:

It is necessary to remember that the growing scale of Communist construction requires a constant exchange of cadres among the people. Therefore any manifestations of national separateness in the *training and employment* of personnel of various nationalities in the Soviet republics are intolerable. (Emphasis added)

The significance of the editorial lay in the fact that it was the first time in at least two decades that the principal organ of the Party had inveighed against anti-Semitism, and had given emphasis to its condemnation by quoting the authority of Lenin. The editorial's importance was further underscored by the fact that it was widely reprinted in provincial newspapers throughout the country. Apparently, Skriabin's warning had been heeded by an increasing number of authorities. Whether the editorial means that new policy directives will be issued to reverse earlier instructions on both a national and local level is, as yet, uncertain.

Patterns of discrimination are also apparent in political life. Representation of Jews in the Supreme Soviet has dropped drastically since the thirties. The percentage of Jewish representation in this body, and even more so in the Supreme Soviets of almost all of the fifteen Union republics (and in local Soviets as well), is far below the Jewish percentage of the total population or that of individual republics. Similarly, available data suggest a pattern of discrimination in agencies involving foreign contact—

the Ministry of Foreign Affairs and the Ministry of Foreign Trade. A policy of exclusion is especially noticeable in the elitist Central Committee of the Party, where until the late thirties the percentage of Jews was high.

Besides banning discrimination on national and racial grounds, Soviet statutes make overt expressions of anti-Semitism a state crime. As early as July, 1918, the Council of People's Commissars issued an order aimed at destroying the anti-Semitic movement "at its roots" by outlawing "pogromists and persons inciting to pogroms." The RSFSR criminal code of 1922 provided a minimum of one year solitary confinement (and death in time of war) for "agitation and propaganda arousing national enmities and dissensions." The same republic's criminal code of 1927 provided for loss of freedom for "no less than two years" for "propaganda or agitation aimed at arousing national or religious enmities and dissension," as well as for the dissemination, manufacture, or possession of inflammatory literature. The present RSFSR criminal code, which went into effect in 1961, reads:

Propaganda or agitation aimed at inciting racial or national enmity or discord . . . is punishable by loss of personal freedom for a period of six months to three years, or exile from two to five years. (Article 74)

This section of the code is based upon Article 11 of the Fundamentals of Criminal Jurisprudence of the U.S.S.R. adopted by the Supreme Soviet in December, 1958.

During the twenties, the Soviet press from time to time reported instances of anti-Semitic activity and the judicial proceedings taken against offenders. At the same time Party organs took a strong condemnatory stand against anti-Semitism and called for vigilant and energetic action against its manifestations. In the thirties, the number of anti-Semitic incidents declined sharply and press reportage of such incidents became infrequent. That anti-Semitism would not, however, be countenanced by the Party was made clear to the public in a speech by V. M. Molotov, Chairman of the Council of People's Commissars, to the Eighth Soviet Congress in November, 1936, and carried in *Pravda*.

By contrast, the immediate postwar period was marked not only by an absence of condemnatory references to anti-Semitism, but in 1949–52, by a campaign against "cosmopolitanism," an open public incitement against Jews that reached its climax in the dangerously anti-Jewish atmosphere of early 1953, stirred up by the "doctors' plot." The death of Stalin and the subsequent exposure of the plot as a fraud, fabricated by the organs of state security, brought an end to the anti-Semitic provocation.

But neither *Pravda* nor any other major organ nor, indeed, any top Soviet official took the occasion then or later to identify the plot as specifically anti-Semitic, or to use it for a public educational campaign against anti-Semitism. Even in Khrushchev's secret speech at the Twentieth Party Congress in 1956, which disclosed some shocking details of the episode, no reference was made to its anti-Jewish character. Indeed, Khrushchev was later to imply in a letter to Bertrand Russell that the plot, in his judgment, did not involve an anti-Semitic policy.

Until recently, no specific editorial condemnation of anti-Semitism has appeared in the principal organs of the U.S.S.R. No specific court cases involving Article 74, if they have taken place, have been reported in the press. And, with one exception, the Soviets have not publicly dealt with charges about incidents or propaganda of an anti-Semitic nature which have been reported in the Western press.

The exception is the book *Judaism without Embellishment*, written by T. Kichko and published in October, 1963, by the Ukrainian Academy of Sciences. The 192-page pamphlet depicts Judaism as fostering hypocrisy, bribery, greed, and usury, and links it with Zionism, Israel, Jewish bankers, and Western capitalists in a worldwide conspiracy. The vulgarities of the text were illustrated in a series of viciously anti-Semitic caricatures. Only after worldwide protests, including outspoken condemnation by leading Western Communist parties, did Soviet authorities finally react with some vigor. The Central Committee Ideological Commission, in April, 1964, criticized the book for "erroneous statements and illustrations likely to offend believers and which might be interpreted in a spirit of anti-Semitism." The wording of the resolution was somewhat vague: the book itself was not specifically identified as anti-Semitic, nor was its author accused of violating Article 66 of the criminal code of the Ukraine (similar to Article 74 of the RSFSR Code).

If some action was taken on the Kichko book, however, nothing was done about a similar book by F. S. Mayatsky, published in 1964, which used source material prepared during the "doctors' plot" to illustrate an alleged conspiracy between Zionism, Jewish bankers, and Western intelligence agencies. During the intense campaign against economic crimes (1961–64), the press on a number of occasions emphasized the Jewish national origin of those charged with and executed for economic crimes. But no prosecutor or newspaper was singled out for criticism by the authorities, and Khrushchev publicly denounced the charge of anti-Semitism, terming it "a crude concoction, a vicious slander on the Soviet people, on our country."

Only very recently have statements condemning anti-Semitism appeared in the Soviet press. In July, 1965, *Pravda* published a speech by Premier A. N. Kosygin delivered at a large rally in Riga, Latvia. The Premier denounced "the manifestation of nationalism, great-power chauvinism, racism, anti-Semitism" as "absolutely alien and in contradiction to our world view." Whether these statements will signal an educational effort to eliminate anti-Semitic manifestations, using the full force of Soviet law, is uncertain. Such an effort might be considered necessary in order to cope with problems impeding national production. For the present, however, the enforcement of laws on anti-Semitism leaves much to be desired.

The constitutional "fiction," to use Lenin's term, which exists in regard to Jewish rights in the Soviet Union has set in motion a paradox which does violence to a principal Communist objective. On the one hand, the "fiction" of nationality rights for Jews serves the higher Party aim of assimilation; but, on the other, the "fiction" of civil rights psychologically stirs a national consciousness, an awareness that one's nationality, as indicated in the passport, really defines one's identity. Those who have spent some time in the Soviet Union have testified that the various discriminatory practices have induced many Jews, particularly the young, who no longer speak Yiddish and know nothing about Jewish history or Jewish culture, to become keenly aware of their Jewishness.

Since the ordinary channels for expressing this Jewish consciousness are severely restricted, it is hardly surprising that substitute forms of expression become manifest. They may take the form of an electrifying response to a reading of Yevtushenko's "Babi Yar," attending a visiting Italian company's production of *The Diary of Anne Frank*, listening to a performance of Shostakovich's *13th Symphony* (based upon the Yevtushenko poem), assembling by the thousands outside the synagogue on *Simhath Torah*, or asking Jewish visitors from abroad innumerable questions about Israel. Clearly, Jewish self-identification remains vibrant despite increasing State pressures, and in many cases precisely because of the contradictory nature of these pressures.

Sovyetish Heymland

BY *Joseph Brumberg*

The name of Aaron Vergelis is little known to the Jewish literary world outside of the Soviet Union. Professor Max Beloff, of All Souls College, Oxford, in a letter to the *London Jewish Chronicle*, published on November 22, 1963, wrote:

American Jews are presumably aware that Vergelis' name has been associated in a circumstantial way with the purge of the Soviet Jewish intelligentsia between 1948 and 1953, of which he is one of the few survivors. . . . Students of the Soviet Jewish scene are seemingly convinced of the truth of these allegations, and they would be consistent with Vergelis' own attacks upon the poets Haim Grade and Israel Emiot in *Literaturnaya Gazeta* on August 8, 1959, and, subsequently, in the *Morgn Freiheit* [Communist Yiddish daily, New York] on September 1, 1959. . . . Vergelis himself opposed the revival of Jewish literature after the end of the purge, and in his limited edition of some Yiddish classics he went so far as to state in his introduction to Sholom Aleichem that this writer's main characteristic was Russian patriotism.

Little is known of Vergelis' biography from official sources. He was born in the Ukraine in 1918. Ten years later, his parents moved to the abortive Jewish Autonomous Province of Birobidzhan. Later he studied linguistics and literature at the University of Moscow. He served in the Soviet Army during World War II and was wounded several times. Subsequently, he became associate editor of a military front newspaper. In 1945, he returned to Moscow. Three years later he turned up again in Birobidzhan, publishing essays and poems in the Soviet Union's sole Jewish periodical at the time, the *Birobidzhaner Shtern*. A few years later he returned to Moscow again. His first Russian-language book was published there, in 1956.

When Vergelis visited the United States, with the sole exception of the editor and staff of the Yiddish Communist daily, *Morgn Freiheit*, no representative of an American Jewish organization would consent to meet with him. Asked by a reporter for *The Day-Morning Journal* to comment on anti-Jewish propaganda in the Soviet Union, Vergelis vigorously denied its existence. He also denied that German nationality groups were being granted the kind of cultural facilities not available to Soviet Jews.

(The truth is that the 1,620,000 Germans in the Soviet Union have two weeklies: *Neues Leben*, published in Moscow, and *Rote Fahne*, published in the Altai territory, as well as a literary magazine, *Hand in Hand*. In addition, there is a regular German-language broadcast over the Soviet radio, and a number of schools have German as their language of instruction. Soviet Jewry, with a population of almost 3 million, have, in *Sovyetish Heymland*, one literary journal and nothing else.)

In view, then, of the singular circumstances surrounding the publication of *Sovyetish Heymland*—the fact that it is the *only* Yiddish periodical in the Soviet Union, and that it was published after a lapse of thirteen years of cultural barrenness—its appearance was greeted with general approval in the West: *The New York Times* went so far as to underline it as a "significant fact—a change in Soviet policy." In the Soviet Union itself, *Sovyetish Heymland* was prominently mentioned in numerous Russian magazines. The illustrated weekly *Ogoniok* featured a photostat of *Heymland's* first page and the table of contents of its first issue. Under a banner headline *Literaturnaya Gazeta* published on August 31, 1961, an interview with Vergelis, listing the contents of the first issue and stressing hopeful prospects. *Sovyetish Heymland's* arrival was prominently announced by *Sovyetskaya Kultura* on the same day, and many other Soviet magazines followed suit.

Sovyetish Heymland is of course under official auspices, being published by the Soviet Publishing House; like *Novy Mir*, it is an official organ of the Union of Soviet Writers. The physical surroundings in which it is edited are lavish. To quote an eyewitness account:

The first impression is very favorable. A building on Kirov Street in downtown Moscow . . . eight-room office . . . soft chairs, desks, telephones. Placards on each door, with the name of the room's occupants in both Russian and Yiddish. Newspapers from foreign countries available (which I unfortunately did not see—they are kept in a closet). I asked one of the staff whether I could read them. The answer was that only editors are permitted to read the foreign press.

The informed Western Jewish press had expected *Sovyetish Heymland* to be used as a Soviet propaganda weapon to refute the widespread charge of the persecution of Jewish culture in the Soviet Union. Within a few months after the periodical began appearing, this expectation seemed confirmed officially by Minister of Culture Furtseva, and by General David Dragunski, who is a Jew. (His "Three Journeys to Paris" was printed in the January–February, 1962, issue.) Both these public figures averred that *Sovyetish Heymland* was being published mainly for foreign consumption, and for purely political purposes. Paradoxically, however, this prognostication was to prove only partly true.

It is important to understand that *Sovyetish Heymland* could not be *essentially* different from any other literary magazine published in the Soviet Union. These may differ somewhat in their approach to works of art; may be more flexible or less flexible in interpreting "party-mindedness" as reflected in literature; may exhibit divergent attitudes toward "formalism" or "naturalism." Some may open their pages to younger poets, such as Yevtushenko, who write honestly about the crimes of the past and the shortcomings of the present; others may attack these same poets for "slandering Soviet reality." Yet basically all Soviet literary journals are expected to adhere to the principles of "socialist realism," and none can afford the luxury of honesty in the sense in which this term is understood in any democratic society. In the past few years, the

Communist Party has tolerated a more heterogeneous situation in the literary field than it did under Stalin. (The journals *Novy Mir* and *Oktyabr* are cases in point.) But it always reserves the right to prescribe the limits of what is and what is not permissible, esthetically as well as politically.

This being so, it was to be expected that a new magazine in the Yiddish language would never defy the dictates of the Communist Party. In fact, given the special sensitivity and past history of Jewish literary activity in the Soviet Union, one might have expected it to be "more Catholic than the Pope." The surprise is that *Sovyetish Heymland* has over the years succeeded in injecting a certain amount of specifically Jewish content into a Yiddish Communist publication.

The very first issue, published in September, 1961, is prefaced by a lengthy excerpt from the Draft Program of the Communist Party of the Soviet Union, entitled "The Bright Future of Mankind," and this "Letter to the Subscribers":

Dear Readers:

We transmit into your hands the first issue of the *Sovyetish Heymland*. Here you will feel the breath of our times, be informed of our literary life, hear the voice of the multi-national Soviet literature. Being a part of this literature will bring honor to the names inscribed on the title page. We are living in a time when the whole Soviet literature is animated with the ideas with which our whole nation is preparing itself for the 22nd Party Congress. . . . [A quotation from one of Khrushchev's speeches about art follows.] Events of gigantic proportions are taking place over the vast expanses of our country. . . . It is [therefore] the holy duty of our writers to find the warm words and lofty feelings appropriate to these historical events.

Solemn are the tasks facing our journal, *Sovyetish Heymland*. It has to illuminate all the aspects of the life of the Soviet nation. . . . The works already submitted to us by Soviet Yiddish writers give us the assurance that this journal will be able to reflect most of the important problems of our time on a high artistic level. The voice of the Soviet Yiddish writers will resound vigorously in the chorus of brotherly literature. . . . The hero of our works is the man who long ago discarded the heavy burden of the past and who is living a creatively productive life together with all builders of Communist society. . . . The fact that Yiddish poets are still deeply interested in poetry is completely in accord with the experience of the multi-language Soviet literature, which teaches us that great journals flourish in great times. We believe that our critics will pay special attention to the new generation of writers who are now active in Soviet Yiddish literature. These, dear readers, are the immediate goals of the journal *Sovyetish Heymland.*

These opening lines do not clarify whether *Sovyetish Heymland* intends to be a "Jewish" magazine. Its avowed aim is to serve the Soviet nation, to be a part of Soviet, i.e. Communist, literature. It offers its readers "a broad picture of Soviet life"—but what about Jewish life? Judging from the opening statement, one would expect to find nothing in the magazine even remotely connected with Jewish interests. Nevertheless, even the very first issue does contain works of meaningful Jewish content.

The first issue contains contributions by twenty-six Yiddish writers. One of these, L. Vaserman, lives in Birobidzhan. One died shortly before the appearance of this issue. Thirteen of the twenty-six were unknown to Yiddish readers in the West. Almost all of them were brought up under Soviet rule. The first issue also includes a fine poem by the liberal editor of *Novy Mir,* Alexander Tvardovski, called "Siberia," as well as poetry by Alexander Prokofiev and Chingiz Aytamatov from Daghestan—all in Yiddish translation, thus setting a precedent that was to be followed in all subsequent issues. Finally, there is a long article devoted to Vissarion G. Belinski, the prominent nineteenth-century Russian literary critic and militant liberal, on the occasion of his 150th anniversary.

Most of the writing shows no special tendency to glorify Soviet achievements. On the other hand, there are no themes that may meaningfully be called Jewish. Some are the usual "construction" stories so abundant in Soviet literature during the 1930's and 1940's. Then there are topical contributions, e.g.: Dora Haikin's "To the Widow in the Congo" (about Lumumba's widow), Motl Gruvman's poem "Leningrad," an ode to the cosmonaut Yuri Gagarin, and similar contemporary verse about Cuba and the Congo, by Motl Grubyan. The veteran poet Samuel Halkin, who died in 1960, is represented by only one poem, *"Gut Yomtev, Mayn Land"* ("Happy Holiday, My Country"), whose title speaks for itself. Like other Jewish writers, this talented Yiddish poet (born 1897) started his literary career in Hebrew, and later turned to Yiddish. Halkin was noted for his deeply Jewish national feelings. Arrested during Stalin's reign of terror, he was released after the dictator's death and allowed to live out his life in comparative peace. According to the editors, Halkin composed *"Gut Yomtev, Mayn Land,"* together with other patriotic poems, shortly before his death.

Then there are some—unfortunately few—honest pieces dealing either with Jewish life before the Revolution, or with the destruction of the Jews during World War II. Outstanding is a poem by Moyshe Teyf, "Song of My Brothers," mourning the fate of East European Jewry. Interestingly enough, the poem contains a reference to Babi Yar, epitomized in the famous poem by Yevgeni Yevtushenko, which has never appeared in translation in *Sovyetish Heymland.* Several other pieces make reference to Babi Yar and similar places of mass execution; there is also a sketch by the non-Jew Boris Prorokov, of three women lamenting at a grave. Yet there is no mention made of the fact that Babi Yar was a specifically *Jewish* tragedy. To do so would presumably not have been in accord with the principles of the "multinational" literature of the Soviet Union.

The first issue's literary quality is mediocre. The stories glorify the "positive hero," single-minded in his devotion to communism. The style is generally in the manner of the stereotyped and tendentious writings of the 1930's and '40's. The stories sound like translations of Russian stories about collective farms, the Russian name of the heroes simply having been replaced by Jewish ones. The poetry is archaic, rhetorical, and declamatory.

Still, not everything published in the first issue is inferior. Abram Gontar, though writing the usual Soviet platitudes, shows genuine talent in his story *"A Geveynlikhe Mishpokhe"* ("An Ordinary Family"); the same is true of Yosef Rabin in his "Rachel and Her Children." There is also a competent literary essay by Elie Falkovich, a lengthy analysis of the writings of the Yiddish classicists.

Every issue concludes with a section chronicling the events in Soviet and Yiddish culture. The first issue concentrates on news about the successful concert tours of the talented Yiddish singer Nehama Lifshitz, which were attended by over 300,000 people, and the tremendous success of the play *"Tevye der Milkhiker,"* by Sholom Aleichem, directed by Vladimir Schvartser. We are told of the more than 125 concerts performed all over the Soviet Union by the chorus of Emil Horevits, and of the "cultural exchange" with Israel (limited to concerts performed by Jewish musicians in Israel).

We also find announcements about the anti-religious works published in Russian in 1961. One, by the "great atheist" Khivi Habalkhi, which saw the light of day no less than 1,000 years ago, contains sixty-six "scientific" theses denying the divine origin of the Bible. Another book highly praised by the editors of *Sovyetish Heymland*, both for its rich language and erudition, is M. Altshuler's *A Discussion on the Day of Rosh Hashanah*, 100,000 copies of which were published.

The second issue was, if anything, even more disappointing than the first one. Again, the lead article was propaganda—this time a greeting to the Twenty-second Congress of the Communist Party in the Soviet Union held in October of that year, followed by Haim Baider's poem "My Party":

> Say but a word, and I am ready again,
> I hear your call and stride toward you.
> Whatever I do, whatever your orders,
> I shall accept them with a serene conscience. . . .

Khrushchev's 1962 campaign to raise more pigs as an inexpensive means of producing more meat is faithfully reflected in a short story by Haim Melamud, "Visiting the Brigade Leader." It tells of an old Jew on a collective farm who, "though not born a Communist," is enthusiastic over his job as a pig-breeder. Max Riant from Birobidzhan is poetically proud as he "carries with love the lofty name of the Soviet man."

So it goes, the theme of love and loyalty to the Soviet homeland repeated again and again, by the more or less talented contributors. Then, for a fillip, we are given something different, namely, the first part of a hitherto unpublished novel by Sholom Aleichem, called *The Mistake*. According to N. Oyslander, one of the editors of the *Sovyetish Heymland*, this novel was never published in full by the Yiddish newspapers in the United States, because of Sholom Aleichem's sharply critical attitude toward what he called "the country of business," and the upper strata of American society.

An important feature is a list of forty-one Yiddish writers who were killed at the front of the German army in World War II. (One is thankful to the editors for publishing these names—thus we know at least that these forty-one writers had not simply "disappeared.") The second issue's current events department is disappointing: most of the items bear no relation to Jewish life or culture. Two items are of interest: an announcement of the publication of a book of seventy songs, with lyrics in Russian and in Yiddish; and information about a Yiddish amateur theatrical group organized by the Council of Trade Unions in Vilna five years earlier. [This group has now been officially designated as a "People's Theater."—Ed.] The troupe, the magazine informs us, had been enthusiastically received. Its most successful production, *Freylakhs*, devoted to the Twenty-second Congress of the Communist Party, had been performed in Riga as well as Vilna.

The March–April, 1963, issue of *Sovyetish Heymland* is unique in that it devotes an entire section to the twentieth anniversary of the Warsaw Ghetto Uprising—in other words, to a singularly *Jewish* event.

Yet lest there be any misunderstanding, let us point out, first of all, that the section on the Uprising is very small indeed. The tone of the issue, which one might have hoped would be *entirely* devoted to this tragic yet heroic chapter in contemporary Jewish history, is introduced by a picture of Lenin on page 1. This is followed by a thirty-page translation of Khrushchev's speech of March 1, 1963, delivered at a meeting of Party and Soviet Government officials with representatives of the Soviet literary and artistic world. Next comes a number of "programmatic" poems, including six by Vergelis, entitled "The Beginning and the End." ("The Beginning" refers to the October Revolution, "the End" to the victory of the Revolution.)

In the *Sovyetish Heymland* version of the Uprising, it was led exclusively by Communists, with Polish workers rendering incalculable help to their Jewish comrades. "The Great Battle Behind the Walls of the Ghetto," by the editor of the Warsaw *Folksshtimme*, Hersh Smolyar, manages to mention the name of one non-Communist leader—Mordecai Anilevich, the commander-in-chief of the Jewish Fighters' Organization, and a member of the left-Zionist youth group Hashomer Hatzair. Other political groupings, such as the Socialist "Bund," are not only not given credit for their part in the Uprising, but are maliciously slandered. Smolyar's more remarkable historical reconstructions include the assertion that Polish Communists not only provided the Jewish fighters with ammunition, but actually engaged the Nazis in several diversionary battles near the Ghetto Walls. He also reports that the Soviet Army helped the Jews by bombarding Warsaw on the night of May 13. (Smolyar seems to have forgotten that the Uprising was already over by that time.)

All in all, *Sovyetish Heymland's* "tribute" to the Ghetto Fighters is in incredibly poor taste, mitigated only by the late Peretz Markish's moving poem *"Der Trot fun Doyres"* ("The March of Generations").

The first few issues, described above, are representative of the bulk of the contributions to *Sovyetish Heymland*. Yet with each successive issue there has been an increase of poems, stories, and novellas bearing little relation to the tedious, stereotyped, and mendacious examples of "socialist realism."

Two of the stories deserve special mention. Y. Rabin's *"Nit Haynt Gedakht"* ("Heaven Forbid!") describes the fate of a Jewish Communist girl who fled Poland to the Soviet Union before the war, only to be accused of spying for Poland. The other, by Irme Druker, called *"Der Vilner Balebesl"* ("The Householder from Vilna"), is remarkable for its nostalgic evocation of the Jewish past. The hero, a young cantor with an extraordinarily beautiful voice, makes the acquaintance of a Catholic organist. Through his new friend, he falls under the spell of the "Gentile" music of the nineteenth-century Polish composer Stanislaw Moniuszko. Gradually, his cantorial melodies take on the tonalities of the Polish composer, much to the horror of the pious Jews, who eventually oust him from the synagogue. With the help of his organist friend, the cantor obtains a job at the Warsaw Opera House—there to be rejected for "Judaizing" the arias of Moniuszko and other Polish composers. Spurned by both Jew and Gentile, the cantor finds himself in a limbo of alienation.

Another aspect of *Sovyetish Heymland* that may be included under the heading of "exceptions" is its important function—all the limitations notwithstanding—as a *Jewish* magazine in providing its readers, through its regular section on current events, with some information about Jewish cultural life both inside and outside the Soviet Union. We find in this section regular reports on the activities of several choral and dramatic groups in the Soviet Union, mostly itinerant, who draw large and enthusiastic audiences wherever they go. The repertoire of these groups consists mostly of traditional Yiddish folk songs and excerpts from Yiddish classics, particularly Sholom Aleichem.

The reader is also supplied with information about translations from the Yiddish that appear in the Soviet Union. We thus learn that in 1962 and 1963, a total of sixty-seven books (more than 8 million copies) were published in five languages: Russian, Ukrainian, Byelorussian, Moldavian, and Azerbaijanian. The figure is impressive, to be sure; but since no breakdown of the titles is offered, and even an eight-page pamphlet is considered a "book" by Soviet standards, it is difficult to gauge the real significance of this data.

In addition, "Chronicles" reflects the changing attitude of the editors of *Sovyetish Heymland* toward "bourgeois" Yiddish writers abroad. While the editorial reports are highly selective and hardly give the reader a balanced picture of Yiddish cultural life outside the Soviet Union, they do indicate that it is no longer obligatory for Soviet Yiddish writers to reject out of hand the works of their "capitalist" brethren.

Thus, the editors noted the death in New York of the "great Yiddish poet" H. Leivick (author of *The Golem*) on October 23, 1963; the 100th anniversary of the birth of the playwright S. Ansky (author of *The Dybbuk*); the 80th anniversary of the noted literary critic S. Niger (pejoratively characterized as a "typical representative of Yiddish bourgeois critics in the United States"); and the anniversaries of the novelist I. J. Singer and the poet Mani Leyb (the latter, as "one of the most prominent representatives of American Yiddish poetry"). All of these authors are "safely" dead.

Of particular interest was the observance of the 90th anniversary of the outstanding Hebrew-Yiddish poet and dedicated Zionist Haim N. Bialik, previously vilified as a "reactionary nationalist." The fact that *Sovyetish Heymland* now pays its respects to Bialik, rationalizing his writing in Hebrew as "just a question of language," may be a straw in the wind. Another even more startling example of the same "liberalism" was the noting of the recent 70th birthday of "the philologist and literary critic" Max Weinreich, the founder of the renowned YIVO Institute for Jewish Research, now living in New York.

In its capacity as the only "representative" of secular Jewish culture in the Soviet Union, *Sovyetish Heymland* plays an important public relations role *vis-à-vis* the outside world and the non-Jewish public within the Soviet Union. Ever since its inception in 1961, its offices have been the second biggest attraction, after the Moscow Synagogue, for the large number of Jewish tourists visiting the Soviet Union. Throughout the year visitors from the United States seek interviews with Vergelis. The latter has shown himself very obliging in this respect, if not always equally candid.

Exactly how the Jews in the Soviet Union regard the new Yiddish magazine is hard to tell. One can only surmise that they have accepted it as the best that could be expected under existing circumstances. The serious reservations of one Soviet Jew may be gleaned from "The Diary of a Jew in the Soviet Union." According to the American Yiddish monthly *Zukunft,* where it appeared, the Yiddish manuscript was delivered to the editors by a highly reliable person. For obvious reasons, the manuscript was unsigned. A few passages are revealing:

The office of the editors is a very useful showplace for tourists—Jews and non-Jews alike. Important visitors are told: "Here you have a Yiddish publication. Here you have Jewish editors." . . . Occasionally, a few Yiddish writers and their wives get together, drink tea, and talk about the state of Yiddish literature, etc. . . . I asked one of the editorial staff whether they intended to publish a primer to teach our children to read Yiddish. For we do have many children who would like to learn the language. The answer was: "This is not a subject for discussion." . . . I left the office of *Sovyetish Heymland* with a broken heart. I saw there soft chairs, beautiful rooms, but unfortunately, neither Jews nor Jewishness.

Whatever the doubts of local Russian Jews, foreign Communist-oriented writers have accepted the journal without any reservations. Their contributions have, if anything, been even more orthodox than those of Soviet Yiddish writers.

Thus, the November–December, 1961, issue contains a section headed "Poems from Our Friends." These "friends," residing in Tel Aviv, Paris, and the United States, contribute poems with such titles as "October" (referring to the October, 1917, Revolution), "Praise the Man of the Wonderful Country," "The Gagarins," "Youth Is Coming," and "Thus It Will Be." The July–August, 1963, issue included works by thirteen Israeli writers, some translated from Hebrew, two from Arabic. Again, revolutionary, patriotic themes recur: a hosanna for the October Revolution that "smashed injustice to pieces," by Alexander Pen; a poem declaring that "The sea of Tel Aviv is lively but the Black Sea is bluer still," by P. Binetski.

93

Whatever the services *Sovyetish Heymland* performs for the Jews in the Soviet Union, they are inconsequential compared to the services it performs for the Soviet authorities. One of them is undisguised propaganda—wholesale defense of Soviet Jewish policy, and attacks on the "calumnies" printed in the "vicious foreign press." In this vein, the November–December, 1963, issue contains a lengthy report of a meeting held at the offices of *Sovyetish Heymland*, attended by "dozens of people, men and women of various occupations, Jews and non-Jews." Here, Aaron Vergelis spoke about the many letters the editors had received from abroad decrying "the great wave of anti-Semitism and racism . . . in West Germany, the United States, Argentina, and other countries." The audience, mostly readers of *Sovyetish Heymland*, expressed its indignation at these deplorable events, then went on to inveigh against the "slanderous campaign directed at the Soviet Union"—that is, the Western press reports of anti-Semitism in Russia. How sensitive the editors of *Sovyetish Heymland* and, of course, the Soviet authorities are to this campaign may be gauged from the fact that this gathering was attended by Roman Rakhumov and Gennadli Terakhov, two high officials from the office of the RFSFR Procurator (more or less equivalent to the Attorney-General's office in the United States). In a speech, Rakhumov referred to Article 123 of the Soviet Constitution as incontrovertible proof that anti-Semitic propaganda was not tolerated in the Soviet Union. Lieutenant-General Hirsh Plaskov, speaking at the same meeting, argued against the existence of anti-Semitism by referring to the large number of Jews in high positions in such institutions as the armed forces.

As might be expected, *Sovyetish Heymland* goes to great lengths to "refute" allegations of Soviet anti-Semitism. The September–October, 1963, issue, for example, reports on an article that appeared in the Russian-language publication *Znamia Kommunizma* (*Flag of Communism*), attacking Israeli "spies" and tourists who spread "ideological poison" in the Soviet Union. One year later, the editors replied to Bertrand Russell, who had asked the magazine to publish a letter from a Soviet Jew which he had received some time before, apparently containing incriminating information about the situation of Soviet Jews. Since the letter was unsigned, the editors informed Russell they could not publish it. They took advantage of the opportunity to lecture the noted British philosopher (generally well disposed to the Soviet Union) on the dangers of giving credence to anti-Soviet propaganda. "The real needs of Soviet Jews and Jewish culture," Russell was assured, "are fully satisfied."

Vergelis does not confine himself to the pages of *Sovyetish Heymland*. His articles on the Jewish "question" have appeared in Russian, Ukrainian, and Moldavian newspapers and magazines. To mention two examples:

The October 10, 1963, issue of *Literaturnaya Gazeta* printed Vergelis' "New York Lament on the Day of Atonement." In this piece, Vergelis assails the "impudent campaign in the reactionary press abroad" that misrepresents Soviet life, and, in particular, the plight of Soviet Jewry. He castigates by name the two largest Yiddish newspapers in New York, the *Jewish Daily Forward* and *The Day-Morning Journal*, as well as Moshe Decter, author of an article printed in *Foreign Affairs*, entitled "The Status of the Jews in the Soviet Union." [1] These "spokesmen" of the Jewish "bourgeoisie," asserts Vergelis, wish "to preserve national identity through a return to the ghetto," absurdly claiming "that the situation of Jews in the Soviet Union is bad because they cannot create the style of life of New York's Williamsburg."

Again, in an article published in the May 16, 1964, issue of *Sovyetskaya Moldavia*, submitted at the request of the editors, Vergelis asserts with pained naïveté: "We, Soviet persons of the Jewish nationality, are bewildered when asked to 'prove with facts' that we enjoy the same rights as Russians, Ukrainians, Moldavians, Azerbaijanians, etc."

Given Vergelis' obvious role as propagandist-at-large for the Soviet regime in regard to its Jewish policy, it is not surprising that he was sent on a tour of the United States.

As noted earlier, representatives of the American Jewish community flatly refused to meet with Vergelis in his capacity as "representative of Soviet Jewry"; Vergelis blamed the American rabbinate for his failure to establish a line of communication. The fact is that Vergelis quickly undermined his own mission by a categorical denial of any Jewish problems in the Soviet Union. Immediately upon arrival in New York, he publicly charged that a campaign was being waged in America over the "so-called

1. This article is included in Part One above.—Ed.

95

Jewish question" in Russia. He then summarized the life of Jews in the Soviet Union as "in a single sentence, the normal life of people in Soviet society."

A reporter from the *New York Herald Tribune* asked Vergelis why there were no cultural facilities for Jews in the Soviet Union outside of *Sovyetish Heymland*. He had a simple, readymade answer: "They are already integrated. They are satisfied with general Russian culture." Why *Sovyetish Heymland*, then? "There is still an element that reads and loves Yiddish." Apparently, Vergelis did not realize that these two statements were not quite reconcilable.

On his return home, Vergelis wrote a long and vitriolic account of his visit to the United States. "Twenty Days in America" appeared in four successive issues of *Sovyetish Heymland*. Jewish life in America, the editor reported to his Soviet readers, is controlled by rabbis, Zionists, and Jewish capitalists.

As might be expected, *Sovyetish Heymland* follows an explicitly anti-religious line. Thus, the March–April, 1962, issue highly recommends Hillel Lifshitz's book *Religion and Church Past and Present*, which devotes a separate defamatory chapter to Judaism. The magazine has nothing but praise for such books which endeavor to "help those who are still believers to rid themselves of the dangerous influence of religion." The January–February, 1963, issue carries a short story by M. Shulman, "*Untervegs*" ("En Route"), in which the author expresses his distaste for informers—such as the Jew who showed him a number of documents proving the existence of speculation and thievery in the local synagogue. Shulman does not need this evidence; "the facts" are generally widely propagated in the Soviet press: Jewish religious leaders are "money grubbers, parasites, thieves . . . using 'the Temples of God' to hide foreign currency. . . . Yes, we must admit that these 'thieves of God' have made considerable progress in the art of swindling."

Passover and *Matzoh*: A Case History of Soviet Policy

BY *Moshe Decter*

A careful examination of Soviet policy on the festival of Passover is valuable both for the sake of the historical record and for what it reveals about over-all Soviet strategy toward the Jews as a group.

As it evolved over the past decade, that policy emerged as a process of encroachment composed of several elements—the ban on the public baking and sale of *matzoh* (the unleavened bread indispensable to the observance of Passover), the concomitant propaganda campaign that harped on themes of anti-Semitism and political subversion, and, finally, the constriction of the scope of the holiday from the broadly historical to the narrowly ritualistic.

This policy of attrition had a multiple impact: It deprived hosts of Soviet Jews of *matzoh*. It made it impossible for religious Jews to observe the holiday properly. It created a miasma of fear among the synagogue

97

Jews. And it established an atmosphere of intimidation against large numbers of non-religious Jews who would otherwise have celebrated the festival in some significant way.

Having accomplished this much, the authorities seem now to have embarked on a new, more refined course of deprivation. The events of 1966 suggest the emergence of a paradox: a new form of attrition characterized by the apparent gradual reversal of the ban on *matzoh* baking in the synagogue. For, on an extremely limited scale in 1966 and in a slightly more expanded form in 1967, a number of synagogues in various cities have quietly been permitted to resume the provision of *matzoh* to their parishioners.

The paradox is only superficial, however. This new turn may well reflect a certain decision very likely stimulated by the pressure of world opinion, taken tentatively in 1966 and now carried forward somewhat more confidently: to tolerate the baking and sale of *matzoh* only on synagogue premises, and to maintain the prohibition for public bakeries. At a stroke, this move would accomplish three ends: It lets the old synagogue Jews have their piece of bread, so to speak. It serves to stifle or blunt the worldwide protest against the *matzoh* ban. And it effectively deprives the great mass of Jews and particularly the new generation of young unsynagogued Jews of the opportunity to participate meaningfully in the festival.

Passover, uniquely among Jewish traditional festivals, represents a cluster of values which Moscow views as inimical. For Passover represents and commemorates the liberation of the Hebrews from Egyptian slavery, the molding of the Jews into a nation, the unbroken continuity of Jewish history from the Exodus onward, the persistence of the Jewish historical memory, the sense of kinship with all Jews past and present, the embodiment of that kinship in the family around which the gala celebration of the Passover feast centers and which even non-religious Jews join in joyously. These values together make Passover the most important link, as it were, between the Jewish past and the Jewish present. For it represents, more clearly than any other holiday, the perpetuation of Jewish historical consciousness and the sense of Jewish identity.

Since it is precisely the Soviet objective to eradicate that consciousness and that identity, to shatter and pulverize the bonds of Soviet Jews with their history and their people, Soviet policy has fixed on the Passover as perhaps the key target of a process of attrition. The very consumption of *matzoh* has been transformed, in the process, from a basic historic symbol for the entire Jewish people into a ritual food of a religious cult.

Certainly Passover is a religious holiday—but it is not only that. And certainly *matzoh* is a religious food—but it is not only that. For large numbers of non-religious Jews, in the U.S.S.R. as in the United States, enjoy this festival because they feel some kind of kinship with Jewish historical, moral, cultural, and family values. For them, Passover stands for the historic freedom of the Jewish people—and it celebrates and exalts the spirit of freedom for all men. For non-religious as well as religious Jews, the eating of *matzoh*, especially at the Seder table, is the tangible way by which they can symbolize that commemoration, that celebration, that exaltation. It is how they symbolize their historic sense of Jewish kinship and of Jewish cultural and spiritual values.

To transform this holiday into a narrowly religious rite observed only by religious Jews means, in the Soviet context, to relegate the observance of Passover and the consumption of *matzoh* to the level of superstition— and to barely tolerate them impatiently while awaiting their disappearance along with the older generation of believing Jews.

This can only result in depriving the masses of non-religious younger Soviet Jews, increasingly aware of their Jewishness, of the opportunity to perpetuate and enrich their historic Jewish bonds. Such Jews would not think twice about buying *matzoh* at public stores and bakeries. But they would surely boggle at exchanging flour and rubles for *matzoh* at the synagogues. A Jew who is a member of the Communist Party or the Komsomol, or who is a government or public official, or is a student or an employee seeking advancement, will keep an absolute distance—for fear of censure, punishment, or retardation of career.

This is nothing if not a subtle means of forcing young Soviet Jews away from even a secularized version of their heritage. In short—forced assimilation.

Against this theoretical backdrop, it becomes possible to evaluate the Soviet policy on Passover and *matzoh* in a meaningful way.

The history of the prohibition on *matzoh* baking in the Soviet Union is instructive. It reveals a gradual process of official encroachment on this key religious practice and national tradition.

In the past, two methods had been used for the public baking of *matzoh* for Passover. In Moscow, for example, a State bakery used to be specifically set aside for this purpose a few months prior to the holiday. In other places, where baking facilities exist in the synagogue compounds —as in Leningrad, Riga, Tbilisi (Georgia), and Kulashi (Georgia)—the *matzoh* had been baked there with flour allotted by the State, and by workers sent by the appropriate State institution.

The ban, as it developed, affected both of these methods. Like an ever-tightening noose, it began in outlying cities and towns as early as 1957, and by 1961 it had gradually come to encompass all but Moscow.

The first restrictions on the baking of *matzoh* can be traced back to 1957, when the authorities refused to issue permits to the Jewish community of Kharkov, which numbers about 70,000 Jews. In 1958, *matzoh* baking was discontinued in those areas where existing Jewish religious congregations were not officially registered—or where, if they had been registered until then, they were dispersed by the authorities during that year. For example: the communities in Shaulyai, Lutsk, Khabarovsk, Kolomyya, Stalino, Brest, Yakutsk. In 1959, the ban was extended to places where registered Jewish religious congregations still existed. For example: Zaporozhe, Rovno, Uzhgorod, Bobruisk, Gomel, Kuibyshevka, Rostov, Saratov, Stalingrad.

It may be assumed, however, that at that time the Soviet authorities were still guided in the enforcement of the ban by the strength of the reaction in each individual community. Thus, though the ban in 1959 was extended to Odessa, permits *were* issued to the communities in Zhmerinka, Berdichev, and Lvov. In 1959, also, Jewish communities were still permitted to receive *matzoh* parcels from abroad.

In 1960, the ban spread to the following communities: Beyala Tserkov, Berdichev, Zhmerinka, Lvov, Zhitomir, Smolensk, Chernovtsy, Bendery, Kiev, Kishinev. The extension of the ban to areas open to foreign tourists —such as Kiev, Chernovtsy, and Lvov—brought the ban on *matzoh* baking to the attention of the outside world. In 1962, with its application to Moscow as well, the ban became total. It covered the production and sale and/or distribution of *matzoh* in both State bakeries and synagogues that possessed *matzoh*-baking machinery on their premises.

The West became aware of the spreading restrictions only very gradually. After a few years it became known to limited circles that, for example, Jewish congregations, synagogue leaders, and ordinary religious people in such places as Kishinev, Riga, Beltsy, Saratov, and Uzhgorod had been arrested, fined, or had special taxes imposed on them for engaging in the "illegal production" of *matzoh*, or for "speculating" and "profiteering" from its sale. But it was only the announcement a few weeks before Passover, 1962, by Rabbi Yehudah Leib Levin, of the Moscow Great Synagogue, that Moscow's Jews were also to be deprived of *matzoh* that made Jewish communities abroad, and to a certain extent world opinion, aware of the nature and scope of the countrywide ban.

For the first time in Soviet history—including even the Stalin period—the ban on organized *matzoh* baking covered the entire country, including Moscow, Leningrad, the Ukraine, Byelorussia, the Caucasus, and Central Asia.

The record of Soviet prevarication and evasion when confronted with protests on this policy is illuminating.

When the first reports began to circulate, early in 1962, that no *matzoh* would be baked in Moscow, official spokesmen angrily denied the reports, calling them anti-Soviet lies aimed at exacerbating the Cold War. By March, 1962, however, Rabbi Levin had to announce that the machines in the State bakery which made the *matzoh* had broken down; the required repairs, it was vaguely intimated, might even be completed in time for that very Passover. No such "repairs" were ever made, and the good rabbi had to urge his flock to do without *matzoh*, and to make do with peas instead. As late as January, 1963—more than half a year after Passover—Novosti Press Agency, one of whose main tasks is to disseminate propaganda abroad about Soviet Jewry, was still imputing the machinery-breakdown "explanation" to Rabbi Levin.

Just prior to Passover, 1963, and for more than a year thereafter, a new explanation was given: It is unconstitutional and illegal for State bakeries to bake *matzoh* and for State stores to sell them, because *matzoh* are a religious article—and the U.S.S.R. adheres strictly to the separation of Church and State.

This of course failed to explain why *matzoh* had been baked and sold in State bakeries *prior* to 1962. It was, moreover, contradicted by an official Soviet document submitted to the United Nations on July 11, 1956, which stated:

By order of the U.S.S.R. Government, on days preceding particularly important holidays—such as Passover in the case of the Jews—the shops of the State trading organizations sell special types of bakery products, *matzoh* for Orthodox Jews, etc., to enable worshipers to perform the appropriate ritual.

Just to prove that no anti-Jewish discrimination was intended, Soviet spokesmen pointed out that State bakeries also no longer produced *kulichi*, the communion cakes used by the Russian Orthodox at Easter.

The analogy with *kulichi* is misleading and defective in several respects. In the first place, though both are symbolic wafers used for religious purposes, the analogy ends there. For *matzoh* is in addition, for Soviet religious Jews, perhaps the basic food they eat for the entire eight-day period of the Passover. In general, under Soviet conditions, the bread product is the basic element in the diet, and *matzoh* is the Passover bread for the religious Jew. Thus, in being deprived of *matzoh*, the Soviet religious Jew is deprived not only of a symbol but of a basic food and, not least, of a fundamental *religious food. Kulichi* are clearly not comparable items.

But even if they were, the analogy is defective on other grounds, which point to the uniquely weak and isolated situation of Jewish congregations in the U.S.S.R. The Russian Orthodox Church, for all that it is, like other religions, subjected to official anti-religious propaganda assaults and practical curbs, is a large, extensive, tightly organized and powerful nationwide structure—in many ways favored by the regime. It is in fact through its nationwide organization that it undertakes and supervises a wide range of activities aimed at providing the wants of communicants. And among its varied institutions are not only churches but also monasteries, academies, and seminaries, all with cooking and baking facilities—which can and do produce *kulichi* in adequate supply for their *symbolic* use.

The provision of an adequate supply for *matzoh* in the U.S.S.R. requires a major enterprise. If the State bakeries are withdrawn from this production, Soviet Jews have no institutions comparable to those of

Russian Orthodoxy to supply their needs. Each synagogue is literally on its own. Even those synagogues that own the appropriate machinery cannot guarantee to produce enough for their own needs, let alone those of neighboring communities that lack such machinery. And those—the large majority—without such facilities have literally nowhere to turn.

(After the institution of the ban in 1957, and until it blanketed the country in 1962, poignant stories emerged from the U.S.S.R. telling of bold, venturesome Jews who dared to travel such long distances as from Rostov to Tbilisi, or from Byelorussia and the Ukraine to Tashkent, to obtain *matzoh* from those synagogues still permitted to bake on their own premises. And such journeys were also branded as illicit by the Soviet press.)

For Passover, 1963, Rabbi Levin was authorized to announce to his flock that they should freely bake *matzoh* in their own homes. He was even encouraged to state, before and during Passover, that this do-it-yourself program was providing more than enough *matzoh* for those who needed it. At the same time, he proclaimed an official rabbinical easement, permitting religious Jews to eat certain items, such as peas and rice, which are normally forbidden on Passover, but which would have to suffice in the absence of *matzoh*—a sad commentary on the officially announced adequacy of home-baked *matzoh* supplies.

This private baking program was tragic in other respects. To begin with, *matzoh* cannot be baked in just any oven. Certainly, strictly religious Jews would not likely find it acceptable. But even if they did, under duress, current Soviet living conditions make it virtually impossible for most people to do so. Housing conditions still require most Soviet citizens to share an apartment, or at least the kitchen and oven, with several families. In such circumstances, baking *matzoh* at home becomes for most people either a physical hardship or a source of social awkwardness, or both.

But, technical difficulties aside, there exists in the U.S.S.R. a general climate of official disapproval of private *matzoh* baking. Again and again, private *matzoh* baking has been exposed and branded over the years in the Soviet press as "illegal production." The "speculative" character of its sale has been underscored. The authorities have even taken stringent measures against individuals who have baked *matzoh* privately, by imposing heavy fines and even arresting some of them—as, for instance, in such communities as Beltsy, Saratov, Uzhgorod, Riga.

The simple fact is that, in the last few years, this dispensation did not work and most Jews went without *matzoh*, or had only some tokens. The authorities did, however, allow the delivery of several thousand parcels of *matzoh* sent to Soviet Jews by their relatives abroad; the permission was not publicized, so that many Jews, who might otherwise have asked their relatives to send *matzoh*, did not know they could. In one instance, a consignment of *matzoh* sent by the Jewish community of Sweden was returned.

In July, 1963, a new climax of prevarication was reached at the trial of four Jews accused of profiteering in the production and sale of *matzoh*. When the news of their arrest first appeared in the Western press, Soviet sources vehemently denied it altogether. But the trial itself showed the value of these denials. At the trial, defense counsel, courageously defending the innocence of their clients, pointed to a serious discrimination: "All churches sell candles and wafers at high prices, and nobody holds them criminally responsible."

Indeed, if Soviet Jewry were permitted the kind of nationwide organization or representative body allowed the Russian Orthodox, the Baptists, and the Moslems, among others, they would have the authorized legal instrumentality by which their sacramental foods and other religious articles would be provided. The absence of such an authorized instrumentality inevitably leads to the creation of an artificial scarcity in Jewish religious articles. It also forces those Jews committed and courageous enough to seek to supply such articles as *matzoh* (and religious calendars, etc.) into the position of involuntary lawbreakers.

At the trial, still more official prevarications emerged. Rabbi Levin was called as a witness for the prosecution—but the import of his testimony was clearly for the defense. Among other things, he testified to a statement made to him by a certain Andreyev, an official of the Committee for the Affairs of Religious Cults:

"Unfortunately," said Andreyev, "this State cannot provide you with *matzoh* at the moment, because it has neither place nor equipment for it. . . ."

Was this conceivable or credible in so advanced an economy—especially since *until 1962* the State had found no difficulty in providing place and equipment?

A year later, just before Passover, 1964, still another new "explanation" was offered, this time by Mr. Leonid A. Gouliev, of the Soviet Mission to the United Nations. In an interview with Jewish students on March 2, 1964, Mr. Gouliev said:

Until 1961 the State baked *matzoh* in State bakeries. But because it was not prepared in a *kosher* manner, the Jewish population would not buy it. In addition, other nationalities began to demand that their traditional foods be prepared. Since this would have been impractical, the production of all religious food was stopped. . . . This past week the government decided to resume baking *matzoh* because they realize how difficult it is for small communities to make *matzoh* on their own.

This was a truly extraordinary statement. It was of course untrue that the Jews did not in years past buy *matzoh* in the State bakeries; they did, in vast numbers—including non-religious Jews. The injection of the newly discovered "demand" of the other nationalities for their own traditional foods is a transparent diversion. The other nationalities never lacked facilities to produce their own foods.

Beyond this, Mr. Gouliev's statement no longer contained, strangely enough, the traditional insistence on the principle of separation of Church and State; it had now become merely "impractical" for the State to produce religious foods. And so, despite the vaunted principle of separation, he announced the government's resumption of *matzoh* baking—out of ostensible consideration for small, outlying Jewish communities.

The government did *not*, in fact, resume the baking of *matzoh* in 1964. Rather, a mere handful of congregations, chiefly in Georgia, with baking facilities on the synagogue premises, were permitted to resume their own baking there. And as a result of the increased pressure of world public opinion, the Moscow Great Synagogue was ostensibly given permission to make special arrangements for *matzoh* baking, at a house some distance from the city. The baking there was stopped almost as soon as it started, on some technical or "sanitary" pretext—after the baking facilities and process were duly photographed by Novosti specialists.

At the same time, Rabbi Levin was authorized to request rabbis and rabbinical organizations abroad to ship *matzoh* parcels urgently, so that they might arrive in time for Passover. Jewish communities in the United States, England, and Israel responded, but were nevertheless unable to provide more than a fraction of what was needed.

The shipments had been addressed to the synagogues in Moscow and Leningrad, and similarly to all other towns where houses of prayer were known still to exist. The security organs, however, forced the Jews to return the *matzoh* and to attach to the returned parcels letters in which the shipments were described as "provocations" and "pressures."

On the very eve of Passover, 1964, it was ascertained that the authorities had allowed just 204 parcels to enter Moscow only, and that these parcels were but a small part of the shipment from London to Rabbi Levin. All the other *matzoh* shipments sent to all other Jewish communities throughout the U.S.S.R. were either returned or impounded, though customs duty had already been pre-paid.

Thus was a cruel cat-and-mouse game played with the needs and sensibilities of Soviet Jews.

For years, a virulent propaganda campaign was conducted against Passover and *matzoh*. It employed the crudest forms of traditional anti-Semitic stereotyping. It charged the Soviet atmosphere with ominous doubts about the loyalty of the Jews. And the very ideological nature of the propaganda assault revealed the central symbolic role which Passover plays in the Soviet policy of attrition of Jewish identity.

The articles appeared in a variety of languages in cities all over the country—in Russian, Byelorussian, Ukrainian, Moldavian; in Moscow, Tallin, Kiev, Zhitomir, Minsk, Alma-Ata. No major city and no major language was excepted—especially in those areas of sizable Jewish population, in those areas of pervasive and endemic anti-Semitism. The assault went beyond the usual ridicule, derision, and contempt poured out on religious beliefs and practices. It reached to and stirred up ancient hatreds.

1. Passover and the Golden Calf. In the case of the baking of *matzoh*, the traditional anti-Semitic stereotype of inextricable connection between Jews and money was a constant and central theme. Here are some choice quotations:

Passover and Matzoh: A Case History of Soviet Policy

For these "saints" nothing is holy! But there is one thing they consider holy: Money, money, money . . . And the flow comes through into the pockets of the parasites of the Jewish synagogue of Alma-Ata. The camera has preserved the picture of the servitors of the synagogue doing a "sacred" deed—the lively activity of making *matzoh*.

Money—this is their ideal. . . . This spring, Fanya Weisman and Sioma Weiner began to bake *matzoh*. Were they motivated by religious feelings? Oh, no! They wanted to profit from the believers.

. . . Stuffing themselves with *matzoth* and *ethrogim*, the preachers of Judaism —Spector, Kotlaryevsky, Shuchat, and Monastryrsky—pray only to the golden calf: how to collect more money from the believers for their own needs and for the militant spirit of the Israeli militarists.

The gods of the servitors of the synagogue are profit and money—"the golden calf."

That phrase—"worshipers of the golden calf"—was the sinister key to the Soviet portrayal of the image of the Jew. On the one hand, as we have just seen, it was constantly used in the atheist propaganda directed against Judaism. At the same time, it was a recurring theme in the enormous press campaign conducted from 1961 to 1964 against economic crime. (In that campaign, incidentally, nearly 55 percent of all those sentenced to death for such alleged crimes were Jews: a grossly disproportionate number, protested the world over as evidence of anti-Jewish scapegoating.)

This odious phrase was never used against non-Jews. But it became the standard journalistic mode for anti-Jewish assaults in the Soviet press. It conjured up, in the minds of large masses of Soviet people not far removed from traditional illiteracy and superstition, the hoary image of the Jew and money, perpetuated through the long, dark centuries of anti-Semitic persecution, until our own day.

2. *Passover and Political Disloyalty.* Even more ominous, however, was the associated theme of ideological subversion and political disloyalty directed against Judaism generally, and against the Passover most specifically.

In the Ukraine, a "scholar" like Karl Y. Yampolsky could write: ". . . The chauvinist Passover slogans stand in direct contradiction to the feelings of Soviet patriotism and boundless love for the Socialist mother-land." (From: "The Origin and Class Essence of Jewish Rituals and Holidays," issued by the Society for the Diffusion of Political and Scientific Knowledge of the Ukrainian S.S.R., Kiev, 1961.)

Also in the Ukraine, another "scholar," by the name of T. K. Kichko, wrote:

Under modern conditions, the Passover holiday harms us in a great number of ways, through engendering disrespect for work and fostering elements of nationalism among the Jewish workers. In celebrating the Passover, the believers do not go to work for several days; thus they hinder production plans and violate work discipline.

The celebration of the Passover is especially harmful because the entire Passover legend, all the prayers, orient the believing Jews toward returning to Israel, which is now the center of Judaism and Zionism. The Passover prayers urge the believing Jews: "May God grant that we meet in Jerusalem next year." Invitations summon the Jews to move to Israel, where they—free workers of our country—will become cannon fodder for Ben-Gurion's clique and for his imperialistic masters.

(From: *Judaism without Embellishment*, published by the Ukrainian Academy of Science, Kiev, 1963.)

Though this book was half-heartedly criticized by Soviet sources, neither Kichko, nor the editors of the book, nor its academic sponsors have ever been punished by the terms of Soviet and Ukrainian law.

In Moldavia, another Soviet "specialist on the Jews," F. S. Mayatsky, could write:

The peculiar characteristic of most Jewish holidays is their clear expression of nationalism. Such festivals as Passover, for example, give rise to nationalist feelings, and poison the minds of Jews by diverting their thoughts to Israel, "the land of their fathers" . . . Judaism kills love for the Soviet motherland. . . .

(From: *Sovyetskaya Moldavia*, official daily government newspaper in Kishinev, capital of Moldavia, July 23, 1959.)

3. The 1964 Propaganda Assault. This vitriolic campaign reached its zenith in time for Passover, 1964, in a nationally co-ordinated and concerted fashion.

On March 17, *Pravda Vostoka* (in Tashkent, Uzbek S.S.R.) violently attacked the shipment of *matzoh* from abroad as "ideological sabotage" and "ideological subversion." It demanded that Jews should forthwith return any such parcels received. And it reported a series of protest meetings in Uzbekistan, at which some Jews were trotted out on stage to urge other Jews to protest the shipments.

On March 21, this article was reprinted in *Izvestya*, the government's central daily paper published in Moscow and distributed nationally. This gave the entire country to understand precisely where the Soviet Government stood.

On March 22, *Sovyetskaya Byelorussia* (Minsk, Byelorussian S.S.R.) lashed out in similar terms, also publishing letters of protest against the *matzoh* shipments—letters ostensibly volunteered by Jewish readers.

On March 23, *Moldava Sochialiste*, a Moldavian-language paper in Kishinev, published an article on "The Essence of the Jewish Passover," in which the sentiment is expressed that this holiday *"undermines the noble feelings of Soviet patriotism."*

On March 24, *Vicherny Leningrad*, the popular afternoon daily in the U.S.S.R.'s second city, described the *matzoh* shipments as a "provocation," an "offense," and "gross interference in our internal affairs." In its view, these shipments were anti-Soviet acts, made "in order to trigger off nationalistic and Zionist sentiments."

On March 25, the distant Siberian Jewish paper, *Birobidzhaner Shtern*, otherwise utterly removed from Jewish life and from Jewish values and interests, also found it necessary to publish a similar article.

On March 26, *Sovyetskaya Moldavia* (Kishinev, Moldavian S.S.R.) followed suit.

On March 28, *Vichirny Kiiv*, a Ukrainian-language paper in Kiev, published a letter from a Jewish pensioner who is made to reject the parcel with the following words: "This gift has simply insulted me; it has debased my dignity as a human being."

On March 28, *Znamia Kommunizma* (Odessa, Ukrainian S.S.R.) also published a lengthy rejection of the parcels: "We know that *matzoh* is not quite as innocent a thing as some people might think. It is, first of all, a means of propagating the Jewish religion. . . . You rabid defenders of Judaism are kindling unbridled Zionist-chauvinist propaganda around the *matzoh* that you send to Jews with a provocative, anti-Soviet purpose."

Though this kind of massive propaganda assault did not carry over to Passover, 1965, it found its echo in a notorious article published February

2, 1965, in *Zviazda*, the leading Byelorussian-language paper of Minsk, capital of the Byelorussian S.S.R. The article was written by still another of the long line of Soviet "scholars" and "experts" on Jews and Judaism, one J. Muraviev. Its very title gives away its intent: "The Shadow of the Synagogue."

One of its many choice items is the following:

Jewish bourgeois organizations are doing their utmost to revive Judaism in our circumstances. Many Israeli tourists disseminate Zionist literature. Every year the Minsk synagogue receives *matzoh* packages from abroad. But the matter doesn't stop at these "gifts" alone. Judaism is trying to create an ideological diversion, to fill the consciousness of working Jews in our country with the poison of bourgeois ideology.

Thus Passover plays a very special role in an ominous propaganda campaign in which Judaism and the Jewish people are linked with a doctrine and a movement, Zionism, which the Soviets consider subversive—and with a state, Israel, which they consider the agent of imperialism in the Middle East.

It is only against Jews and Judaism that such ominous political suspicion has been raised in Soviet propaganda, and such themes as ideological subversion, lack of patriotism, and disloyalty exploited. Even a non-religious Jew would be offended and perhaps even intimidated. Indeed, this is precisely what is involved in the process of attrition against Passover and *matzoh*—to atomize Soviet Jewry. For the objective of the policy is to erode the Jewish spirit and to eradicate Jewish values.

Undoubtedly as a result of consistent, systematic worldwide protests—including many from Western Communist parties—a certain shift of emphasis in the policy became discernible in 1966 and apparently continued into 1967. The virulence of the propaganda, for one thing, has substantially abated. For another, the number of synagogues being permitted to produce *matzoh* has very gradually grown. In 1966 *matzoh* was baked by congregations in Moscow, Leningrad, Odessa, Kishinev, Tbilisi, and certain Central Asian towns, and in 1967 probably in even more.

But it must be noted that this shift is seriously defective in three major respects. First, the lifting of the ban on *matzoh* baking is far from being nationwide, so that a large number of Jews—perhaps the majority—are unaffected by the glacier-like forward movement. Second, *matzoh* production is restricted to the synagogues, thus depriving the great number of unreligious and younger generation Jews of any tangible means of observing the holiday. Third, even in the synagogues the procedure for obtaining *matzoh* is inefficient and even demeaning. All told, then, the situation is far removed from the *status quo ante* 1957, when *matzoh* was freely available in bakeries throughout the country.

A word about the procedure for obtaining *matzoh*. To do so, Jews must bring flour to the synagogue. Flour is not the easiest thing to get in the Soviet Union. Moreover, the finished product is very expensive. Above all, when bringing the flour to the synagogue, Jews must register their identity, in order to place their *matzoh* request in advance. In a situation where the security police still plays a substantial role, especially in the affairs of the synagogues, this procedure can only arouse apprehensions. Although it may be perfectly safe for the registrants now, the fact is that their names are known to the police—and the future is uncertain.

Thus, the process of attrition against Jewish culture, religion, and identity persists. Soviet Jewry represents the last great remnant of a vast East European Jewish community devoured by the Nazi Holocaust—the last residue of what was once the matrix of a rich and ancient Jewish heritage, from which sprang all that is best in modern Jewish life everywhere in the world.

The Soviet policy of forcible assimilation, as reflected in the treatment of Passover, conjures up in the minds of Jews the specter of the involuntary loss of this community to the Jewish people and to Jewish historical and cultural values. It is this which is at the heart of the Jewish people's anguish over the fate of Soviet Jewry.

THREE

Popular Anti-Semitism

Soviet Jews as Economic Criminals

FROM THE *Journal of the International Commission of Jurists*

For Jews, Lvov has important historical connotations. A Jewish settlement dating back to the thirteenth century, when it was rebuilt from the ashes by the Polish kings, it served for more than six centuries, with its multinational population (including, in addition to Jews, Armenians, Tatars, Moldavians, Ukrainians, and Poles, large settlements of Scots and Huguenots), as the antemural of Western civilization. Lvov, although coveted by Russia, remained outside the confines of the Russian Empire, and until World War II escaped Soviet domination. Not only were the Lvov Jews mostly former Polish citizens, attached to Jewish religion and culture, but they were a branch of Western European cultural experience. In addi-

The International Commission of Jurists, which issued this survey as a staff study, is a private agency with headquarters in Geneva. It has consultative status with the United Nations and is supported by almost fifty thousand lawyers in 108 countries.

tion, they have lived under Soviet rule less than half as long as the rest of Russia's Jews. And yet in spite of all these circumstances, which for the Soviet regime were full of ideological dangers, the existence of 30,000 Jews in Lvov was of no political consequence for the Soviet Union. The city's former inhabitants were either deported to Russia, decimated by the Germans, or evacuated to Poland after the Teheran Conference assigned the city to the Soviet Union. The remnants of the once numerous Jewish community were surrounded by new inhabitants. In the new social setting the spiritual comforts of religious practices were for the majority of the Lvov Jewry of singular significance.

The Lvov affair was the subject of an extensive press campaign. In the period from February 25, 1962, to November 1, 1962, seven articles attacking the synagogue and its leaders appeared in *Lvovskaya Pravda*.

In addition, an important letter entitled "Letter from Lvov" was printed in *Voyovnichy Ateist*, a paper published in Kiev, which demanded that the Lvov Synagogue, exploited for anti-Soviet activity, be closed. The synagogue was pictured as the center for illicit currency dealings. Jewish speculators from Lvov and foreign towns met and carried on their trade and concluded their transactions. Not only was the synagogue abused for such a purpose, but the synagogue leadership consisted of speculators entrenched in important positions in its administration, including its highest body, the *dvatsatka*, the Council of Jewish Elders. The leading figure in the synagogue and in the ring of speculators was, according to *Lvovskaya Pravda*, the ritual slaughterer Kontorovich, who made religion and its rites the source of his personal income. In contravention of the State wine monopoly he made religious wine, which he sold at exorbitant prices, for the celebration of religious festivals.

The misdeeds of Kontorovich and his accomplices finally resulted in a trial, which was held in March, 1962, and resulted in the death sentence for Kontorovich and Sapozhnikov, both members of the synagogue's council. They shared the dock with three other defendants, Chernobilsky, Sendersky, and Cherkas, who had acted as their accountants, salesmen, and agents. The general purpose of the trial was to link the synagogue and its leaders to the machinations and speculation with currency and gold which were the object of court proceedings in other Soviet cities. The activities of Benjamin Gulko, executed for currency transactions and trade operations in Odessa, were brought in evidence to seal the fate of the defendants. Although he was dead, his alleged depositions for his own trial were read as evidence in court.

"For several years," wrote *Lvovskaya Pravda* of March 9, 1962, "the accused had engaged in large speculative deals, purchasing and selling gold, foreign currency, and jewels. Acquaintances and 'business relations' were established within the synagogue walls, the heads of which—members of the so-called *dvatsatka*—were Sapozhnikov and Kontorovich."

A sort of "black market" was active in the synagogue. "This was where currency speculators from other towns gathered, among them the aforementioned Gulko, as well as Sh. Kuris and others. It is here that Kontorovich and Sapozhnikov transacted their deals. And here too came Sendersky, not to pray, but to receive orders from Kontorovich and subsequently to depart on regular trips for the purchase of foreign currency."

The second theme is that religious rites provide an opportunity to conduct trade with objects connected with the cult:

One member of the synagogue's administration, Belenitsky, drew profit from the sale of prayer books and other religious literature. Another member of the synagogue elders traded in places in the synagogue, and unless a proper donation was made to the synagogue the place was denied. Other members of the synagogue services also carried out their functions to receive their share. They sold penicillin and other medicine at fabulous prices. In this atmosphere of concern with money and profit from religion they also took large sums from believers for *matzoh*. It is no wonder that the synagogue was the scene of unseemly brawls, which find their end in court.

Lvovskaya Pravda of September 1, 1962, reported a brawl started by a candidate for the position of the synagogue cantor, who is paid a salary of 340 rubles.

Press reports and anti-religious propaganda culminate in a number of letters from the readers who add their bit to charges against Jewish religious practices in Lvov. A reader writes of concern that in the Lvov synagogue "humility" and "long-suffering" were preached, which helped the American imperialists, who planned to impose the blockade on Cuba. This ideology was harmful to Jewish interests, and the synagogue must be closed. In another article it was claimed that the synagogue was visited by representatives of the Israeli Embassy, who distributed Israeli propaganda material. It was also the place from which gold and foreign currencies were exported abroad.

Court proceedings involving people connected with the Jewish synagogues in the Soviet Union continued in the following year. In July, 1963, three Jews were sentenced in Moscow for baking *matzoth* for sale to their co-religionists. The convicted Jews were Golko Bogomolny, forty-nine, a ritual slaughterer, who was given a one-year sentence, and two illiterate women who received six months' imprisonment each. It was alleged that the women received 10 kopeks (eleven U.S. cents at the official rate of exchange) for over two pounds of *matzoth*, while Bogomolny sold it for 2.5 rubles a kilo (*The New York Times*, July 18, 1963).

The last reported case in this study concerned three Soviet citizens, including Rabbi Gavrilov, sentenced to death in August, 1963, for trading in gold and foreign currencies in Pyatigorsk Stavropol region, while six other persons were sentenced to various terms of imprisonment (*Sovyetskaya Rossia*, August 19, 1963). The death sentence was commuted later by the U.S.S.R. Supreme Court to fifteen years' imprisonment, according to the *Guardian* of January 28, 1964, on the basis of a Reuters dispatch quoting reliable Jewish sources in Moscow.

A standard picture presented to the public shows how the nefarious activities of the defendants were brought to light. Even at that stage of the proceedings the public is told of the activities which are declared criminal, even before the court has a chance to examine the evidence and to pass on the case. The next stage is an account of the trial. This usually includes a description of defendants in the dock, in such a way as to leave little doubt that the criminals have committed the crimes with which they are charged, and also that their dishonest trade and criminal activities are easily recognizable from their mien and demeanor. Then comes the closing act of the court drama. The court, faced with the evidence presented in the course of the trial, and in response to the public demand for a severe and just punishment, imposes such a punishment, and society is rid of the nest of rats, ring of criminals, embezzlers of people's wealth, and so on. The style and technique of reporting in the Soviet press is not to furnish data and information on which to form an opinion, but to form such an opinion.

The same technique is used in incidental propaganda, which provides a counterpoint to the main theme. One of the important points which the Soviet press is anxious to make is the danger which the Jewish minority represents owing to their contact with foreigners and foreign countries. The case of the Lvov synagogue, and of the central synagogue in Moscow visited by the members of the Israeli Embassy, underlined the undesirable aspects of the continued existence of Jewish institutions. Even individual members of the Jewish community may be sources of considerable embarrassment for the good name of the entire country.

So, for instance, *Sovyetskaya Moldavia* (July 8, 1962) reported that a certain Jewish lady, Frieda Holzman, who lived in Moldavia, had relatives in the United States, Brazil, and France. "From time to time she wrote letters to them complaining of her difficult lot." She said that she lived in poverty, that she dressed worse than a homeless old woman. In other words she begged for help. So these relatives and friends from abroad sent poor Frieda parcels of gifts on many occasions. Holzman immediately sold the contents of these parcels on the black market at speculative prices. She was also an unauthorized seamstress on the side. This form of private enterprise also brought her a sizable income. The evidence of Frieda Holzman's nefarious activities was her wealth and a few gold coins which she bought with her earnings.

Another article, in *Vechevnaya Moskva*, exposed a confidence trickster, a certain Grigori Abramovich Tennenbaum, who engaged in promoting artistic photography studios in various local institutions, such as houses of culture, district committees, etc. His aim was to gain official status for his shady operations. He exploited the belief that genuine safety measures could be replaced by a system of posters. In the words of *Vechevnaya Moskva*, "the State allots large sums for labor protection and safety engineering. However, there are economic executives, who are ready to pour all these millions into picture posters such as: 'Do not stand under the tap!' and 'Do not lie under the press!' Isn't this much easier than genuine safety engineering? Such people were a godsend for private operators. Tennenbaum managed to sign a contract for 3.5 million rubles with the Glavgaz enterprise alone."

What irks the author of the report is that machinations of this sort "have legalized the residence in Moscow of a large group of parasites who do not wish to encumber themselves with work useful to society. Let us mention just a few of Tennenbaum's assistants: Gorokhovsky, Heiman, Pulver, Leder, Shulman, and others."

Another example of similar literature is an article in *Partiinaya Zhizn*, which discussed the efforts of a group of Jewish Party members, Freint, Nikonova, Kreins, Rosengurt, Zetser, who dealt with the case of a certain Oksengendler, who was sentenced for theft of government property and expelled from the Party. After Oksengendler's release, not only was he made head of the tableware section in a government store, but the local Party organization decided to change his expulsion into reprimand and reinstate him in the Party ranks, which demonstrated the well-known fact that Jews will go to any length in order to help their kind.

Then there are three cases of a slanderer, a professional complainer, and an informer, who, by denouncing his chief, endeavored to hide his own misdeeds and avoid criminal liability.

The slanderer (according to *Izvestya*) wrote false accusations, signing other people's names, thus causing serious trouble to innocent people against whom the accusations were directed, and whose names were used: "Yakov Zakharovich Frishter, a former economist at the Ministry of Trade, saw life in dark colors, reacting to every achievement in Soviet life by vile slander." *Vechevnaya Moskva* published a letter by Comrade Sudakovaya entitled "The house in which I live" and an anonymous letter arrived immediately; "allegedly the whole thing is lies, we all live in cellars, with ten people per room . . . in Moscow, people dress in rags, and even worse than that in other cities . . . Epidemics, but there is no medicine. The achievements of Soviet literature are mentioned—Yakov Zakharovich immediately deprecates and derides the works of leading writers, bringing various calumnies and aspersions against them. The entire world rejoices at the launchings of space ships, but Frishter at this time was pouring buckets of refuse upon the cosmonauts."

Finally, there was the case of the technical engineer Roman Lazarevich Isakov, who denounced the director of the Krasnovodsky Bread Enterprise. The director stole bread and other materials from the enterprise, and mismanaged the affairs of the bakery. At the same time, the inquiry revealed that Isakov was not without blame. The quality of the bread was poor, there were frequently tons of substandard bread produced, and loaves of bread were found to be underweight. The press report suggests that Isakov reported on his chief in order to hide his own crimes. However, the investigation by the control agencies revealed his own deficiencies.

As the reporter tells his public, Isakov's denunciation, which by itself would be an honorable act, was not motivated by the public interest. It was hinted that Isakov acted from spite and sought revenge. The report speaks darkly of "punishment which was leveled" at Isakov, to which he did not reconcile himself. In addition the report unmasks Isakov as an "impostor":

During our conversation, you bragged about how much of a specialist you are. In supporting your claim, you referred to an invitation extended to you to go to Daghestan. You would have gone, but the Council of National Economy did not let you go. Here, we have to clarify something. The Council of National Economy answered that they would not detain you. Anyway, could they have bothered about such a chief engineer, who does not even have a secondary education? (*Turkmenskaya Iskra*, October 31, 1962.)

On occasion the Soviet press has dropped strong hints that contact with those members of the older generation who were former owners of factories and commercial enterprises might be a source of ideological contamination. The children of such people were singularly exposed to this type of influence, which almost ruled out their chances of becoming useful members of Soviet society. Although the State gave them higher education in Soviet universities, gave them decent and well-paid jobs, it happened all too frequently that young descendants of the former bourgeoisie participated, albeit only passively at times, in the crimes of the older generation. A full analysis of such pernicious parental influence is the subject of a lengthy article which appeared in *Moskovskaya Pravda* (July 13, 1962) under the suggestive title, "How the Son Grew into a Pig."

The hero of this "story of a criminal case" is Israel Konstantinovich Eidehand, a young man who scurried around from job to job, enriching himself fraudulently. The article presents the "characteristic" sins of the Jew. In spite of higher education, which the State provided for him, he avoided socially useful work. He forged his personal documents; his real purpose in life was to acquire wealth. The title of the article was drawn from a poem by Mayakovsky in which the poet described the consequences of the bad education a man received in his youth at home.

And indeed, the article described his home background, where he was reared in an atmosphere of dishonesty by the parents, whose highest aspiration was to "get rich quick." His father is depicted as an illegal dealer in building materials and in alcoholic liquor. The young man himself tells of his father's corruption: how he once got a bicycle for the boy by illegally diverting building materials and trading them for the bicycle; how he bribed school officials to obtain good marks for his son; how he bribed other officials to get his son an easy job during the war, while other loyal young citizens went into the army and fought for the fatherland. Indeed, Jewish alleged unwillingness to serve in the army during the war is stressed over and over again.

The tale of Jewish dishonesty and shady dealings crops up even when the Jews are not the object of an immediate attack. *Sovyetskaya Moldavia* of July 12, 1962, reported the doings of two Orthodox priests. They are portrayed as debauched drunkards and fornicators, who exploit the faithful in order to practice sins which they denounce in church. Though the emphasis is on the clergy of the Russian Orthodox Church, the secondary characters, who assist the debauchery of the priests, are an elderly Jewish couple, who act as pimps and procurers of illicit pleasure. Their Jewish home in Kishinev, where priests come to enjoy life, is the center of their activities. The old Jew, described as an habitué of the underworld and a pickpocket, provides the "entertainment" for the priests. The article projects the traditional anti-Semitic stereotype of the clever, cunning Jew who outwits even the clever exploiters of human naïveté.

This analysis ends with two more samples from the Soviet press propaganda campaign at the time, when the Soviet apparatus of criminal justice has centered its attention on economic crimes: both are on a more general theme, in all probability describing fictitious situations. A *feuilleton* entitled "The Golden Key" in the trade-union paper *Trud* (September 12, 1962) described a merry-go-round of the parasitic machinations. The story started with how a certain Kaplan poses as a poor man in order to hide his illegal acquisition of a house and his diversion of State funds to his own purposes. Dvoskin, another Jew, imitated Kaplan and began to divert government funds to his own advantage. Dvoskin's doings caused a non-Jew, Murygin, to seek illicit profit, and finally another Jew, Abram Mendelevich Snovsky, learned crime from Murygin. At last Dvoskin and Murygin were found out. But the Jew was shown to be cleverer and more cunning than the non-Jew, for Dvoskin had the foresight to register the house which he acquired from his illicit operations in his sister's name, and she could not be touched. The moral of the story was that Jews are a source of demoralization in business and that their doings, particularly when they own property, bear watching.

The *feuilleton* published in *Sovyetskaya Byelorussia* of September 16, 1962, "Newcomers to the Backwater," dealt with a situation in a factory. The Jewish director surrounded himself with Jewish personnel placed in jobs for which they had no qualifications, so that they could milk the factory for their own advantage. The director and his associate, the factory's chief engineer, began their activities at the factory with the selection and placement of personnel. The factory was expanding, being reorganized, and improving technological processes. Therefore, suitable personnel were necessary. Under no conditions could progress fall behind. But these personnel, in the opinion of Polyakov and Zholnarkevich, must be obedient and industrious, taciturn and apathetic. This is why the selection of such personnel was delegated to a nurse, Ida Borisovna Akselrod. The principle of selection was that a person had to have higher education, but in a field different from that in which he was working. If he was a failure in his specialization, then his papers were adjusted accordingly. So a lawyer was given the job of chief of the labor and payroll office, a timber specialist that of an engineer technologist, a teacher that of an engineer, a mathematician that of a construction engineer, and so on. The director uses his influence to promote his associates to higher positions by providing them with higher education; they receive additional advantages in the form of reconstructed houses, and entertainment is organized at the State's expense. There is no specific description of illicit deals or of embezzlements, nor is it hinted that the factory is not run efficiently, but obviously the lot of the Jewish employee is much better than in other factories, and that, in the eyes of the author, is a grievous and suspicious situation.

The Soviet press deals with the Jew both in terms of individual characteristics and as a member of his national collective. The Jew as an individual is fundamentally anti-social, as his sense of values does not permit him to accept fully and without reservation the rules of life in a socialist society. His loyalty, instead of to his Soviet fatherland, is primarily to his family; instead of to the high ideals of Leninism, to radical kinship; instead of to honesty and justice, to the protection of the interests of other Jews. Authors of press articles indicate that Jews in government apparatus and in Party positions need closer supervision than other members of Soviet society. Officials in the administration of justice, in social services, police, State, and financial control are warned that their watchfulness must be greater when the affairs of a Jew come within their purview. In the press story covering the career of the speculator Gulko, the reporter thinks that the manager of a Lvov theater had demonstrated a lack of proper watchfulness as she did not inquire into Gulko's past, although Gulko's job as a ticket salesman was only temporary, and apparently he was satisfactory in his work. Similarly, a housing administration employee failed in his duty when he registered without thorough investigation a change in house ownership involving a transfer of rights between members of the Jewish community. Some authors of articles published in the Soviet press seem to deplore that Jewish property rights, or their standing *vis-à-vis* the Soviet authorities, are under the equal protection of the law.

The Jews are portrayed as people "whose only God is gold," who flit through the interstices of the economy, cunningly manipulate naïve, unvigilant non-Jewish officials, prey upon honest Soviet workers and cheat them of their patrimony. Over and over again, the Jews are depicted as the initiators and masterminds of the criminal gangs; the non-Jews, primarily as the recipients of bribes and as accomplices of the Jewish ringleaders. The Jews hoodwink not only the innocent non-Jews—but even Jewish accomplices. Even in their mutual relations the Jews lack honesty.

This propaganda in both timing and content seems to bear a direct relationship to the economic crimes trials. Sentences are shaped in the image of the criminal schemes presented to the public at large in the Soviet press *feuilletons*, which ponderously and piously educate the public in the art of crime detection. As a result, as Soviet trials demonstrate only too frequently, the criminal activities of the Jewish defendants are highlighted, while many non-Jewish principals are hidden from the public eye.

There is no doubt that the concentration of law and propaganda on the suppression of economic crimes evidences a serious moral malaise in Soviet society at a time when the stage reached in post-revolutionary development of a Communist State should, in theory, have eliminated the kind of cupidity that has been rampant. It is obvious, too, that private enterprise, honest and dishonest but in both cases illegal, has been carried on in the very heart of public enterprises. It is also clear that there has been an insidious and sometimes subtle propaganda campaign directed against the Jewish people of the Soviet Union, specifically against those charged with economic crimes and also against the supposed general characteristics of Jews that have been reiterated for centuries. If the reports of trials for economic crimes are even reasonably complete, the number of Jews receiving death sentences and severe terms of imprisonment is greatly disproportionate to their number as a minority group.

The charge has been raised of Jewish persecution, linking their difficulties over synagogues or Passover bread with the unwelcome attention which Jewish defendants have received in the press in connection with economic crimes. But it is considered that the link between anti-Semitism and the suppression of economic crimes is indirect only. There is anti-Semitism in the Soviet Union, but there is not a sufficient amount to warrant an accusation of organized discrimination or persecution. Jews have been made the target of a dangerous propaganda campaign, and Jewish participation in economic crimes has been highlighted if not actually magnified.

The religious difficulties faced by the Jews in the Soviet Union are in many respects shared by people of other religious faiths. Spiritual ties that run counter to the tenets of atheistic communism have long been discouraged. There is undoubtedly also a certain amount of anti-Semitic prejudice at all levels of Soviet society, as there is in many others where the State itself would not seek to discriminate or persecute. The traditional activities of Jews in history—finance and commerce—are not activities which are warmly welcomed in a Communist society. It is a simple matter to link the picture of the money-grubbing Jew of anti-Semitic fancy with the picture of the arch-villains of capitalist cupidity. This has certainly been done by the Soviet press, but the most that can safely be said is that the picture painted of the moral malaise in the Soviet Union diverts attention toward Jews because the primary object of the Soviet policy is to divert attention away from the real truth, to find scapegoats. The real truth is a veritable cancer in the vitals of ideology—capitalistic corruption even within the Party and in local economic administration and a spectacle of amazing fortunes made quickly. That unpalatable fact explains the severity of the laws on economic crimes, even to the extent of reversing a highly publicized trend in the new penal policy. It is a tragedy for the Soviet Jewish people that they have been made the scapegoat for the transgressions of those whose guilt it would be dangerous to make public. They are victims of the "highest interest of State," the need to bolster up belief that the Communist way is the right way and the successful way, and that capitalism is both evil and less successful.

The latent anti-Semitism in the U.S.S.R. is possibly being used by the Soviet authorities as a weapon to render unpopular economic offenses which appear to be rampant. This is probably the most charitable view which can be taken of the apparent anti-Semitism which seems to have influenced Soviet policy. It is earnestly hoped that even if this were the dominating factor which influenced Soviet authorities in this regard, they have and will continue to realize the real and grave injustices which must result from such a course. Anti-Semitism represents the most dangerous form of racialism in the world; no question of expediency can ever justify its use as a political, social, or economic weapon.

The Forgotten Martyrs of Babi Yar

BY *William Korey*

Babi Yar, once a steep ravine on the outskirts of Kiev, just behind an old Jewish cemetery in the Lukianovka district, became a common grave for perhaps as many as 100,000 Jews who were massacred there. The site is now filled in, surrounded by housing projects. Five years ago it was still a wilderness, eloquently captured in Yevtushenko's famous poem:

> *There is a rustling of wild grass over Babi Yar.*
> *The trees look fearsome, like judges.*
> *Everything here screams in silence.*

A large part of Kiev's Jewish population was ordered to the ravine on September 29 and 30, 1941. In the course of two days, *Einsatzgruppe* C, Extermination Command 4-A, performed the record-breaking task of machine-gunning 33,771 Jews (according to German figures; Soviet and Jewish sources say it was two to three times greater). The gas chambers of Auschwitz and Treblinka, at their most efficient, could not equal this achievement. (The Nazis built no gas chambers on Soviet soil; Jews trapped by the German occupation army were simply shot.)

Three days before, the Nazis had posted notices throughout Kiev instructing all Jews to report at a major road junction at eight o'clock on the morning of September 29. Told that they would be resettled elsewhere, the Jews were advised to bring their valuables, warm clothing, underwear, and food for three days. Failure to report was punishable by death.

Unaware of the Nazi extermination policy, apparently believing that they were to be resettled and fearful of the death threat for disobedience, the Jews assembled by the thousands. Ilya Ehrenburg records, in a moving section of his recently published memoirs, how "a procession of the doomed marched along endless Lvovskaya; the mothers carried their babies; the paralyzed were pulled along on hand carts."

An eyewitness report, recorded in an official account, related the grim finale of the procession as it reached the Lukianovka area:

They were ordered to deposit on the ground in a neat pile all the belongings they brought with them and, then, in tight columns of one hundred each, were marched to the adjoining Babi Yar . . . I could see well how at the ravine's edge the columns were stopped, how everyone was stripped naked, their clothes piled in orderly bundles. Then they were put in a row at the very edge of the ravine and shot in the neck by machine guns; children were thrown alive into the ravine.

According to an authoritative Soviet source, the technique of mass extermination required the first group selected for shooting to lie down at the bottom of the ditch. After they were shot, the Germans shoveled a little earth over their bodies, and "the next group of people awaiting execution was forced to lie on top of them and was shot in the same way, and so on."

Tremors in the Earth

Ostensibly the action was taken as retaliation for a land mine explosion on September 24 which had wrecked the headquarters of the Nazi army's rear area command. The town commandant was determined to make an example of the Jews. He called in SS Colonel Paul Blobel, whose *Einsatz-*

gruppe C had achieved an extraordinary record of mass murder (for which Blobel would be formally condemned by the Nuremberg Tribunal and executed on June 1, 1951).

During the next two years, Babi Yar became the execution point for thousands of captured Russian and Ukrainian soldiers and workers. But it was particularly identified as a symbol of the anti-Jewish fury of the Nazis. Colonel Blobel, answering a Gestapo agent, Albert Hartel, as to why the surface of Babi Yar seemed to shake from pressures below, replied that in Babi Yar "my Jews are buried." Blobel explained the tremors as the release of gases from thousands of decaying corpses.

Fearful that the butchery might come to the attention of the world, the SS also assigned Blobel the task of erasing all traces of the Babi Yar mass burial. In August, 1943, his unit dug up the area, examining each corpse for rings, earrings, and gold teeth. Huge crude crematoriums were built, the bodies stacked alternately with logs and doused with gasoline. Each pyre took two nights and a day to burn. Human bones that were not incinerated were crushed, mixed with earth, and scattered over the area. The blazing fires lasted almost six weeks, the stench suffocating the entire Lukianovka district.

The macabre evidence could not be completely suppressed. The Soviet public learned the shocking details from the reports of *Izvestya's* military correspondent, Yevgeny Kriger, and from Ehrenburg's Stalin-prize novel, *The Storm*. Documentation was also provided in 1945 in a book by K. Dubina and the findings of an official inquiry were also made public, although the special martyrdom of Jews was blurred.

The Unbuilt Memorial

In 1959, Soviet novelist V. Nekrasov wrote that a prominent architect, A. V. Vlasov, had designed a memorial, "strict, simple, in the form of a prism," to stand at Babi Yar as a symbol of Nazi genocide, and that the artist B. Ovchinnikov had developed sketches "dedicated to Babi Yar." The plans, if they existed, were soon shelved, and mention of Babi Yar disappeared from the Soviet press. The anti-cosmopolitan campaign with its strong nationalist and anti-Semitic overtones could hardly tolerate consideration of Babi Yar as a symbol of Jewish martyrdom. (Ten years earlier, *Literaturnaya Gazeta* had condemned a wartime poem about the Babi Yar holocaust by the Ukrainian-Jewish writer Savva Golovanivsky as "nationalist slander" and "defamation of the Soviet nation." Golovanivsky was accused of saying that Ukrainians and Russians "had turned their backs on an old Jew, Abraham, whom in 1941 the Germans had marched through the streets of Kiev to be shot." Another Ukrainian-Jewish poet, Pervomaisky, was also denounced for "repeating Golovanivsky's defamation of the Soviet people.")

Yet Babi Yar could not be erased from the minds of Soviet Jews. Many were familiar with a recording popularized by the Yiddish singer Nehama Lipschitz which told of the grief of a Jewish mother unable to find the remains of her child who had perished at Babi Yar. Some courageous Jews would stealthily visit the site of Babi Yar on Yom Kippur eve to mourn the martyred.

Nor would the conscience of the Soviet intelligentsia be stilled. When Nekrasov learned that the Kiev Town Council planned to flood and fill the ravine, then "turn the site into a park, to build a stadium there," he bitterly commented: "Is this possible? Who could have thought of such a thing? To fill . . . a deep ravine and on the site of such a colossal tragedy to make merry and play football? No, this must not be allowed!" (*Literaturnaya Gazeta*, October 10, 1959.) Nekrasov noted that other sites of Nazi atrocities had been transformed into memorials, and "lest people ever forget what happened," he demanded similar "tributes of respect" for the Kiev citizens who had been "beastly shot in Babi Yar."

Two months later, *Literaturnaya Gazeta* published a letter, signed by a number of inhabitants of the district near Babi Yar, supporting Nekrasov's plea for a memorial. The signers welcomed the idea that "a park be first planted in Babi Yar," and then "a monument erected in its center." The letter omitted any mention of martyred Jews. This appeared to signal an eventual halfway response by authorities to the outraged conscience of the intellectuals: A Babi Yar monument yes, but one not specifically dedicated to Jews.

Some months later, *Literaturnaya Gazeta* reported (March 3, 1960) that the deputy chairman of the Kiev Town Council Executive Committee, in reply to the Nekrasov article, had explained that the monument had not yet been erected because of "lack of reclamation of the region."

He promised that after afforestation of the slopes of the ravine and a public park were completed, "an obelisk with a memorial plaque to *Soviet citizens* exterminated by the Nazis will be erected in its center." (Emphasis added.) This commitment, it might be noted, was "a resolution adopted by the Ukraine Government in December, 1959," three months after Nekrasov had raised the issue. The novelist had, it seemed, pricked the conscience of the Kiev community.

Impact of a Poem

A much larger community, twenty years after the massacre, extending beyond Soviet borders, would be stirred by Yevtushenko. In an autobiographical sketch published in the French newspaper *L'Exprès*, Yevtushenko explained how he had come to write his courageous and moving "Babi Yar." He had waited a long time, he said, to publish a poem on anti-Semitism, but an appropriate form had not presented itself until after he had visited Babi Yar to see and sense the holocaust. On his return to Moscow he wrote the poem in "a couple of hours." In it, the young poet identified himself with "each man they shot here," "every child they shot here," and, in his profound mourning, he felt himself transformed into "one vast and soundless howl."

On the evening of September 16, 1961, Yevtushenko recited "Babi Yar" to 1,200 students at the Polytechnical Museum. He was "so nervous" that he kept the text in front of him. The reaction of his listeners was overpowering:

When I finished there was total silence. I just kept folding the paper in my hands, scared to look up. When I did, the entire audience stood. Suddenly the applause began and continued for nearly ten minutes. People rushed up onstage and embraced me. My eyes were full of tears.

Yevtushenko was uncertain whether the poem would be published. However, the editor of *Literaturnaya Gazeta* agreed to do so, although not without a last-minute warning to Yevtushenko: "No telling what may happen. Are you prepared for it?" The poet replied, "I am." The poem, published September 19, became an international sensation.

It also set the doctrinaire apologists in motion. On September 24, *Literatura i Zhizn*, organ of the Writers' Union of the Russian Republic, carried a crude attack by Alexei Markov, who asked "what sort of real Russian" was Yevtushenko. Because the theme of the poem was the martyrdom of Jews at Babi Yar, Yevtushenko was accused of defiling (with a "pygmy's spittle") "Russian crewcut lads" who had fallen in battle against the Nazis. An echo of a former period resounded when Markov flung the epithet "cosmopolitan" at Yevtushenko.

A less vulgar if more trenchant accusation by a leading conservative critic, Dmitri Starikov, appeared in the same journal three days later. It challenged the view that Babi Yar symbolized the martyrdom of Jews. The "destinies of the persons who died there cry out" against the idea that Babi Yar was "one of history's examples of anti-Semitism," wrote Starikov. To underscore his argument, Starikov appealed to the authority of Ilya Ehrenburg, one of Russia's leading literary figures and a Jew as well. Quoting selected extracts from Ehrenburg's wartime articles on Babi Yar, Starikov contended that Ehrenburg "did not stress the fact that it was Jews who were killed there."

Ehrenburg promptly repudiated the contention. His reply, published on October 14 in *Literatura i Zhizn*, said:

I consider it necessary to state that D. Starikov quotes arbitrarily from my articles and poems, cutting the quotations short to make them correspond to his thoughts and contradict mine.

Yevtushenko became the center of a political and literary controversy. A prominent literary spokesman of the regime, N. Gribachev, pointedly charged at the Twenty-second Party Congress that *Literaturnaya Gazeta* had manifested "irresponsibility" by publishing "cheap sensations." But "Babi Yar" also received unexpected artistic support from one of the U.S.S.R.'s most prestigious cultural figures, Dmitri Shostakovich. In late 1962 the composer completed his *13th Symphony*, a musical and choral setting of five poems by Yevtushenko, "Babi Yar" among them. The work received its first performance in Moscow on December 18, 1962, and was accorded a tumultuous reception. Yet no review appeared in any major Soviet newspaper.

Khrushchev's Denunciation

Official reaction to the Shostakovich symphony was not surprising. The day before its debut, at a special meeting in Moscow of top Party leaders and leading Soviet intellectuals, the Party's principal ideologist, Leonid Ilyichev, reportedly criticized Shostakovich for choosing an undesirable theme and failing to serve the true interests of the people. Public performances of the symphony temporarily ceased.

To answer the Party's thrusts, Yevtushenko made two additions to his text. At one point, he added the line: "Here together with Russians and Ukrainians lie Jews." A second insertion read: "I am proud of the Russia which stood in the path of the bandits." Yevtushenko vehemently denied in a Paris interview (February 1963) that he had capitulated to Party pressures. "I am not a man to take orders," he said. All that he had done, he maintained, was to make a slight addition without changing the sense of the poem. The addition, he insisted, was the result of a letter he had received, after the poem's publication, which described how a Russian woman had saved the life of a Jewish child threatened by the SS. Shostakovich incorporated the revisions in the symphony, performances were renewed, and *Pravda* observed that it was a truly "Russian" work (February 10, 1963).

But Soviet authorities, even with the compromise, were not happy. At a Kremlin conference on art and literature on March 8, 1963, Premier Nikita Khrushchev denounced the poem, accusing the author of depicting events at Babi Yar as if only the Jewish population had fallen victim to the fascist crime. The Premier charged Yevtushenko with political immaturity.

On April 2, a Minsk newspaper, *Sovyetskaya Byelorussia*, repeated the condemnation in a political critique of the Shostakovich symphony. It was "indisputable that the crimes of fascism in relation to the Jews are monstrous," the newspaper said. But why did the composer "look only here," at Babi Yar, for "material revealing the bestiality of fascism. . . . Why was fascism terrible only and first of all because of anti-Semitism?"

For the next three years there was silence on the issue in the Soviet press. The proposed memorial remained an unfulfilled promise. Yet the clamor for a monument could not be stilled and early in 1967 it was announced that the Ukrainian architects' club had placed on exhibit some 200 designs and thirty large-scale detailed plans for a memorial at Babi Yar. Visitors to the exhibitions were invited to express their views. The announcement added that entries would be judged by a special tribunal of municipal and governmental authorities and representatives of the Academy of Sciences and other cultural institutions.

The inscriptions on the designs avoided any reference to Babi Yar as a symbol of Jewish martyrdom. Instead, they read that "in this place," more than 100,000 "Soviet citizens, Russians, Ukrainians, and Jews, were murdered." An architect of Jewish origin, Abraham Miletsky, was reported to have submitted a plan bearing a Yiddish inscription which he was asked to withdraw. Another report said that a group of Kiev Jews had expressed to the municipal committee responsible for the exhibit its disappointment that the designs were without Yiddish inscriptions.

If the Russians needed more evidence that Jews specifically were singled out for murder at Babi Yar, it was provided in a recent issue of the Soviet literary journal *Yunost,* which carried the first installment of the documentary novel on Babi Yar by A. Kuznetsov. The author asserts that the Nazis had intended only to liquidate the Jews on September 29–30, 1941, and that the slaying at that time of a number of Russians and Ukrainians was a result of either confusion or Nazi fears that they had seen too much.

It now seems evident that some kind of monument will be erected at Babi Yar.[1] The Moscow correspondent of the *London Daily Telegraph* cabled in 1967 that he was told "emphatically" in Kiev that the memorial would be completed in time for the fiftieth anniversary of the Russian Revolution in 1968.

But it is not likely that the monument will particularly memorialize the Jewish martyrs of Babi Yar.

1. The memorial to the martyrs of Babi Yar has still (1968) to be erected. A temporary plaque at the site fails to note the unique Jewish tragedy, reading only: "A monument to the Soviet people, victims of fascism in the years of the temporary occupation of Kiev in 1941–43, will be put up here."—Ed.

Judaism Without Embellishment

BY *Moshe Decter*

For years the Soviet press has been full of articles that have systematically exploited traditional anti-Semitic stereotypes to project a viciously distorted image of the Jews and Judaism. This has been accomplished chiefly through atheist propaganda directed against Judaism as such and by the nationwide press campaign against economic crimes in which alleged Jewish criminals have been the main culprits.

But now an unprecedented volume has appeared, encapsulating all the anti-Semitic themes characteristic of the Soviet press. It is *Judaism without Embellishment*, by Trofim Korneyevich Kichko. The book was published in late 1963 by the Ukrainian Academy of Sciences in Kiev. What makes it startlingly unique is its extensive series of anti-Semitic caricatures, be-

With the withdrawal of Kichko's notorious work, the world thought it had seen the last of his name in print. But suddenly, in the wake of the 1967 Six-Day War, there he was again, disseminating his anti-Semitic fabrications. That he had in fact returned to the limelight was made clear in a January 20, 1968, article in *Pravda Ukrainy* in which it was reported that the chairman of the Supreme Soviet of the Ukraine had awarded Kichko the Diploma of Honor of the Supreme Soviet of the Ukraine "for his work for atheist propaganda."

ginning with the blood-curdling cover in color, which are worthy of nothing as much as Julius Streicher's *Der Stuermer*. The caricatures obviously speak for themselves; it should only be pointed out that nothing like them has appeared in the U.S.S.R. for decades, and one has to look to the Nazi regime for their like.

The book is also significant in various other aspects. Its size, for one thing. Atheist pamphlets attacking Judaism have appeared from time to time but never approximating the length of this one—192 pages.

Occasionally an atheist institute or a society for the dissemination of political knowledge would publish an item of this sort in one or another Soviet city. But this is the first time that such a publication has appeared under the official aegis of an Academy of Sciences. This sponsorship removes the anti-Jewish slanders from the rubric of propaganda and gives them the distinction of officially approved "science." Even the *Stuermer*-type cartoons thus become "scientific" documents.

Of course, the fact that this book appears in the Ukraine has its own special significance. For the Ukraine, of all the fifteen Soviet republics, is the one in which anti-Semitism is perhaps most deep-rooted and widespread. And this book appears in the Ukrainian language, for all to understand. It can be said that this volume bases itself on, and climaxes, the tradition of Ukrainian anti-Semitic literature that stretched back far beyond the Revolution. One may imagine how the Ukraine's one million Jews, and not least the approximately one-quarter of a million in the capital city of Kiev, where the book was published, must feel when confronted with such a volume. All the more, when we consider the fact that the Ukraine has the highest rate of inflicting capital punishment on Jews for alleged economic crimes. For the U.S.S.R. as a whole the Jews constitute 50–60 percent of the victims; in the Ukraine, they represent 80–90 percent.

Its importance is enhanced by the fact that it is published in an edition of 12,000—quite a large number for a "scientific" book from the Academy. Doubtless, the authorities wished to make sure that this science was well disseminated, for it is explictly intended for party cadres and educators, as "a valuable manual for propagandists of atheism in their daily work. . . ." If this is how science is written in the ivory tower, it is not hard to imagine how it will be used by the grass-roots cadremen and propagandists "in their daily work. . . ."

Judaism Without Embellishment

A word about the author, T. K. Kichko. This is not his first venture into "Jewish scholarship." A non-Jew, he has apparently become the leading Ukrainian "spetz" on all things Jewish. In 1957 he wrote a pamphlet entitled *The Jewish Religion, Its Origins and Essence*, published by the Kiev Society for the Dissemination of Political and Scientific Knowledge. It already contains all the seeds of the current blossom. It was on the whole well received by Ukrainian critics, though taken to task for occasional careless formulation and lack of profundity in certain matters. Presumably he has corrected these faults in his latest effusion, since his work has graduated from a propaganda society to the Academy of Sciences.

By 1962 he was a lecturer in the Technological Institute of Kiev. Precisely what he lectured on can only be surmised—undoubtedly political topics such as Marxism-Leninism, atheism, political economy. The quality of the instruction may perhaps be inferred from the fact that early that year he was awarded the degree of "Candidate in Philosophy"—the equivalent of the master's degree in England or America—for a dissertation on contemporary Judaism on which he had worked for three years. And in December, 1962, he published a lengthy study, *What Does Jewish Ethics Teach*, in the official atheist organ of the Ukraine.

All these earlier efforts may be regarded as precursors of the expanded scientific volume now at hand; his years of preparation have culminated in *Judaism without Embellishment*, a volume whose scholarship as such— quite aside from its anti-Semitic style, tone, and content—can only be described as puerile, irrelevant, or actually non-existent. Its scholarly "apparatus"—some footnotes based on a meager bibliography of secondary or tertiary sources—can fool only the willfully ignorant.

This virulent tract, a crude amalgam of falsehoods and distortions, purveys variants of two traditional anti-Semitic themes, one ancient and medieval, the other comparatively modern. The old one may be described as the "Shylock Theme"—the intrinsic connection between Judaism and money. The more modern one is based on elements of the notorious *Protocols of the Elders of Zion* (whose nineteenth-century Russian origin is doubtless familiar to Kichko and his fellow Academicians)—the worldwide Jewish conspiracy of Judaism, Jewish wealth, Zionism, Israel, and Western capitalism. In fact, of course, the two themes interlock and reinforce each other. The following excerpt from the book's Foreword touches on most of the variants of these themes:

Among the other religions which obscure the consciousness of the workers, not the least is Judaism. As is known from history, it always served the interests of the wealthy classes, using them to distract the attention of poverty-stricken Jews from struggling against social injustice. In recent times Judaism has acquired particularly reactionary coloration after the establishment of the State of Israel, where it was proclaimed the official religion.

Deceived by the enticing promises of bourgeois agitators, people fom seventy-four countries assembled there. Although all are Jewish by descent, they have nothing in common except the Jewish religion. . . . Therefore, the Israeli government, more than any other, is assisting the flowering of religious obscurantism in every possible way, in the hope that it will aid in uniting the different groups of immigrants into "one" nation. On this platform, Judaism is not only closely tied to Zionism, but is, so to speak, the trump card in the dirty game being played by the Israeli bourgeois politicians who are trying to ensnare the greatest possible number of faithful common people: after all, the new capitalistic state needs cheap labor; it needs soldiers to accomplish its aggressive military plans.

Here the double theme that runs through the entire book is already announced: Judaism is reactionary and subversive not only historically but also contemporaneously, through its connection with Zionism, Israel, and imperialism.

But now to history. Here is a characteristic segment (page 34) which, in two short paragraphs, hints at the politically subversive nature ("religio-nationalistic spirit") of Judaism, and elaborates the ancient anti-Semitic doctrine that Jews are encouraged to steal from non-Jews and to exploit them:

The Mishna consists of six chapters according to thematic principles. . . . The most important part of the Mishna is the Abot (Sayings of the Fathers)—a treatise "concerning principles." The texts here, just as in other treatises, are written in a religio-nationalistic spirit. . . .

Quite characteristic is the interpretation of the Decalogue—the Ten Commandments of the Bible: You may not steal from or cause any other damage to your *khavers* (neighbors) only—i.e., the Jews. As to how this applies to "goyim," to those of different religions, the Jews are free to take from them because, as Judaism teaches: "Jehovah delivered all of the wealth of non-Jews to the use of the Jews. If the Jews did not take everything into their hands, it was because in doing so they would have been deprived of many productive forces with the help of which the Jews profit from non-Jewish peoples without exerting any particular effort."

These plaints have echoed down through history from the medieval inquisition to Nazi propaganda. One may well wonder how, and on what basis, it found its way into the scholarship and propaganda of a "progressive socialist society."

We find another similar interpretation on pages 91–92—with the addition of the charge that Jews may also bear false witness, a hoary and cruel accusation particularly painful to the historical memory of Jews whose ancestors many centuries ago were tortured and murdered by the hundreds of thousands, with that charge flung at them by their executioners:

The Jews like to talk a great deal about the Commandment which forbids them to bear false witness. However, when the welfare of a Jew is in question, false witnessing and even false oaths are permissible. . . . While giving a false oath, it is only necessary, the "Holy Scripture" teaches, to negate the oath in the heart and soul, and therefore the oath is meaningless. But this must be done in such a manner that "the glory of the name of the God of Israel, the honor and worth of the Jewish religion and the people of Israel do not suffer."

One of the Commandments of Judaism is "do not steal." However, as the *Khoshen Mishpat* interprets it, it is only from *khavers* (i.e., from your Jewish neighbors) that you must not steal. But you may steal everything from others —because, as it is written in the "Holy Scriptures," Jehovah handed over to the Hebrews all the wealth of the non-Jews. If the Jews did not take everything into their own hands, it was because they did not want to lose the labor power of non-Jewish workers. Moreover, Judaism teaches the believer that his exclusive purpose is to study the Torah, and if the Jews always engaged themselves only in studying the laws of Moses, then God would force other people to work for them.

Although the commandments of Judaism teach not to steal, nevertheless in many places of the Old Testament recommendations are made for the people to resort to common theft.

The following passages sharpen and clarify the theme of the inextricable relationship between Judaism and money. But this is not a matter of mere theory and doctrine; these same passages bring the doctrine closer down to the everyday reality recognizable to a Ukrainian anti-Semite. From page 37:

In humiliating working people, the Talmud at the same time glorifies persons of wealth; in downgrading agriculture, it praises trade and usury. According to the Talmud, even the prophet Moses made a fortune through trade machinations which he practiced by speculating with community property. "Moses grew rich by selling pieces of sapphire which broke off during the cutting of the stones for the Ten Commandments," says the Talmud.

The Talmud morally corrupts people, instilling in them the spirit of commerce and extortion. An example of practitioners of extortion are the priests themselves, the teachers of the law—the rabbis, who supervise adherence to the religious prescriptions which permit common people "to be cleaned like fish."

In his daily newspapers, the Ukrainian reads countless stories of present-day descendants of Moses who allegedly "made a fortune through trade machinations practiced by speculating with community property." Now he learns here that it goes all the way to the beginning with Moses. It is, thus, no mere accident. . . .

From page 40: "The Talmud is saturated with contempt for work and for workers, for the common people. . . . The Talmud takes an especially negative position toward the work of peasants. . . ."

No less "contemporary" and succinct is the following brief passage from page 93:

The ethics of Judaism do not condemn such disgraceful actions as hypocrisy and bribery. The well-known commentator on the Talmud, Rashi, teaches: "Based on Biblical teachings, the Jew at the very outset must work with bribery in order to tempt his enemy, and in other cases he must resort to a variety of artifices."

And now, finally, to the nub of the matter, from pages 86–87:

Judaism considers a person to be moral if, not working for the good of society, he devotes all of his free time to prayer and to the performance of religious rites. For Judaism, not work but prayer is the highest manifestation of morality. Furthermore, all of Judaic ideology is impregnated with narrow practicality, with greed, the love of money, and the spirit of egoism.

"What is the temporal basis of Judaism?"—wrote K. Marx. "Practical necessity, self-interest. What is the temporal cult of the Jew? Commerce. Who is his temporal God? Money. What was the actual basis of the Jewish religion? Practical need, egoism. The God of practical need and self-interest—is money. Money—is the jealous god of Israel before whose face there must not be any other god."

The entire Judaic cult—is the translation of trade and commerce into religious language. The sale of matzah, the auction of chapter-readings of the Torah ("Aliye"), burial rites, circumcision, marriage and divorce—in all of these money is of prime importance, as is contempt for productive work.

What is alarming in all this is of course *not* that Karl Marx should have written that egregious passage (for whatever twisted psychological reasons), but that in the country where he is venerated as the omniscient Founder of the Faith, a contemporary writer should deem it necessary to quote *this particular passage* in a treatise on Jews and Judaism. The intention is unmistakable, the implication undeniable: Money, money, money —is the god of the Jews today, as it was in olden times and in Marx's time. So the following passage from page 96 is but one of the many contemporary reflections of the Jew's quintessential commercial spirit:

Speculation in matzah, pigs, thievery, deception, debauchery—these are the real characteristics of many synagogue leaders. Shrewd operators convert the synagogues from religion into their own personal feeding-grounds; they make free with the contributions of the believers, and become wealthy from them.

Strewn about all the above pages are various sorts of anti-Jewish caricatures, such as those on page 94 and page 96. The caption under the former reads: "All sorts of swindlers and cheats find refuge in the synagague." It shows a *Stuermer*-style Jew wearing a phylactery [a religious article used by Jews at prayer] on his forehead—with his hand in the money plate. . . .

The caption under the latter reads: "The swindlers in religious articles brawl among themselves over the division of the spoils in the synagogue." And the caricature shows the synagogue Jews fighting—under the sign of the Jewish Star, the Mogen David. . . .

Or the *Stuermer*-style caricature that accompanies the chapter title, "Opium for Some—Pocket Money for Others," on page 123—showing a religious Jew wearing a *yarmulke* (skull cap) and a *tallith* (prayer shawl) on his shoulders.

141

The ancient stereotype brought up to date will unquestionably be familiar in a Ukrainian context. It is calculated to infuriate, to incite to hatred of the Jew in more or less traditional terms. But the second theme —that of the Jewish conspiracy—is calculated more to frighten and unsettle the audience. And this is perhaps the more ominous impact, for it gives rise to the truly primitive notion of the Jew's alienness, it conjures up fears of political infiltration and subversion, and makes the Jew quintessentially suspect. The following passage (page 61) sets the stage for this theme:

The Talmud sanctified and continues to sanctify dividing people into masters and slaves: it developed legislation for the caste system; it divided people into distinguished persons and common people who were limited in their rights. The Talmud implants the thought that poverty is supposedly a method of obtaining a better fate in heaven, in the other world, and to cast off poverty— is a sin.

In the hands of the rabbis, these ideas are the chief spiritual weapon with whose help even today reactionary ideas are propagated, nationalistic illusions are implanted about the exclusiveness and God-like image of the Jewish people—which in essence supports an ideology inimical to our people.

The ground is laid—with such weighted words as "nationalistic illusions," "exclusiveness," "inimical" to "our" people—for the presentation of the Jew as the stranger, the alien, with aims other than "our" own. . . . This attitude is surely not far removed from that revealed by the Soviet leadership in explaining, several years ago, the increasing exclusion of Jews from a wide range of professional employments—on the ground that the Jews had to make way for "our own" intelligentsia. After all, the Jews have been living on what is now Soviet soil for many centuries; how long does it take for them to become considered native . . . ?

Here now, in the same spirit, is Kichko's treatment of the ancient rite of circumcision (page 144):

The cruel rite of circumcision has been filled with a reactionary meaning by the Jewish religion. It proclaimed circumcision as a unique mark of Jewish nationalism itself; in other words, it endowed it with a clearly expressed religious-nationalistic character. It is not difficult to substantiate the latter again by texts from the Bible. Acquiring a mark of belonging to "their own people," to the Jews, a mark which would simultaneously inoculate them with contempt and even hatred toward those who do not possess this rite—this is the basic meaning of the rite.

This unconscionable distortion comes with the most ill grace from a Soviet propagandist or "scholar." For the U.S.S.R. is, after all, a country that prides itself not least on having solved its nationalities problem—by encouraging the nationalities to retain and take pride in their national character and distinctiveness. It encourages all, that is, but the Jews, who, if they dare abide by an ancient sacred rite of *their* distinctiveness are accused of thereby showing contempt and hatred for non-Jews.

Another of the great Jewish traditional observances—the holiday of Passover—is assaulted on two grounds here (page 135):

Under modern conditions the Passover holiday harms us in a great number of ways, through engendering disrespect for work and fostering elements of nationalism among the Jewish workers. In celebrating the Passover, the believers do not go to work for several days; thus they hinder production plans and violate work discipline.

The celebration of the Passover is especially harmful because the entire Passover legend, all the prayers, orient the believing Jews toward returning to Israel, which is now the center of Judaism and Zionism. The Passover prayers urge the believing Jews: "May God grant that we meet in Jerusalem next year." Invitations summon the Jews to move to Israel, where they—free workers of our country—will become slaves, will become cannon fodder for Ben-Gurion's clique and for his imperialistic masters.

In the above passage, more clearly than before, is the theme of potential Jewish disloyalty subtly injected: Passover, Israel, Ben-Gurion, imperialism. Passover is indeed the crucial holiday asserting Jewish identity, which is why it, more than any other holiday, is subjected to such virulent and ominous abuse—why it is subjected to a process of attrition even to the extent of denying *matzoth* (unleavened bread indispensable to the holiday's proper observance) to the Soviet Jews.

The book moves inexorably toward its climax, first linking Judaism and Zionism and so making the Jews a security risk. From page 143:

Foreign Judaists, together with Zionists, are attempting in every possible way to activate nationalistic propaganda among the believers in our country. . . .

143

The Israeli Zionists are openly striving to use Judaism for the activization of Zionism, are trying to incline believing Jews toward a useless expectation of a fictional Messiah, toward cosmopolitanism and anti-patriotism, and are trying to divert the believing Jews of our country from the cause of building communism.

There we have it—two of the deadliest words in the Soviet lexicon: "cosmopolitanism" and "anti-patriotism." No one who remembers or knows of the use of the word "cosmopolitanism" to cover the wicked anti-Semitic purges and liquidations of Stalin's last five years can see the word in the present context without the greatest qualms.

And now, the climax of the doctrine: the massive interlocking world Jewish conspiracy; international Jewish capital; the Rothschilds; international Jewry and Zionism; oil, Palestine (Israel), and Western bankers. The amalgam is complete; it might well have been taken from a pre-Revolutionary anti-Semitic tract (pages 171–72):

Taking advantage of the legends of the Old Testament, the Jewish capitalists and their ideological parasites—the Zionists—together with the rabbis in Israel, kindle religious-nationalistic passions, and incite the Jews against other peoples who inhabit Palestine. . . .

A union between the financial oligarchy of the West and Zionism has been in existence for several decades. As is known, the English and American monopolists subjugated Zionism when it first appeared, when it only dreamed of creating a bourgeois Jewish state in Palestine. Long before the Second World War, after the reorganization in 1929 of the executive committee of the International Organization of Zionists which began to call itself the "Jewish Agency," the Rothschilds, Jewish bankers, backed the Zionist organization in England. They also financed the French Zionists. Oskar Wasserman became the supporter of the "Jewish Agency" in Germany; he was the director of the German bank which at one time controlled the concession for constructing the Baghdad railroad. All of these Zionist businessmen invested their capital in Palestine with the aim of obtaining colonial gains at the expense of the Jewish as well as Arab population.

American bankers, just like their English, German and French partners, viewed Zionism as a convenient colonial business. Founding in 1926 the syndicate, "Palestine Economic Corporation" (PEC), the American-Zionist colonizers engaged in creating a modern state of Israel.

The history of relations between American capital and Zionism cannot be understood if one does not consider the affairs of the billionaire Rothschilds, who for several decades had been attempting to grab a part of Palestine—the Negev desert and its oil deposits. In 1919, immediately after the First World War, an agent of the American Petroleum Combine, "Standard Oil," and a technical employee of the commission for developing American policy for Palestine, declared that although England would obtain a mandate in Palestine, with the help of the Zionists the U.S.A. would actually rule there.

And that is what happened. After World War II, the Zionists in Palestine discontinued recognizing the supremacy of English imperialism, while the Rockefellers became strongly entrenched. At the present time, Israel, and its Zionism and Judaism, is considered as its outpost by American imperialism, as a reserve cannon for bombarding the Arab world.

What is this if not an updated and refurbished version of the *Protocols of the Elders of Zion?* And to drive the point home, another *Stuermer*-style caricature of the Jewish capitalist-imperialist and the religious Jew accompanies the chapter heading "Life Denies the Zionist Lies."

Unquestionably the most unspeakable of the caricatures is that on page 161, showing the Jew . . . servilely about to kiss the Nazi boot. The theme is reminiscent of the incredible story Chairman Khrushchev told at the meeting of the Party leadership and the intelligentsia on March 8, 1963—of the Kiev Jew (Kogan, a former Komsomol leader, no less) who served as an interpreter for the German Marshal von Paulus at Stalingrad. Khrushchev introduced the story by saying, "There were cases of treason on the part of people of different nationalities. I can mention the following instance." And he went on to cite the only one he could think of—the Jew, Kogan. . . .

From Moscow to Kiev, it would seem, it has become permissible—nay, fashionable—to be both anti-Nazi and anti-Semitic at the same time. The fact that Soviet anti-Semites were also anti-Nazi during the war is precious little consolation to the contemporary Ukrainian Jew. For his religion is uniquely depicted as the embodiment of the spirit of capitalism and subversive nationalism; and the character of his Jewishness is also uniquely viewed as alien, suspect, and actually or potentially disloyal.

FOUR

Soviet Jewry and Israel

When the State of Israel
Was Proclaimed

BY *Joseph B. Schechtman*

When the State of Israel was proclaimed on May 14, 1948, the Kremlin granted *de jure* recognition within two days (Washington's *de facto* recognition preceded it by forty-eight hours). On August 17, *The New York Times* correspondent reported from Tel Aviv: "The State of Israel rolled out the red carpet for Pavel I. Yershov, Minister of the Soviet Union, who presented his credentials":

Prime Minister David Ben-Gurion and Foreign Minister Moshe Shertok donned high hats and striped trousers. Bands played the Hebrew and Soviet national anthems and a guard of honor stood at attention.

During Israel's struggle against the invading Arab armies, badly needed arms came from Czechoslovakia with Moscow's tacit approval and in defiance of the United Nations' embargo on the introduction of arms and fighting men into the Middle East. Arms deliveries were paid for in cash, so there was no "philanthropy" in this action. Moreover, a report issued in April, 1948, by the International Committee for the Study of European Questions, established that Israel was not the only beneficiary of Czechoslovakia's well-paid help: Arabs were simultaneously receiving arms deliveries from the Skoda works for use in Palestine. Nevertheless, at that time, arms—from whatever source and at any price—were a matter of life or death for Israel, and seventeen years later, in 1965, Katriel Katz, Israel's new Ambassador to Moscow, when presenting his credentials to the Soviet Head of State, Anastas Mikoyan, stressed that the Jewish people in Israel would never forget the deep understanding which the Soviet Union revealed during the struggle for its establishment as a sovereign state; the Soviet Union occupied a special place in the history of Israel.

The advocacy of Jewish statehood by the Soviet U.N. delegation was widely publicized in the entire Soviet press, reawakening long suppressed Zionist feelings and expectations.

The anthology *Struggles of a Generation* includes eloquent and touching excerpts from letters sent to Israel from various parts of Soviet Russia. Some of them were in Hebrew—a proof that the language had not been extinguished in spite of the long separation from Hebrew press and literature.

In a postcard from Odessa, dated May 17, 1948, G.V., a former Zionist deportee who had served his term in the distant parts of Northern Russia, wrote:

Today, with great joy, I heard the tidings about the rise of the State of Israel. With all my heart and soul I send you, the whole *Yishuv* and the whole Jewish people my blessings and the greeting, *mazel tov,* at the commencement of a new epoch in the history of our people. May the Lord give you strength and courage to surmount all the obstacles in your difficult way. . . . Many thanks to the Soviet Government for the good deeds of kindness for Israel.

A Hebrew letter from Kharkov, written on October 14, 1948, said: "Now a miracle has occurred in the midst of a miracle. Yesterday there was neither people nor state, and overnight there is a state with a government. And the next day, while the state was literally still in infancy, there was an enemy attack which you overcame. Is there such example in all history?"

When the State of Israel Was Proclaimed

An inmate of a concentration camp in the remote Komi district of Northern Russia, who worked in a large factory employing considerable numbers of Jews, wrote:

The evening of the 15th of May was unforgettable. While I was lying on my wooden bunk I heard the last news from Moscow over the loudspeaker. The announcer reported the official statement that the Jewish State had been proclaimed in Tel Aviv. Warm tears of joy streamed from my eyes. All the exiled non-Jews who were there with me became silent with astonishment. Then they rose from their bunks and spontaneously shook the hands of the Jews and congratulated them. A sweet joy pervaded my whole body. The sadness and bitterness which filled my heart vanished away, and I suddenly felt as though reborn.

We ran at once to the other Jews in the camp to tell them the news and rejoice with them.

. . . In honor of the festive occasion each of us produced the little food in his possession and we camp Jews held a feast together. We could not sleep all night long. In our hearts and thoughts we were at the front with our brothers and sisters who had begun a bitter war, rifle in hand, against the invading Arabs immediately after the proclamation of the State.

There was much satisfaction and jubilation in non-Zionist circles as well. It was reported that when in a small, intimate group of intellectuals the conversation turned to Gromyko's speech at the United Nations, Solomon Mikhoels recalled a passage in one of the Yiddish classics by Mendele Mocher Seforim in which a Jew asks a Russian peasant to point him the way to the Land of Israel. "Gromyko," said Mikhoels in exaltation, "is that good Gentile who shows us the way to the Land of Israel." After the proclamation of the state, the poet David Hofstein, who was both a loyal Soviet patriot and an exalted Jew, sent a telegram to the vice-chairman of the Ukrainian Academy of Science suggesting the establishment of a chair in Hebrew. When Dr. Chaim Weizmann was elected president of Israel's Provisional Council, he received the congratulations of the Chief Rabbi of Moscow. The government-sponsored Jewish Anti-Fascist Committee, whose organ *Ainikkeit* referred to the State of Israel not by its own name but as *Malchus Yisroel*, the Realm of Israel, also dispatched a congratulatory cable. While praising the policy of the Soviet Government, which "ceaselessly fought for a just solution of the Palestine problem," the committee sent Dr. Weizmann and the Jews of Eretz Israel its hearty good wishes on the establishment of the Jewish state. This event is regarded as one of the most important in the history of the Jewish People. . . . With all our hearts we wish you and the working people in the State of Israel a victory over the aggressors, quiet and fruitful work for all freedom-loving peoples and for the Jewish people itself.

All this individual and collective evidence of reawakened Jewish national consciousness sounded dangerously akin to the long banned "Zionist spirit." Those in the Kremlin were apparently becoming apprehensive lest things go "too far," and felt that a halt must be called to further displays of Soviet Jewry's involvement in the renascence of Jewish statehood. Ilya Ehrenburg, a gifted Soviet author of Jewish origin and a seasoned and willing weathervane of the regime's changing attitudes, bestirred himself to publish in *Pravda*, mouthpiece of the Russian Communist Party, a four-column article (September 21, 1948) condemning the Zionists as "mystics," and denying that there was any affinity between Jews in different countries. While the Soviet Union was sympathetic to Jewish aspirations for statehood, it had no sympathy for Israel's "bourgeois" government; the workers in Israel "must fight not only against the invaders, but against the bourgeoisie for whom war, as for all bourgeoisie, above all, means profits."

Ehrenburg's obviously officially inspired article was meant as a stern warning to Soviet Jews to dampen their enthusiasm for everything Israel and Zionism stood for. It was certainly no coincidence that it appeared almost simultaneously with the arrival in Moscow of the first Israeli Legation, headed by Mrs. Golda Meyerson (Meir). They took temporary lodging at the Metropol Hotel, which unfurled the white and blue flag of the State of Israel, which is identical with the Zionist banner. Though no mention of it was made in the press or over the radio, the Jews of Moscow soon found out and, disregarding Ehrenburg's warning, were in the thousands crowding the sidewalk by the hotel or across the street, eager to see with their own eyes the symbol of Israel reborn. Parents raised their children onto their shoulders for a better view of the flag.

When, on October 16, Mrs. Meyerson and her staff went for the Jewish New Year service at the Choral Synagogue in Moscow's Spassogei-niczevsky Pereulok, tens of thousands of fervid worshipers solidly packed not only the synagogue and the courtyard but also the street, overflowing into the side streets. Joseph Newman, Moscow correspondent of the *New*

York Herald Tribune, described this event as "unprecedented" during the thirty years of the Communist rule: "Men and women cried from emotion, exclaiming—'We were waiting for this all our lives. For Israel! Next year in Jerusalem.' The synagogue was decorated with banners; on one of them was inscribed in large Hebrew letters, 'Israel Is Born,' on the other, 'Eretz Israel is Reborn.' "

The atmosphere in the synagogue was charged with emotion. Necks were craned to catch a glimpse of the ambassador in the women's gallery. During the service and on the way out, men and women pressed to get as close to her as possible. Hands reached out to touch her sleeve or dress; those who got close enough kissed the edge of her sleeve or the fringe of her shawl, as though they were sacred objects. On the way to the hotel, Mrs. Meyerson and her secretary were followed by a crowd of Jews, thronging the sidewalks and street. Exclamations such as *"Am Yisroel Hai"* ("The Jewish People Lives") arose from the crowd. A police detachment accompanied the procession, but did not interfere. A similar demonstration took place a week later after a Day of Atonement service. The news of the inspiring encounter betwen the Israeli Legation members and the Jews of Moscow spread with lightning speed throughout provincial Jewish communities. Very soon, Jews started applying to the legation for visas and asking for its co-operation in obtaining exit permits from the Soviet authorities.

Young Soviet Jews, though largely assimilated, were becoming restive and started posing disturbing questions. A Czechoslovak officer of Jewish origin, who visited the U.S.S.R. at that time, later related in the *Jewish Daily Eagle* of Montreal (March 18, 1949) a confrontation he witnessed at one of the weekly lectures on international affairs held at a large hall at the Khlebny Pereulok No. 5. This particular lecture was devoted to the United Nations' decision of November 29, 1947, and was widely advertised in advance. The speaker was E. Yermolayev, well-known editor of *Pravda*. The large audience was almost exclusively Jewish.

They were treated to the time-worn arguments that Zionism was "the instrument of British imperialism," that Palestine was not a solution to the Jewish problem, which exists in the capitalist countries only, because it had disappeared in socialist states. Following the usual pattern of such gatherings, the chairman called for questions from the audience, which had to be submitted in writing. A flood of questioning notes followed. Yermolayev started reading them—and exploded in anger: "How do you dare to pose these kinds of questions, they are sheer provocation?" And he quoted some of them: "Can you deny that Zionism has transformed deserts into fertile soil and thus performed a useful deed?" Or: "Do you admit that Communist theoreticians who had asserted that the Jews were not a nation, proved to be wrong, and that it was Theodor Herzl, the founder of Zionism, who was right?"

Yermolayev refused to answer the questions. The youthful inquirers loudly protested. The chairman hastily closed the meeting. Before being permitted to leave the hall, everybody had to present his or her identity card; particular attention was paid to those who had submitted the questions. Subsequently, more than twenty of them were arrested, transferred to Kuibyshev, appeared in a public trial, and received sentences of fifteen to twenty years in a "re-education camp."

Arrests and deportations of Zionists were resumed on a large scale.

The Kremlin's renewed anti-Zionist "hard line" had almost immediate repercussions in other "popular democracies." As early as December 4 and 5, 1948, Rumania's militantly pro-Communist Jewish Democratic Committee forcibly occupied club houses and other headquarters of various Zionist organizations in Bucharest and Yassy. The Zionists, whose membership among the 240,000 Rumanian Jews reportedly totaled 160,000, vigorously resisted. But a week later, the politburo of the official Communist Party joined the anti-Zionist crusade, publishing a violent attack on Rumanian Zionists who were "hindering the Jewish masses" from attending to the country's constructive work; the statement decried the "idea of Jewish unity" and branded Zionism as "a political, nationalistic, reactionary current of the Jewish bourgeoisie, which strives to prevent Jews from fighting with progressive forces against capitalism and their own bourgeoisie." In Hungary, where till the end of 1948 the Jews could obtain an exit visa for Palestine with comparative ease, it "has been made difficult," reported John MacCorman to *The New York Times* on January 10, 1949. On March 13 the National Council of the Hungarian Zionist Federation "unanimously decided to terminate its activities," the Communist-sponsored "Committee for the Liquidation of the Hungarian

Zionist Federation" triumphantly announced. Two months later, ten Zionist leaders were arrested for organizing "illegal" immigration to Israel.

Soviet support in the United Nations for the creation of a Jewish State
was motivated primarily by the desire to eliminate Great Britain from
Palestine, to weaken the British position in the Middle East, and to enable
Soviet penetration into this strategically important area. However, Israel
showed no inclination whatever to become a Soviet satellite. On the
other hand, while not interfering with mass emigration of Jews from the
Soviet bloc countries (between May 15, 1948, and May 15, 1952, a total
of 296,813 immigrants from Poland, Rumania, Hungary, Czechoslovakia,
and Bulgaria landed in Israel), Moscow from the very beginning barred
emigration to Israel of its own Jewish citizens. From May 15, 1948, till
the end of 1951, only four old women and one disabled ex-serviceman
were permitted to leave for Israel.

Nevertheless, in the early stages, hostility to Zionism rather than to the
State of Israel appears to have been the dominant feature of the Kremlin's
policies. In the years 1948–53, the Soviet Government on the whole re-
frained from active interference in Middle Eastern affairs: there was for
some twenty months no Soviet reaction to the tripartite Anglo-French-
American declaration of May 25, 1950, guaranteeing the integrity of the
existing frontiers and the "balance of armaments" between the Middle
Eastern states. This significant move of the Western democracies was for
the first time mentioned, in a casual way at that, in the Soviet statement
of January 28, 1952. The attitude toward Israel during this five-year
period could be best defined as "unfriendly indifference," the element of
"unfriendliness" being largely motivated by considerations of internal political nature. The Jewish minority in the U.S.S.R., with its deep-seated
sentiment for Israel, its weakened but still potent Zionist background, and
its strong sympathies for the West with its numerous Jewish communities,
was viewed as inherently "unreliable" and Israel was regarded as a major
"diversionary" source of this alleged unreliability. Anti-Jewish, anti-
Zionist, and anti-Israel tendencies of the Soviet regime were organically
interconnected. When on January 13, 1953, *Pravda* unrolled the infamous
"doctors' plot," the six Jews among the nine indicted physicians were
charged with being in league, not only with American and British agents,

but also with "Zionist spies." The same day, *Izvestya* berated "the dirty face of the Zionist espionage." This piece of anti-Zionist demagoguery provoked an angry reaction in Israel. On February 9, "unknown persons" planted a bomb in the Soviet Embassy in Tel Aviv. Accusing the Israeli police of complicity, Moscow three days later broke off diplomatic relations with Israel.

Four weeks after Stalin's death, "Moscow Radio" announced on April 4 that the "doctors' plot" was a provocation and that the charges against the physicians were false. Broadcasting from Jerusalem, the "Voice of Zion" expressed "gratification." "It follows then," said the broadcast, "that the accusations against the Zionist movement . . . must be completely invalid. . . . The government of Israel will press its just demand that the Soviet Union permit the emigration to Israel of those Jews who so desire."

During the short-lived post-Stalin regime of Georgi Malenkov, the tension somewhat subsided. Diplomatic relations were resumed on July 20, 1953; the Soviet Mission in Tel Aviv and the Israeli Legation in Moscow were converted into embassies. There also was a more co-operative response to individual pleas for emigration permits: between July, 1953, and September, 1955, some 125 immigrants from the U.S.S.R. (almost exclusively from the areas annexed in 1938–45) reached Israel and were reunited with their families. These immigrants were all old people; the average age of the twelve who arrived up to September, 1954, was sixty-five.

A glimpse into the innermost feelings and attitudes of Soviet Jews in the years immediately following the emergence of Israel is afforded in a notebook, written in Hebrew, by an aging Zionist between November, 1952, and the end of 1955, which by a circuitous route came into the hands of a correspondent of *Davar*. We read in an entry dated May 16, 1953—the fifth anniversary of Israel's Independence Day:

There are thousands like me, I am sure, everywhere in the U.S.S.R., men and women of all ages for whom Israel Independence Day is a day for clandestine rejoicing. To meet en masse on these occasions would be sheer madness. A public Jewish celebration in the U.S.S.R. would be a treasonable act. Yet kindred souls somehow manage to cluster together on this day. A few of us, members of three families, have been meeting regularly since 1949 on the pretext of celebrating a birthday. On the first occasion, in 1949, we were somewhat reckless, I am afraid, and our loud singing and dancing aroused the neighbors' suspicion. We have since learned better. Walls have ears, and birds may be police informers. We now discourse quietly, and do not sing, except for *"Hatikvah,"* which we only whisper as we adjourn our gatherings.

In mid-1954, Malenkov was replaced by Nikita S. Khrushchev, under whose regime the Soviet Middle East policy became more aggressive and pro-Arab, more anti-Israel, and more anti-Zionist. It reached a climax in the wake of the Sinai Operation (1956). The Soviet envoy in Tel Aviv was recalled to Moscow as a "warning that should be properly assessed," and returned only in April, 1957; in February, 1957, the delivery of Soviet oil to Israel was stopped.

Nevertheless, a 200-member Israeli delegation was permitted in July, 1957, to participate in the International Youth Festival in Moscow. And once again huge and enthusiastic Jewish crowds—both local Muscovites and thousands of guests from the provinces—were bold enough to give an overt and passionate expression to their irrepressible attachment to the reborn Jewish state. They ardently applauded the Israelis, accosted them in the streets, asked for Israeli postcards, match boxes, stamps, pins as keepsakes; invited them to their homes.

A high price was paid for this emotional outburst. During the festival, the police did not interfere. But shortly after the foreign delegations had left, retaliation began. Hundreds—some estimates speak of thousands—of Jews guilty of the offense of "fraternization" were removed, on various pretexts, from their jobs. Many were arrested, some were sent to the Vorkuta hard-labor camp in Siberia. Nobody knows the exact scope of these reprisals. It is possible that popular imagination exaggerated their extent, but the lesson is still fresh in the memories of Russian Jewry.

Israel in the Soviet Mirror

FROM *Jews in Eastern Europe*

There is a singular repetition in the Soviet press of references to the term "Paradise." Here are some random titles: "Hell in the Israeli Paradise," describing how wives of new immigrants were forced into prostitution to earn bread for their families, how Jewish capitalists feel the muscles of laborers looking for work as if "buying a horse," and how the distance between "Israeli chauvinists and the Nazis" is "no greater than a sparrow's beak"; "No, This Is Not Paradise," which reports that a great many immigrants leave Israel because of vast unemployment, bad housing, and general disillusionment; "Wail from Paradise," "Do Not Believe the Fabrication about the Israeli Paradise," "The Man from Abroad: the Truth about the Israeli 'Paradise,' " "Tears in Heaven," "For Whom It Is Heaven in Israel" also deal in the same themes.

Outside the Soviet Union it would hardly be necessary to tell Jews that

Significantly, the accusations leveled against Israel in this selection were published before the Six-Day War. Denunciations of Israel after the war greatly exceeded the absurd descriptions presented here.

conditions in Israel are not idyllic. Information freely available to them makes it clear that the country has difficult social, economic, and political problems, and many Jews have seen conditions there with their own eyes. But cut off from disinterested sources of opinion, prevented from traveling as tourists, and suspicious of the material provided by Soviet propaganda, Soviet Jews apparently have a sufficiently idealistic picture of conditions in Israel to make the term "paradise," even if employed ironically, relevant.

A One-Sided Dialogue

If one assumes that there is a correlation between the intensity of a press campaign in the Soviet Union and the degree in which it reflects official concern—in other words, that it is rationally motivated—then on indirect evidence alone the attraction of Israel for Soviet Jews must be enormous. The articles and political comment represent, of course, a one-sided dialogue, but the silence of the absent participant has its own paradoxical eloquence. What is not being said, because none are permitted to say it, can be inferred by the repetitive insistence upon certain key themes by Soviet publicists, as we have already pointed out in the constant satirical play upon the term "paradise."

It can be assumed that Soviet Jews have a picture of conditions in Israel derived from a number of sources. First, there would be letters to relatives from people who once lived in the U.S.S.R. and settled in Israel. The information contained in these would be passed from one to another and so come to the knowledge of many Jews, sometimes in the form of extravagant rumor. (One such rumor a few years ago was that Israeli scientists had discovered a cure for cancer and that Israel had offered the secret to the Soviet Government in return for Soviet Jewish emigration.) Another source of information is Jewish tourists from abroad, many of whom have also visited Israel, and tourists from Israel itself, who are able to tell relatives at first hand about their experiences. A further source is references to Israel in foreign broadcasts and in the occasional foreign newspaper brought in by tourists.

Znamia Kommunizma of January 4, 1963, in "On the Wrong Side," describes the experiences of Julia Karpovna Bukhanko, who married a Polish Jew, Leonid Davidovitch Hokhman. In October, 1957, they left for Warsaw with their two sons, Valeri and Stanislaw, and from there emigrated to Israel. Mrs. Hokhman and her sons subsequently returned to the Soviet Union without her husband. When they arrived in Israel, the newspaper said, they were met "in an unfriendly way" and were taken to Kibbutz Mishmar Hasharon. Although Julia Karpovna Bukhanko's husband was a skilled shoe-cutter he had to work in the fields while she washed dishes. Two months later the man found work in the Donna shoe factory in Tel Aviv and the family moved into a primitive "asbestos hut." They suffered because "for ten months it is very hot." To make ends meet, the husband had to find a second job and worked for "twenty hours a day." He became almost blind and his health suffered before they found a flat, having paid key money and I£26 a month. A third son, Aron, was born and life became more difficult. The husband had to work even harder, they were forced to buy food on credit "at the kiosk of Peter Froidt in Ramat Yosef," and they sold all their possessions. "We and our neighbors, the Meir Rostovskys, could scarcely make ends meet." Prices escalated, taxes escalated, and the army of unemployed soared. "Even the president of the national bank of Israel admitted in the pages of the official bulletin that over 600,000 are half-starving or starving. And," Julia Karpovna Bukhanko is reported as saying, "is not 600,000 almost the entire population of Israel?" (Israel has a population of 2,300,000.)

The ordinary Soviet reader who may take these articles seriously is unlikely to feel admiration for any of the characters featured in them. The emigrants, re-emigrants, and those still pleading to return were people who "ate Soviet bread" while dreaming of a foreign "paradise." Now they were trying to crawl back into the favor of the authorities. The relatives of such people, even brothers and sisters, were indecently willing to denounce their own kin. The Israelis tell outrageous lies that Soviet people go about in rags, while they themselves were racialists dividing their own brethren into black and white, and waged armed aggression against their peace-loving Arab neighbors on the orders of the imperialists. Their tourists came to the U.S.S.R. for purposes of speculation, to make anti-Soviet propaganda and to spread ideological subversion.

It will not escape the notice of the general Soviet public that all these protagonists—both in Israel and the Soviet Union—are Jews, and some

A collection of typical Jewish publications which appeared in the Soviet Union before World War II. Today only one monthly periodical, *Sovyetish Heymland*, is allowed to publish. Soviet authorities argue that Jews are no longer interested in reading periodicals of strictly Jewish interest.

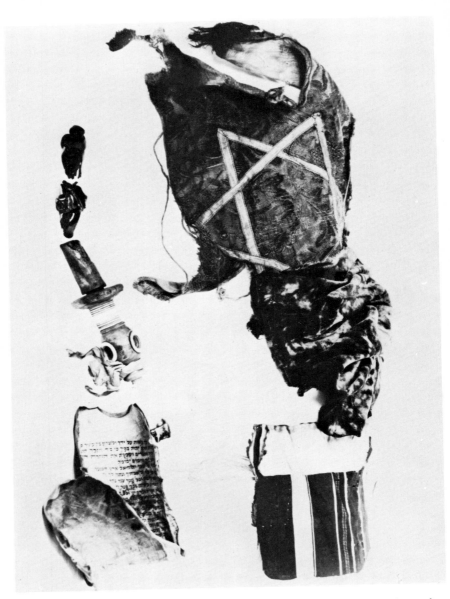

Burned fragments of the Torah remaining after the desecration of a synagogue in the Georgian Republic, 1962.

A Jewish cemetery in ruins in Minsk.

Kazakhstanskaya Pravda

Dayan to Hitler: Move on!

Pravda

Anti-Israel cartoons which appeared in the Soviet press at the time of the Arab-Israeli war in June 1967. (Courtesy of the Conference on the Status of Soviet Jews)

Interior of the Moscow Central Synagogue, popularly known as the
Choral Synagogue.

Sabbath morning service at the Choral Synagogue, to which tourists are taken. (Photograph by Meyer Levin)

The only remaining synagogue in Odessa, on a side street between two factories. As in all other cities, one finds a bare *minyan* of aged people. (Photograph by Meyer Levin)

A poster announcing a performance by Anna Gusica, one of the last of the Jewish entertainers in the Soviet Union. The poster is at the foot of Gorky Street in Moscow, in the area of the tourist hotels. (Photograph by Meyer Levin)

will no doubt recall that whenever there is something about these people in the newspapers, it is always unsavory.

This is certainly the impression given by *Sovyetskaya Moldavia* of June 21, 1964, in an article by "special correspondent L. Bakal" (the form of designation that often indicates an article written under the direct supervision of the KGB) entitled: "You were looking for happiness in the wrong place, Genia!" It commented on three letters, one from a newly arrived immigrant to her former friend and neighbor in Bendery, Nina G. Fuks-Devina, the neighbor's reply, and the neighbor's letter to the editor's office enclosing this correspondence and urging its publication. The Jewish names are all spelled out, even when not directly appropriate. For example, we are told that Nina's husband is Pinkus Srulevich Fuks, although he is not material to the story. Nina's covering letter said that in April, 1964, her neighbor Genia—or Faya—Nakhymovna Bidnaya, and the neighbor's husband, Abram Davidovich Gleizer, had left for permanent residence in Israel. "With all her heart Genia had desired to leave her homeland, but after she found herself in the so-called 'paradise on earth for Jews' she weeps and asks advice as to what she can do."

Genia's letter, written fifteen days after arrival in Israel, is filled with homesickness and depression. She was writing to Nina not as a neighbor but as a sister. There was not a single day that she did not cry for what she had done in leaving her home. She wanted all the news of Bendery. Her brother in Israel took her in for three days, then demanded payment. Now she lived in a hut with a cement floor, and her temporary house (presumably in the Soviet Union) had been a thousand times better. She was cooking on a kerosene stove and her luggage would not arrive for months. She was working, otherwise she and her husband would not be able to make a living, and her friend Nina should ask their friend Ivan not to give any of their property away because they might yet return.

That is, substantially, all. There are no general complaints about "nightmare" conditions, about anti-Soviet prejudice, unemployment, racialism, and the other Israeli "evils" common in the Soviet press. In fact, it is simply the letter of a very new immigrant roughing it before permanent settlement, bewildered by unfamiliar conditions and experiencing homesickness. But Nina's letter to her former friend is sharp and hectoring, full of civic indignation toward someone who had lived almost parasitically at the expense of the Soviet people. "Greetings, Faya!" it begins. "I have received your letter and was much surprised because when you left you hadn't even said goodbye to me and now, as you write, I have suddenly become your sister and your bosom friend. . . . You abandoned your homeland which gave you food and drink, gave you free education, made you an equal member of society, offered you work according to your choice. All this you brushed aside so carelessly and this is the miserable result: you live in a hut with a cement floor, you sleep on cots and, in some sort of way, you are cooking your food. How well you lived in your new stone house! What didn't you have: modern furniture, a television, a refrigerator, and gas, as well as water installed in the house! What convenience did you lack? You ask what life in Bendery is like. Don't you know it? You had plenty of food. You were clothed and shod. You didn't work but your husband had enough money for everything. . . . Your brother, by his behavior toward you, has at once shown you all the bad sides of life there. You don't know Hebrew and anyone can sell and buy you, you are now as if you are dumb."

This shrill dressing down of an ingrate who had brushed aside all the generous blessings of her homeland proved well justified when *Sovyetskaya Moldavia* sent the writer of the article to Bendery. "It is clear from everything that Abram Davidovich and Genia Nakhymovna hadn't lived badly. The house is just like a maid about to be married—festive, well proportioned, full of light. It has three large rooms. Gleizer and Bidnaya had all the conveniences at their service, a bathroom with shower, a refrigerator, and a washing machine. Also everything a man needs for relaxation, a television, a wireless set, and a cozy garden . . . 'They lived in Bendery like in God's lap.' " But in Israel "they were welcomed as they say in an old Moldavian proverb: 'A brother is a brother, but pay money for the goat cheese.' " Why had they left? "The Gleizers, in their naïveté, believed the Zionist propaganda about 'a paradise on earth' in Israel that crept in from abroad," the writer declares; he quotes a report about "a wave of strikes in Israel" from the *Naie Presse*, pointing out that this is a Yiddish newspaper in Paris but omitting the fact that it is Communist. The impression is thus given that the Jews themselves, even in the capitalist world, have to admit that conditions in Israel are dreadful.

The Israeli Diplomats

One considerable factor in the Jewish situation in the Soviet Union is the existence of an Israeli presence in the country, in the strictly formal sense of an embassy and diplomats representing a sovereign state officially recognized by the Soviet Government.[1] Its existence could be described as an ideological embarrassment, since it contradicts the well-known doctrinaire attitudes of Soviet theorists to Jewish nationality and peoplehood.

According to the classic formulations of Stalin and other ideologists, Jews were not a true nation because they lacked, in addition to other properties, a common territory and a national economic existence. These deficiencies are supplied by the State of Israel, although it would no doubt be argued that they have been supplied artificially. Israel's presence in Moscow can also be seen as the triumph of an ideology with which the Soviet Communists have been in conflict—vindication, at least in part, of the Zionist philosophy and its viability as a solution for those Jews who labor under a feeling of discrimination and lack of national fulfillment.

But it is on a more intimate level than the political that the Israeli presence is regarded as awkward. There is no doubt that many, possibly the majority, of Soviet Jews regard the Israeli Embassy as their "Embassy," the Israeli Ambassador as their "Ambassador." It is not exclusively a Soviet phenomenon. Jews in all countries where Israeli diplomatic missions function are inclined to see themselves as having a special relationship to these missions. They cannot regard the ambassador of Israel as just one of many foreign plenipotentiaries; their interests and his coincide on too many levels. They worship in the same synagogues; they share a common language, tradition, and history even if many Jews do not know the language or remember much of their history and traditions; the birth of a Jewish state is a major factor of their own contemporary history, as was the Holocaust, and they cannot regard it as of no special concern; they have close family ties with people who live in that state and it would be unnatural for them to regard these blood relatives as "foreigners"; they also

1. Diplomatic relations between Israel and the Soviet Union were broken off in the wake of the Six-Day War and have not been restored at this writing.—Ed.

163

share with the ambassador of Israel and the people of his country a special interest in Jews whoever they are and wherever they may live. The Soviet authorities are, therefore, confronted by a situation where many of their own citizens have a strong sense of affinity with a foreign mission on Soviet soil, in the heart of the Soviet capital.

For all the analogies there are in the attitudes of Soviet and non-Soviet Jews toward the Israeli presence in their countries, there are also important differences. Jews elsewhere have no obstacles in their access to Israeli members of their families. They can exchange visits with relatives, maintain free correspondence with them, read a wide range of articles about Israel in the Jewish and non-Jewish press, and freely receive material from Israel in the form of newspapers, magazines, travel literature, religious articles, and so on.

Non-Soviet Jews have no difficulty in accepting Israel as a distinct political and social entity, which does not necessarily coincide with their own expression of Jewishness. They have their own communal organizations of every kind, religious, social, cultural, political, and economic, through which common group interests—and even rivalries—with Israeli organizations can be channeled. These preserve the necessary distinctions between themselves as citizens of various nationalities and Jews who are citizens of the politically constituted Jewish nation.

In the Soviet Union, on the other hand, organized identity is represented only by the synagogue and by the embassy of the Jewish State. The latter, therefore, exerts a powerful attraction upon those who need a secular expression of their Jewishness, as the great majority of younger Soviet Jews do. The more they are deprived of national self-expression by the authorities, the greater the influence of Israel as a symbol of that which they are denied. Israel also supplies a vital element of national pride which is entirely absent for them in the Soviet Union—where public reference to the history, religion, traditions, and customs of the Jews is always derogatory, and individual Jews are featured in the press as social parasites, speculators, and religious obscurantists.

Nauka i Religia (No. 4, November–December, 1959), in "Judaism and Zionism," while attacking profiteering, corruption, etc., by rabbis and "Jewish religious activists," declares: "Some members of the Israeli Embassy in the U.S.S.R. also engage in . . . 'philanthropic' activities. Regardless of repeated warnings from several representatives of the Jewish clergy 'not to violate the order established in the synagogues and not to distribute prayer books, shawls, and calendars to believers,' the Embassy people frequent synagogues in various towns of our country and distribute their 'holy' donations. On the 10th October, 1959, an Israeli Embassy member visited the Lvov synagogue, was present at morning and evening prayers, distributed prayer books and calendars to believers, and, on leaving, bestowed two ritual citrus fruits, two palm twigs, a bottle of wine, and 400 rubles for 'synagogue needs.' Another 'philanthropist' from the Israeli Embassy tried to give religious 'souvenirs' to the Tbilisi believers, who, however, refused his presents. Side by side with prayer books and calendars, the 'wandering' Embassy members often distribute articles to believers of far from a religious character."

Lvovskaya Pravda, on February 16, 1962, in "Prayer and Speculation," concerned with "criminal affairs under the synagogue vaults," refers to the "foreign visitors" at the "holy shrine" who are courteously received by the synagogue officials. "Members of the Israeli Embassy in Moscow come as a rule to the synagogue in Lvov, but not to pray to the Almighty. They try to distribute to believers prayer books, calendars, and propaganda pamphlets on the 'Israeli Paradise' edited in the State of Israel."

Trud, which frequently concerns itself with this theme in articles signed "N. Ehrlich," believed to be a Jewish-sounding pseudonym chosen for the purpose, published "The Hangers-on" on June 9, 1963, attacking a group of Jews for allegedly "telling foreigners spurious tales about the conditions of life in our country" which were subsequently published in the Israeli press. It mentions a man named Chernukhin, who was said to have been doing this "as far back as 1949": "This hanger-on of declining years just loves embassy receptions. It is a passionate love and he tries not to miss out on a single one. Thus this love of his led him, a semi-literate hardly able to read or write, to a reception at the Israeli Embassy held in honor of writers, artists, and scientists who arrived from Israel to Moscow to attend the World Congress of Universal Disarmament and Peace. No conversation on methods of literary and scientific development occupied Chernukhin on that evening. Creeping like a snake from one foreigner to another, he begged for knickknacks, surreptitiously stuffing his pockets and lining his clothes with little booklets of dubious contents which were lavishly strewn on the tables. He did not bypass oranges or sweets, either."

Of another Jew, Roginsky, the newspaper says: "On October 17, 1962, the Israeli Embassy organized a reception on the occasion of the Jewish New Year. Of course, Roginsky was there. The guests were talking and exchanging news while Roginsky was skipping around the tables, well stocked with *talliths*, prayer books, books, journals, records, postcards, etc. The longer he skipped around these tables, the thicker his pockets got and the wider swelled his sides."

"Sheyfer," the article goes on, "prefers to 'work' at the synagogue . . . suffice it for a foreigner to show his face at the synagogue—Sheyfer is right there at his side begging for *talliths*, literature, and other foreign knickknacks. . . . Just a short while ago, on June 1, Sheyfer (for the umpteenth time) became the hero of a scandalous incident. During the service at the Choral Synagogue he sneaked into the box where the foreigners sat and begged for 'souvenirs.' A member of the congregation, Rabinovitch, told him off. In answer to this, such a torrent of abuse poured out of Sheyfer's lips that even an edited version would be too indecent to print. . . . Hangers-on like Chernukhin, Roginsky, Sheyfer, and their ilk do not act out of friendly feelings toward foreigners, nor out of a desire to help them to know our country and the life of Soviet people better. Avarice, groveling servility before everything foreign, spiritual waste, lack of pride in our motherland—these impel the Chernukhins, Roginskys, and Sheyfers into the embraces of sometimes not entirely blameless foreigners."

The "Price" of Reparations

The University of Moscow in 1965 published a textbook entitled *Modern History of the Countries of Asia and Africa*. It consists of almost 600 pages, each country being dealt with by a different expert. One chapter, consisting of four pages by G. S. Nikitina, is concerned with Israel. This is what Mme. Nikitina has to say about Israel-West German relations:

"The ruling circles of Israel conduct a policy of rapprochement with the revanchists of West Germany. In September, 1952, the government of Israel, with the support of the U.S.A., signed the essentially illegal agreement on reparations with West Germany under which Israel obtains, mainly at the expense of the Jewish population in other countries which had been the real victim of the Hitlerite horror, what is described as general reparations amounting to $822 million. The agreement is spent on the militarization of Israel. In return, the rulers of Israel appear as defenders of the militarists in West Germany and assist in the spreading of the monopolies of the German Federal Republic." Also, "the policy of enslavement of Israel by the imperialists of the U.S.A., and of the rapprochement with West German militarists, finds its completion in the anti-Soviet policy of the rulers of Israel. . . ."

In general, this so-called textbook of Moscow University represents Israel as an eager lackey of Western imperialists and colonialists, but the passages quoted above are typical of the way the Soviet press links Israel with all that is most reactionary and sinister in postwar Germany. In addition to articles, the point has been underlined in a number of crude newspaper cartoons showing Israeli leaders making deals with Nazi-type Germans at the expense of the victims of Hitler's concentration camps, and this preoccupation with Israel as a disreputable ally of neo-Nazism is one that creates profound misgiving among Jews in the U.S.S.R.

Nazi practices in occupied Soviet territory surpassed in frightfulness anything in other conquered countries and have left bitter memories. Few things could be more demoralizing to Jews who themselves suffered at the hands of the Nazis than to be confronted by "evidence" that Israel is a cynical collaborator with the heirs of Hitler, and nothing is more likely to feed the surviving anti-Jewish prejudice in certain sections of the Soviet population. It is, of course, cynical and dishonest to describe German reparations to Israel as obtained at the expense of Jewish populations in countries which had been the victims of Hitlerism, or to state that reparations were spent on militarizing Israel. Most of the surviving Jews in these countries settled in Israel after the Holocaust. German reparations were used to resettle them and to assist in building up Israel's economy in order to absorb them.

The legend of Zionist collaboration with the Nazis is an old one and has been repeated on a number of occasions in the Soviet press, as in the version given by *Trud* (May 26, 1959) that Kastner, "one of the

Zionist leaders who collaborated with the Nazis in World War II and was charged with the death of hundreds of thousands of Hungarian Jews," was murdered by "the Okhrana of Ben-Gurion" for fear that he would divulge the names of his associates, "beginning with Ben-Gurion." The standard Soviet textbook on Israel by Ivanov-Sheinis extends this alleged collaboration into the present and has been in constant use as a source book by Soviet newspapers. *Leningradskaya Pravda* of November 12, 1959, taking its material from the book, claims that the Israeli Government passed a resolution to plant a park in the name of Adenauer, thus hurrying "to immortalize his name on Israeli soil." (This was a distortion of the fact that a group of German-Jewish emigrés in America donated money to the Jewish National Fund to plant a grove in Adenauer's name as a gesture of appreciation for the latter's part in negotiating the German-Jewish Reparations Agreement.) It also states that the West German banker Herman Abs, who is called a war criminal—"one of those who fed Hitlerism with golden rain and whose plants produced gas for the gas chambers and soap from Jewish corpses"—paid a secret visit to Israel in May, 1959, to negotiate the investment of German capital in the country. (The facts were that Abs did visit Israel for discussions with the Finance Minister; this was raised in the Israeli Parliament by the Communist Party; the Finance Minister pointed out that Abs had *not* been named as a member of the Nazi Party and had *not* been incriminated for his conduct during the Nazi regime. No one—not even the Israeli Communists—suggested that the German banker had been attached to factories manufacturing gas and soap.) The same newspaper asserts that "the Israeli rulers have neither been disconcerted by the past of the German racists nor by the present revival of Nazism and anti-Semitism in Western Germany."

In these standard interpretations of Israel-West German relations, the Israeli leadership is represented as having made a deal with the "Bonn revanchists" whereby the role of Nazis and their successors in West Germany is concealed. This interpretation was emphasized in the relatively infrequent Soviet commentaries on the trial of Adolf Eichmann in Jerusalem. At first the Soviet attitude was reserved and undecided. During the first two weeks after the Nazi war criminal was brought to Israel, when the world's press discussed the event from every conceivable angle, nothing appeared in the Soviet Union apart from a brief news item from Jerusalem in *Sovyetskaya Rossia* (May 25, 1960), and another from Athens in *Pravda* (June 1, 1960). Before long, however, a general political formula emerged. This asserted conspiracy between the Israeli Government, Adenauer, and the U.S. State Department to protect Eichmann's accomplices and suppress evidence at his trial that might lead to the exposure of prominent Nazis in the West German Government.

The considerable aid given to Israel by West Germany under the 1952 Reparations Agreement has been consistently represented by Soviet spokesmen as payment for dubious services rendered by Israel to West German "revanchists" in the Middle East, or as the price paid by neo-Nazis for Israel's silence on their activities. The amount of space allocated to this theme and its variations is colossal in relationship to a country of only 2.3 million people. Hundreds of radio and press commentaries, articles, and news reports on Israel could be gathered from the Soviet press in a single year and it has justly been noted that Soviet propaganda often devotes as much hostile attention to Israel as if it were some powerful enemy.

The charge that Israel had made a deal with Adenauer to suppress the names of Globke and others at the Eichmann trial may have been totally discredited at the trial itself, but this has not prevented Soviet newspapers from continuing to repeat it whenever a suitable opportunity occurs. In late February and in March, 1965, the crisis that developed between the Arab States and West Germany over the latter's supply of arms to Israel and the visit of Ulbricht to the U.A.R. provided just such an opportunity. A spate of articles appeared representing the "secret arms agreement" as the price paid by the Germans for the Eichmann trial "deal."

Here are some representative comments. *Sovyetskaya Latvia*, on March 14, 1965, in "The Price of Silence": "During the trial in Jerusalem of the fascist butcher Adolf Eichmann in 1961 a strange thing was noticed by many observers: the Israeli authorities and the court itself carefully avoided even a mention of any connection between Eichmann and his spiritual acomplices who have burrowed in Western Germany. At the time this remained a riddle. The underlining of this matter has been quite unexpectedly revealed. At the time when Bonn was artificially arousing hysteria over the invitation of the chairman of the State Soviet of the German Democratic Republic, V. Ulbricht, to the U.A.R., there appeared reports in the press about the clandestine agreement between the F.G.R. and Israel. As far back as 1960, in the luxurious hotel Waldorf-Astoria, a meeting took place between the then West-German Chancellor Adenauer and the former Israeli Prime Minister Ben-Gurion. No information of the meeting was given." [Although the impression is deliberately given that the meeting was held to discuss the trial of Eichmann, it actually took place before Eichmann was even captured.—Ed. *Jews in Eastern Europe*]. "Meanwhile, the partners there made a deal which, for understandable reasons, they decided to keep strictly secret. . . . Adenauer promised to supply Israel with armaments to the value of 320 million marks free of charge. But this 'largesse' of Bonn was made conditional on by-no-means insignificant reservations. The fact is that the government of the F.G.R. was anxiously contemplating the then approaching trial in Israel of the Hitlerite criminal, A. Eichmann. . . . At the trial the accomplices and assistants of Eichmann, now successful in the Bonn Reich, might possibly be named. It is sufficient to mention the then secretary of Adenauer, Hans Globke . . . co-author and commentator of the Hitlerite racist laws. . . . These two names are irrevocably linked. One cannot speak of Eichmann's crimes without putting Globke on the same level, and vice versa.

"In exchange for the supply of armaments by Western Germany, the government of Israel had given Bonn a guarantee that Globke would not be invited as a witness to the Eichmann trial. In Tel Aviv they kept their given word. Globke was not only not invited as a witness to the trial, but the court also did everything it could to prevent his name being mentioned at the trial. This conspiracy of silence cost the West German taxpayers the sum of 320 million marks."

The note of alarm was again sounded when Israel and West Germany finally reached agreement on exchanging ambassadors. Moscow's Arabic broadcasts to the Middle East, which are notably uninhibited, represented the agreement as a threat to the Arabs. An Arabic broadcast to the Maghrib on July 12, 1965, was typical of this interpretation. It was entitled: "An Imperialist Conspiracy against the Arabs" and referred to the fact that "the Israeli Government has welcomed the appointment of the former Hitlerite officer Rolf Pauls as West German representative in Israel. . . . The establishment of diplomatic relations is a new step in the rapprochement between the revanchists of Western Germany and the militarists of Israel."

"There is no doubt," the broadcast continued, "that the Israel extremists, who have sent a representative of the military clique to Bonn as Ambassador, hope to continue expanding their military co-operation with the German Federal Republic. The Israeli extremists are prepared to do everything to strengthen their military potential with the help of the F.G.R., thus creating a new threat to the Arab states." These "Israeli extremists" were not disturbed by the fact that the West German Ambassador in Tel Aviv "is a man who served in the fascist army, the army which destroyed millions of people, including the Jews annihilated in the Second World War." The "Israeli extremists" were seeking to strengthen their military, political, and economic relations "with the Western imperialists" and attached great importance to their relations with Bonn. "At the same time, West Germany, like the U.S.A. and other NATO allies, looks on the territory of Israel as an imperialist base in the Near East and a bridgehead from which it might be able to implement its expansionist schemes not only in the Arab East but also in the Afro-Asian countries." All this confirmed the concern of the Arab states that the strengthening of relations between "the militarists of Israel and the imperialist states" constituted a direct threat to their independence and security. "The provocative incidents organized by the Israel Army along the borders with the Arab countries show that the extremists in Israel are seeking to increase tension in the Near East in order to please their NATO masters."

On August 18, 1965, Moscow's Arab service again spoke of the menacing implication of ties between "Israeli extremists" and Bonn "imperialists." "Obviously Bonn is concerned first and foremost with its new imperialist aims: at the same time, however, it has set up close contacts with the Israeli militarists who, as is well known, play the part of the imperialists' assistants in the Middle East."

Israel, in fact, is cast in a contemptible and sinister role by Soviet propagandists. As in this specific instance, nothing is ever said either internally or in foreign reports to qualify the impression of Israel as a mercenary predator retained to do the dirty work of Western imperialists. "Washington is transforming the Israeli state more and more into a major base of its own, through which it pursues its imperialist policy in the Arab East," said Moscow in Arabic on February 8, 1965. "This anti-Arab activity is not a feature of the open support Israel gets from the Western states in general and the U.S.A. in particular, but arises from the fact that the men in Washington have been using Israeli ruling circles for a long time as a striking force against the independent Arab states. In doing this they have two objectives: firstly, to conceal their anti-Arab policy, and, secondly, to keep Israeli territory as a bridgehead for their constant pressure on the Arab countries. . . . To achieve these two objects Washington balks at no means and will ally itself to any element."

Israel is, of course, the "any element" so contemptuously referred to. The propagandist exaggeration would be farcical if the consequences were less alarming.

Israel as a "Great" Power

There is an apocryphal story in the Soviet Union about the little Jew who rushed into his home after a lecture in Minsk on foreign affairs and cried: "Bluma! Bluma! Wonderful news. Israel is conquering Africa!" The joke reflects the paradox. The Soviet press ascribes a degree of ambition and aggression to the small State of Israel that would be presumptuous in a nation with forty times the population and infinitely greater territory and resources. It is represented as performing these functions on a lackey basis for Western imperialism and the image that finally emerges is both grotesque, exaggerated, and contemptible.

Anti-Israel propaganda of this kind has been a constant feature of the Soviet press for years, but a typical example is an article in *Bakinsky Rabochy* of February 23, 1965, "The Hotbed of Military-Political Tension," by S. Halatrian. After arguing that Israel is one of the most developed countries in the Middle East only because it is under the control of foreign capital, S. Halatrian states: "Israel often attracts the attention of the world. It is one of the centers of world tension, one that constantly threatens to become a hotbed of war at any moment. The source of this is the Arab-Israeli conflict. . . . There are differences between militaristic Zionism and the Arab national liberation movement. From the first days of the appearance of Israel its ruling circles performed more than one act of aggression against the Arabs. The most chauvinistic bourgeois circles of the country, leaning on the military and financial assistance of the U.S.A., quite often come out with calls for territorial invasions with the aim of creating the so-called 'Big Zionist State' stretching from the Euphrates to the Nile."

This extract is worth a moment's examination if only as an illustration of the crudely partisan approach used in Soviet publications when dealing with the Arab-Israel problem. These do not speak of differences between Israel and the Arabs, but between *militaristic* Zionism and the Arab national *liberation* movement. The invasion of Israel by seven Arab states when the Jewish state was created in May, 1948, becomes aggression by Israeli ruling circles, "from the very first days," against the Arabs. The "so-called 'Big Zionist State' " is so-called by whom? As for Israeli bourgeois chauvinists aiming to set up a Jewish state from the Nile to the Euphrates, this is a concoction, which scarcely anyone takes seriously, lifted intact from the Cairo press.

To describe Israel as the most insidious weapon of imperialism would suggest that the imperialists' arsenal was unimpressive, but that is not the intention of V. Vladimirov, the author of *Mezdunarodnaya Zhizn's* article "Israel's Policy in Africa." He hopes to persuade his readers that Israel is a major threat to the independence and integrity of African states and projects a giant role for the less than 2½ million population of that country.

"In recent years," he writes, "imperialism has been coming up against ever greater obstacles in its expansion in Africa. That is why it has been forced to seek for new means and devious ways to achieve its aims. Israel, which is heavily dependent on the Western powers, notably the United States, is being actively used by the imperialists as a vehicle of their neo-colonialist policy in Africa. The imperialists have been encouraging its militarist aspirations in the Middle East and in North Africa, and have been supplying it with weapons and munitions."

It will be immediately noted that the alleged activities of Israeli "militarists" have been inexplicably extended here. But in what countries of North Africa has this extraordinary extension of militarist aspirations been observed? Are the Israelis contemplating aggressions against the Algerians, the Tunisians, the Libyans, the Moroccans? The author, naturally, does not specify. In fact, he immediately shifts to the more general charge that the Israelis are performing a subversively economic role.

"In contrast to the Arab East, Israel's drive in the countries of tropical and Southern Africa is being conducted on an economic basis," allowing "Western propaganda" the pretext of advertising this as "altruistic" and "special." However, says *International Affairs*, there are numerous facts indicating that in this case as well, Israel's policy dovetails with that of the "imperialist powers." The numerous facts are in reality sparse—two quotations out of context from alleged statements by Ben-Gurion in 1960 that "Israel was the chief bulwark of the West in Africa" and that her influence in Africa and Asia were of "great importance" for the West, also that this idea (of Israel's policy dovetailing with that of the imperialists) "has been repeatedly stressed in their negotiations with the Western governments on various questions."

But it would, "of course, be wrong to assume that . . . Israel is merely doing the will of the imperialist powers. Israeli ruling circles themselves have a big stake in the penetration of the African continent," namely, to secure the support of the African states in the Israeli-Arab conflict. "Israeli leaders prefer to camouflage their true aims in the political and economic expansion in the African countries" by stressing that their aid is selfless and "not based on ulterior motives," having "nothing to do with colonialist purposes."

Mezdunarodnaya Zhizn complains that some African leaders were inclined to regard Israel, "whose economic and social 'successes' in a relatively short time have been widely advertised," as a model for their own countries. But the "Israeli ruling circles" had "deliberately obscured" the fact that large investments in Israel's economy "are known to have come chiefly in the form of capital from the imperialist powers," the United States and West Germany. The Israelis were advertising in Africa their "para-military agricultural settlements, the organization of military service, and military training for young people. . . . Israeli ruling circles have displayed a special interest in establishing military ties with the developing countries and in building up their influence in the armed forces of the latter." The Israeli press has reported that Israel had extended aid "in that sphere" to fourteen African countries, the article states, and, in particular, "a large military training center has been set up by Israel in the Congo (Leopoldville), the Republic of the Ivory Coast, Dahomey, and other countries."

FIVE

The Aftermath of the Six-Day War

Soviet Jewry and the Six-Day War

BY *Abraham Brumberg*

The questions to which I should like to address myself are the following:

1. What has been the nature of the propaganda campaign waged against Israel by the Soviet Union and what does it tell us about certain attitudes of Soviet officialdom toward the State of Israel on the one hand, and Jews—or Judaism—in general on the other?

2. What explains this attitude, or these sets of attitudes?

3. Assuming that the Soviet Union is not oblivious to world public opinion, what has been the impact of the Soviet propaganda campaign on public opinion outside the U.S.S.R.—specifically, on left-wing and Communist circles in the West and on Russia's allies in Eastern Europe?

4. What has been the reaction within the Soviet Union itself, and what does this reaction augur for the immediate future of Soviet Jewry?

5. Finally, what, if anything, can an organization [such as the National Community Relations Advisory Council], or American Jews in general, do to help Soviet Jews in this particular instance?

Let me start, then, with the first question—the nature of Soviet propaganda against Israel. There is no need to tell you, of course, of the official position of the Soviet Government, the speeches by the Soviet delegate at the U.N. Security Council, Dr. Nikolay Fedorenko, with their unrestrained condemnations of Israel and tasteless references to "Judge Goldberg," the nature of Premier Kosygin's speech at the U.N. General Assembly, and so on. What seems not to be generally known in this country, however, is that the blistering attacks on Israel's "aggression," "atrocities," and "inhumanities" have hardly been confined to the air-conditioned chambers of the U.N. headquarters in New York. Rather, they were mere echoes of a campaign of incredible vilification conducted throughout the length and breadth of the Soviet Union, through all the media of communication and social control at the disposal of the Soviet authorities—newspaper articles, radio broadcasts—both domestic and directed at foreign audiences—television shows, countless mass meetings, "unanimous" resolutions, statements, and collective threats.

These were no mere general condemnations of Israel and no mere vague references to Israeli atrocities against the Arabs. No attempt has been made to present a balanced and judicious picture either of the background to and causes of the Israeli-Arab war or—which is what I am primarily concerned with here—of the treatment accorded the Arabs by the victorious troops of Israel.

We are not dealing here, I should like to emphasize, with distortions or exaggerations of the, say, many instances of looting or cases of individual brutality which we know *have* taken place, and which have been widely reported in the Western press. No, what we are dealing with here are the crassest fabrications, stories that clearly defy credibility, fantasies of a well-nigh pathological nature. Here are a few representative samples taken from the Soviet press and radio broadcasts over the past two weeks:

In the Sinai Peninsula, unarmed Egyptian soldiers were driven to the West by Israeli tanks. Those who were not fast enough or were exhausted perished under the tank tracks. . . . Refugees said that all who refused to leave the villages were shot by the occupiers. Many inhabitants of Hashaya were killed in a mosque. . . .

Israeli aircraft bombed hospitals and motor ambulances carrying wounded from the battle fields. The invaders fired in cold blood against soldiers with their hands up. . . . The inhabitants of the Surian village of Mansourah were put in a house and after having soaked it with gasoline, the Israelis set fire to it. . . . The militarist elite in Tel Aviv . . gave orders to its troops not to take prisoners. And obeying this cannibalistic order, the Israeli tanks ran over disarmed men, while aircraft machine-gunned them in low-level flight. . . .

Again and again, Israel has been accused of committing "Nazi-like atrocities," "following in Nazi footsteps" by staging a "blitzkrieg," and even of surpassing the Nazis in bestiality. Thus a reporter for Izvestya, the government newspaper, sent a dispatch from Rome on June 16 in which he quoted an unnamed Italian colleague just returned from the Middle-Eastern battle front as follows:

Israeli troops poured gasoline over the live bodies of Arab prisoners of war and set them on fire. . . . I cannot help comparing the Jewish girl Anne Frank who was tortured to death by the Hitlerites and whose dramatic diary shook the whole world, with General Dayan, whose actions have surpassed those of the inhuman Nazis!

(I might add, parenthetically, that the credibility of this report can easily be challenged, not merely on grounds of plausibility, but on the basis of the term "Hitlerites," allegedly employed by the unnamed Italian correspondent. I know of no country today that still uses this term, rather than "Nazis," except the Russians.)

I have also mentioned the well-organized "spontaneous" demonstrations that have been taking place all over the U.S.S.R. Let me indicate the flavor of the newspaper reports on these meetings by quoting just one excerpt from Pravda of June 13:

In the factories of the industrial town Zharkov, the "KHTZ," the electro mechanical factory "Hammer and Sickle," and others, protest meetings were held against the Israeli aggression. Master comrade Khudiakov of the "Hammer and Sickle" Factory, metal craftsman comrade Kuts, milling machine operator comrade Ivanov and others brand with shame the Israeli aggressors and their accomplices. "We are full-heartedly with the Arab peoples," they say. "Loyal to our international duty, Soviet people will not abandon the Arabs in these trying hours!"

Now the question I am addressing myself to here, you will recall, is that of the character of the Soviet campaign against Israel and its implications for the Soviet attitude toward Jews or Judaism in general. Which of course raises the problem of anti-Semitism. To what extent does this bleak picture reflect anti-Semitic tendencies or stereotypes? Here I recognize that we tread on more uncertain terrain. For what conclusive evidence is there that these sickening tales are motivated, either predominantly or partially, by hostility toward the Jews? It is the old story: for every closed synagogue Soviet spokesmen will cite a requisitioned church; and for every unfavorable quote about the Jewish religion, a suitable counter-quote about Roman Catholicism or Baptist rites can be produced.

"Wehr eine Jude isst, das bestimme Ich," said the anti-Semitic Austrian mayor upon being questioned as to why he played chess regularly with the town rabbi—"Who is a Jew *I* decide." And I suppose that in this case it is largely up to us—or to myself—to determine who is an anti-Semite. Nevertheless, I believe there are fairly good objective criteria for substantiating the charge of at least *partial* anti-Semitic motivation:

1. The phantasmagoric nature of the campaign, which in its intensity has no equal in recent Soviet history. Even the attacks on American behavior in Vietnam have seldom reached such heights of vituperation. The images conveyed by Soviet media of Arabs being herded into homes and set on fire, the use of terms such as "cannibalistic" and others —all remind one uncomfortably more of the indecent absurdities of the *Protocols of the Wise Men of Zion* than of even the most obnoxious political polemics.

2. The occasional use of more recognizable and explicit anti-Semitic stereotypes—such as "the petty merchants of Tel Aviv" (instead of "the Israeli Government"); the open reference to a possible collusion between the United States and Israel in view of the fact that "Arthur Goldberg, the head of the United States delegation, belongs to one of the rich families in New York"; and occasionally the substitution of the term "Israelites" for "Israelis."

3. Finally, and perhaps most disquietingly, the rash of cartoons that have appeared in the Soviet press, portraying hook-nosed Israeli soldiers with blood dripping from their hands, and committing sundry unspeakable crimes, either on their own or under the benign protection of "Anglo-American imperialists." I have here the June 24 issue of *Pravda,* which I should be glad to circulate among you. On page 1 you will

find a brief announcement regarding the Kosygin-Johnson meeting that was to take place the same day in New Jersey. On page 4, however, there is a cartoon portraying two *Stuermer*-like Jews in military uniforms, one with the Star of David on his helmet, carving out a huge slice of Arab territory from a map, and measuring a Nazi uniform hanging upon a skeleton. I rather doubt whether the significance of this drawing was lost upon its viewers.

Let me turn now to the second question: Why did the Soviet Government decide to embark upon this unsavory campaign? It obviously would be a gross oversimplification to say that the Soviet policy is now dictated by anything more than political considerations. There is the emotional bitterness on the part of a power that had long played with fire, encouraged the Arabs, apparently became alarmed when the Arabs maneuvered themselves into a position from which there was no retreat, and then found all its work reduced to ashes in a matter of days—indeed hours. There is the desperate desire to rebuild Soviet prestige, sorely damaged by mutual bungling. There are the accusations, hurled daily by the Chinese, of unfulfilled promises made to the Arabs, of lack of revolutionary zeal. There are all these reasons, then, why Moscow had decided to turn the tables on Israel, to transform the intended victim into an aggressor, and the real aggressor into an innocent victim.

Furthermore, there are political explanations for the manner in which the campaign has been waged, too—reasons that are grounded in a type of behavior that is as old as Communism itself. Ever since Lenin, back in 1906, openly announced that in a fight against an enemy all means are justified as long as they help—as he put it—to "wipe the enemy off the face of the earth," Soviet communism has employed the technique of the "big lie," which is not merely that of distortion and obfuscation but which aims, in the apt words of Maurice Samuel, "at the subversion of intelligence." Ever since then the technique has been to harness public opinion in the service of the "big lie," to attack the enemy from all sides, to create an impression that he is isolated, ostracized, engulfed by wrath and indignation.

The term "it is no accident" is an old Communist cliché. And it seems to me, ladies and gentlemen, that it is no accident that even Yugoslavia, which certainly has traveled further on the road to liber-

alization and democratization than any other so-called socialist state—
even Yugoslavia, when faced with the collapse of its ally, Egypt, and
with the threat to its ambition to be the leader of the so-called "non-
aligned world," instinctively resorted to the same method. We know
for a fact that a good part of the leadership of the Yugoslav League
of Communists was opposed to the indiscriminate policy of friendship
between Tito and Nasser. We have evidence that the majority of the
people in Yugoslavia, both inside and outside the party, were amused
by the charges that a country of 2½ million decided to commit what
the Yugoslav Communists have termed "genocide" against their nearly
100 million Arab neighbors. Yet so important has this issue been to the
Yugoslav leadership, and so powerful is its apparatus of control, that
even there not a single newspaper has as much as questioned the wisdom
of the party's policy, but instead joined the chorus of condemnations.
Even there the familiar technique of "mass demonstrations," "indignant
meetings of simple workers," "unanimous resolutions" were employed
with monotonous uniformity by the party authorities.

Yet when all this is said and done, the gnawing question still remains
—why the anti-Semitism? The answer to this question, it seems to me,
is relatively simple: it is *natural* for some of the orchestrators of this
campaign to fall back upon anti-Jewish stereotypes, to see the Israeli—
the Jew—the Zionist—in the most unflattering colors, to portray him in
the most despicable terms. I do not wish to exaggerate this aspect of the
anti-Israel campaign. I should not like to assign to it more weight than
it probably has. But it seems to me that we must see it, at least to some
extent, in the context of the over-all attitude toward Judaism and Zionism which the Soviet authorities have exhibited for so many years.

It is true that within the past few years the situation of Soviet Jews
has improved. The drive against "economic crimes" in which Jews had
been so disproportionately singled out has come to an end. The notorious book by Trofim Kichko, *Judaism Without Embellishment,*[1] which I
am sure you have heard about, was criticized four years ago by the
Ideological Committee of the Soviet Communist Party, and quietly withdrawn from circulation. Emigration to Israel has increased, albeit im-

1. For an analysis of this book, see the article by Moshe Decter in Part Three
above.—Ed.

perceptibly, Yiddish cultural activity has been given a somewhat freer hand, and Premier Kosygin, who at his press conference in New York last Sunday denied that anti-Semitism either exists or had ever existed in the Soviet Union, had himself found it necessary, in July, 1965, to criticize its manifestations in the Soviet Union, as did the Party newspaper, *Pravda*, two months later—the first time in decades.

Yet the sad fact is that, though improvements have taken place, the fundamental Soviet hostility to the entire syndrome of "Jew-Judaism-Zionism-Israel" has remained the same. Over the past two years the Arab case against Israel has been presented with almost no qualifications whatsoever, and Israel has been portrayed again and again as an outpost of American imperialism, an aggressive country bent on the destruction of its Arab neighbors, a land of inequality, class distinctions, and chauvinism. After a brief spell, newspapers have again taken to describing Israeli diplomats as "spies" and warning Soviet citizens against them. More, while the vicious anti-Semitic lampoons of Kichko have been taken off the shelves, other essentially similar works have taken their place. Let me cite excerpts from two books about Judaism which have appeared within the last two years, and direct your attention to the close link between the Soviet attitude toward Judaism as a religion on the one hand, and toward Israel on the other:

Judaism sows mistrust and enmity towards other people. . . . Jewish nationalism has exploited this idea . . . arguing that . . . while the others are doomed to perish . . . Yahve has predestined the Jewish people to rule the world.

In Israel the clerical parties, which lean on Judaism, support the chauvinist policy of the government of Israel, hostile to the progressive movements in the countries of the Middle East and playing into the hands of the imperialist powers.

> *Fundamental Questions of Scientific Atheism*, edited by Professor I. D. Pantskhava, Moscow, 1966.

. . . Indeed, the very invasion of Palestine is described in the Bible as a direct order of Yahve. . . . God orders the annihilation of the indigenous population of the country without mercy. . . . The bloodthirstiness also characterized the subsequent wars of the Jews, in which, as expressed in the Bible, they "put to death all that breathed." . . . God only forbade the annihilation of a few of the neighboring peoples, and this was not at all from a feeling of pity, but in accordance with a sly calculation. They were left to serve as an instrument for testing the Israelites in the future, as a sort of training material on which Israel could practice the art of war. . . . It must be said that the Israelites exploited this living material left in reserve for them: later, after they occupied the whole land, they continued their unbelievably cruel raids and the slaughter of peaceful inhabitants. Yahve incited them to this and punished any softening of the heart. . . . King David, the favorite of the God, did not simply kill off all the inhabitants of the lands and the cities he conquered, he did this with a special sadism.

> *Religion in the History of the Peoples of the World,* by Sergei Alexandrovich Tokarev, Moscow, 1965.

I turn now to the next two questions—reactions abroad and reactions in Russia. And here I should like to sound a more hopeful note, which perhaps will seem strange to you after all those rather dispiriting quotes to which I have just subjected you. For it is a fact that by and large, Soviet propaganda against Israel—and certainly its grossest aspects—has not met exactly with the kind of response that the Soviet leaders no doubt wished or expected. I am referring here specifically to left-wing and Communist reactions, of course, for it is to those sectors of public opinion that Moscow has proved most vulnerable over the past few years.

First, what about Russia's East European allies? Poland, Czechoslovakia, Hungary, Bulgaria, East Germany, and Yugoslavia all signed a statement on June 9 and then one by one broke off diplomatic relations with Israel. Not surprisingly, Poland followed in Russia's footsteps by giving wide prominence to charges of Israeli "atrocities," and party First Secretary Gomulka, in a speech delivered on June 19, warned "Polish citizens of Jewish nationality" not to forget their "duties toward People's Poland" and not to get carried away by enthusiasm over Israel's victory. "We cannot remain indifferent," said Gomulka, "toward people who in the face of a threat to world peace . . . come out in favor of the aggressor, for the wreckers of peace, and for imperialism. Let those who feel that these words are addressed to them . . . draw the proper conclusions"—an ominous warning indeed and one that no doubt pleased those elements of the party which have long advocated a complete purge of Jews from important positions in public life.

Yet there is evidence that even in Poland, where there has long been widespread anti-Semitism, these words may have had an opposite effect from that intended either by Gomulka or by his reactionary advisors and contenders. Reports from tourists recently returned from that country indicate that popular sentiment is overwhelmingly on the side of Israel, because of Poland's suspicion of the Arabs, respect for Israel's military feats, perhaps a certain sense of collective shame with regard to the Jews, and last but not least because of the profound hostility toward Russia which is seen as the instigator of a policy for which there is no domestic rationale whatsoever. According to one story related to me, a pro-Arab meeting of Asian and African students in Warsaw brought the astounding cry, "Long live the Jews!" from some of the Polish bystanders —perhaps the first time such a slogan has ever been heard in this traditionally anti-Semitic country.

Nor has Yugoslavia's stand been an unmixed blessing for Moscow. For though virtually forfeiting its claim to an independent role by rushing to Moscow and signing the statement of the "fraternal parties," and although repeating some of the repellent nonsense that has emanated from Moscow, Yugoslavia has at times adopted a more moderate position. Prior to that country's break of diplomatic relations with Israel on June 12, *Borba*—the Party newspaper—went so far as to declare that the defeat of the Arabs makes "the military and economic aid and the strong political and diplomatic ties of the Soviet Union with the Arab world worthless," a statement which reflects, as is widely reported, the views of the vast majority of people in Eastern Europe, and was surely received with less than full enthusiasm in Moscow.

Hungary behaved similarly—generally repeating Soviet formulas, but being careful not to embrace the Soviet charges of brutality and inhumanity. Indeed, an editorial in *Magyar Nemzet,* the government organ, on June 12, after dutifully branding Israel as the aggressor and demanding that the "Tel Aviv government should renounce its ambition for the acquisition of territory," nevertheless came out for "sober and wise negotiations" immediately after the cease fire, aimed at "solving the enormous pile of political, diplomatic, international, judicial, economic, and human problems, including such questions as the future of the Gulf of Aqaba." (It should be recalled that the question of negotiations was studiously avoided by Kosygin both in his blistering speech at the U.N. General Assembly and the more "grandfatherly"—to quote a Washington newspaper—appearance before the press.) Perhaps sensitive about the possible reaction to the Soviet onslaught, both Hungary and East Germany specifically disclaimed any "anti-Jewish" intent, and some of the East European countries emphasized their recognition of Israel's existence—this long before Kosygin allowed the same in his U.N. speech. As in the case of Poland, reports from Hungary and Czechoslovakia speak of an overwhelming pro-Israeli sentiment on the part of the populations at large, and of a contemptuous attitude toward their governments for having allowed themselves to be drawn into supporting the Arabs.

But if the Soviets could be only partially satisfied with the cooperation of their East European allies (excluding the maverick Rumania, which, by declining to join in the chorus of condemnations and by criticizing "extremists on both sides" for refusing to realize that "war cannot solve" the problems of the Middle East, came close to supporting the Israeli position), it certainly found little comfort in the general reaction of the Communist parties outside the Soviet orbit. No longer mere tools of Moscow's foreign policy, some of the parties underlined their dissent and alarm by refraining from making any statements at all. Other parties adopted more equivocal positions and some, though to be sure very few, came out directly in suppport of Israel.

In France, Communist Party member Picasso joined with Sartre, Simone de Beauvoir, and others in signing a statement (May 26) rejecting the "opinion [which] takes for granted the identification of Israel with an imperialist and aggressive camp, and that of the Arab countries with the socialist and pacifist camp." The Party position has been, of course, considerably more pro-Soviet, but has avoided any charges of atrocities against Israel. In the Italian CP, confusion ran rampant: According to a report in the *London Economist* (June 10), *Unità* came out with an anti-Israeli headline on May 29—a day after Nasser announced the blockade—while the independent Communist paper *Paese Sera*, edited by a Jew, "set up a front page denouncing Egyptian aggression. After a first class row, it was never printed." Even after the outbreak of hostilities the Italian party continued to show signs of internal strife: a statement of June 6 made no reference to Israel's "aggression," and the Italian Government was urged to maintain "complete neutrality" in the conflict. Two days later, General Secretary Luigi Longo accused the "Israeli leaders" merely of "failing to understand the reasons and nature" of the Arab struggle against imperialism. At the same time, Longo criticized "certain trends of exaggerated nationalism which have manifested themselves in certain Arab quarters." The British CP issued a lukewarm statement in support of the U.S.S.R., as did the U.S. party.

In Latin America, only Havana came out in full—in fact fulsome —support of the Soviet stand, replete with accusations of "aggression" and "atrocities." The Chilean party, on the other hand, in a statement published on June 6, associated itself mildly with the U.S.S.R., while firmly declaring its support for the "legitimate right to the existence of the state of Israel." Back in Europe, the Swiss CP, in a letter to the Israeli party, associated itself with the latter's stand, which came out strongly against any position that sees in the alliance between King Hussein and Faisal on the one hand, and Syria and Egypt on the other, anything but a "front . . . of pan-Arab nationalism" bent on the destruction of Israel. A similar letter was sent by the Norwegian Communist Youth Club. The Austrian party virtually endorsed Israel's stand (June 10). As for Socialist parties throughout the world (including Nenni's party in Italy), they made no effort to conceal their opposition to the Soviet stance, both its substance and form.

Finally, what of the reaction inside Russia? As I have tried to indicate earlier, the horror propaganda, with its clearly anti-Semitic overtones, was as much a result of political considerations and habits as of an instinctive bias on the part of a considerable segment of Soviet officialdom. As such, it could not but cater to the similar bias of many average Soviet citizens, and intimidate the already cowed nearly 3 million Jewish population of the U.S.S.R., which still remembers the almost open anti-Semitic campaigns waged both by Stalin in the late 1940's and by Khrushchev in 1962–63. Yet evidence is accumulating that in Russia, too, the Party is having a difficult time in persuading its citizens that its position is valid, that the Arabs are innocent victims of a premeditated and unprovoked attack, that Soviet policy played no part in bringing about the hostilities, and that Israel has embarked upon a policy of mass extermination of its neighbors. Indeed, there are signs that the propaganda campaign is creating more sympathy for Israel than for the Arab states. To this date the Soviets have not succeeded in enlisting a single intellectual of any standing whatsoever in their campaign against Israel. A Dutch journalist who has just returned from Moscow told this writer of attending one of the public lectures in Moscow designed to acquaint the public with the Soviet position, and give the reasons for it, at which the speakers were confronted with skeptical questions and almost open derision on the part of many members of the audience. In particular, caustic questions were asked about the nature and extent of Soviet military aid to the Arab countries. A "spontaneous" demonstration took place in front of the British Embassy in Moscow on June 10, in which most of the demonstrators did not even join in the chanting led by a "cheerleader" with an electric megaphone. Some laughed, some went passively through the motions expected of them, then quietly dispersed at the first opportune moment. It seems clear that Soviet citizens are not convinced of their government's newly found passion for the Arab states: it was only a few years ago that an article in *Komsomolskaya Pravda*—the organ of the Communist Youth organization—warned Russian girls against marrying Arab students lest they find themselves languishing in harems upon arriving in their husbands' homeland. Nor do the Russians rely exclusively on Soviet media of information: the BBC, the Voice of America, and other radio stations are listened to avidly by millions of Russians. And their resentment at being in fact forced again to pay for the military and economic rebuilding of states for which they feel no sympathy in the first place may well become more vocal in months to come.

What, then, may be said in conclusion regarding the impact of the Soviet position in the Middle East on the status of Jews in Russia, and what can the outside world do about it? My feeling is that while local anti-Semites in the Soviet Union have undoubtedly been encouraged by this outburst of hatred, chances are that the context in which it has taken place—that is, unqualified support for the Arabs and the obvious fiasco of Soviet policy in the Near East—will lessen and possibly even neutralize the deleterious effects in the long run. Public reaction abroad, not to speak of Soviet inability to push through its original resolution in the U.N.—and last but not least, Soviet disillusionment with the efficacy of its Arab allies—will also contribute to it.

Already some straws in the wind indicate that the campaign may be entering a new phase. The invective has not stopped. On June 25, *Izvestya* carried pictures of Israeli "atrocities," including that of "wild dogs pulling apart the bodies of Arab prisoners of war who had been cast out to the mercy of fate by Israeli military and had died of thirst in the desert." On the other hand, four days earlier the editor of *Sovyetish Heymland*, in a broadcast speech in Yiddish beamed at Israel, reminded his listeners—of all things—of Albert Einstein's pleas for "neutrality in the East–West cold war" and in almost dulcet tones urged the Israelis to live in peace with their Arab neighbors. Another broadcast, also in Yiddish, to Israel urged Israeli citizens to be on guard against the extremists who wish to liquidate completely "democratic freedom and order"—a rather curious formulation, when you remember that Soviet propaganda has never allowed that there was any "democratic freedom and order" in Israel. And on Saturday, June 25, a Polish language broadcast assured the listeners that Soviet policy is motivated only by a desire to assure "a peaceful life to the Israeli people and its future." To be sure, the same has not been said to Soviet citizens, and thus far the authorities seem to be playing a double game. But the fact that Moscow feels compelled to moderate its tone, however inconsistently, is of itself an indirect testimony that its policy of unrestrained hostility and prevarication has misfired—that the line has not been "bought."

Which brings me to the very final comment: What can the outside world do about it? My answer, I am afraid, isn't very novel, for what can be done now is not much different from what could be, and indeed has been, done until now—namely, bringing pressure to bear on public opinion abroad and upon, hopefully, the Soviet authorities—but pressure that is based squarely and intelligently on *facts*—on documented, provable facts. It isn't very helpful to have the correspondent of the *London*

Jewish Chronicle ask Mr. Kosygin when he stopped beating his wife. "Isn't it true that there is a *new* wave of anti-Semitism?" the correspondent asked. Mr. Kosygin's reply was to be expected, and no one came off any better or more informed in the exchange.

There is little doubt that for the past five years Soviet leaders have been far more sensitive about their image abroad, especially in liberal and left-wing circles, than was Stalin. There is little doubt that the reaction of these circles to the most alarming outcropping of Stalinist mentality and methods has forced the leaders either to ameliorate or to abandon some of their policies. That is what happened in 1963, when both a new wave of repressions against Soviet writers and intellectuals and blatant displays of anti-Semitism were quickly toned down after adverse reactions among liberals and left-wing groups became evident. As in the past, so now, too, public opinion can play a vital role in improving the status of the nearly 3 million Jews in the U.S.S.R. And the better informed that public opinion is, the more effective it will be.

Moshe Adolfovich Dayan

FROM *Krokodil*

Guess who it is? One-eyed like Admiral Nelson and cruel like Adolf
Hitler. As recently as May nobody would have guessed. But now everyone will tell you: But of course this is the Israeli warrior Moshe Dayan.
The picture of the man with a black patch in place of the left eye does
not leave the pages of the American–English press. The general with the
appearance of a gangster stares at the reader with one eye from magazine
covers. Dayan is in vogue. Dayan is the idol of the overseas "hawks."

In New York, on Coney Island, in the museum of wax figures—there
is a joyous commotion. The museum's curator announced: "We are

Searching for a precedent for Israel's alleged "militarism" and "bloodthirstiness"
during the Six-Day War, the Soviet hate machine seized on the Nazi symbol, equat-
ing Jews with their Nazi victimizers. The following attack on Israeli General Moshe
Dayan appeared in *Krokodil*, July, 1967.

193

going to remove the wax figure of Hitler and erect in its place the hastily modeled figure of the Israeli Defense Minister Moshe Dayan."

It seems a trifle, but it is worth much! Just imagine, not in place of some fading basketball star or a king of gangsters, but on the pedestal of the raving corporal. You are greatly honored, Dayan! Bravo! Dayan's New York admirers, slobbering with emotion, are joking. Johnson must send a black eyepatch to Westmoreland in Vietnam.

The round black celluloid eyepatch has become for the mad exactly the same symbol as the slanting black forelock and the little rat mustache of Dayan's German forerunner. It certainly means something when the loudest acclaim for Dayan comes from Auschwitz's yesterday stokers. Yes, such is the paradox—the cheers addressed to Israel are coming from Bonn's camp of bestial professional anti-Semites. Karl Zerf, S.S. *Brigadenführer* in the past, and now chief of the "mutual help organization of former S.S. men," enthusiastically appraised Israel's act of brigandage: "Splendid! Not for nothing have they in their libraries our military regulations."

Somebody else would have taken offense, would be filled with indignation, considered himself insulted, tried to disprove it. But Dayan is flattered. Judging by direct mental affinity, he could fully consider himself as Adolfovich. By the way, his stooges do not refute it at all. "The Voice of Israel" commented on Dayan's "blitzkrieg" on June 8, as follows: "For decades Israel's air operations will be studied with admiration in military schools, as the best example of the art of war, which could be compared only with the decisive success of Germany's *Luftwaffe* during the attack against Poland in 1939."

If they would only remember that Hitler's "blitzkrieg" against Poland was followed by ghettos and murder buses, ditches and gas chambers where millions were killed, including the relatives of Tel Aviv's present warriors and politicians . . .

It is ill-omened when a country's policy is blind in one eye. Moshe Adolfovich is able only to discern how to act according to his order and Hitler's regulations, *"Erste Kolonne marschiert, zweite Kolonne marschiert."* But completely dazzled by his own "blitz" successes, he fails to see the fatal consequences of his shameless robbery. In the time free from aggression Moshe Dayan takes a great interest in archeology. This is, so to speak, a hobby. He collects archeological specimens. There is nothing to be said against it, a quiet occupation. However, Moshe Adolfovich's bandit adventures can have the results that he will not collect any specimens at all. None whatever—neither antique nor modern. Like his spiritual daddy who was discovered under the ruins of the Reichkänzlerei.

The Death of Charles H. Jordan

BY *Robert H. Estabrook*

New York—Did the Czechoslovakian secret police kidnap Charles H. Jordan on orders of the Soviet KGB and dump him unconscious into the Voltava River to drown? Was he murdered by Arab extremists who were being taught in clandestine Czech training schools to regard Jewish voluntary agencies, which Jordan represented, as instrumentalities of American and Israeli "aggression" against their countries?

These are two of the more prominent theories that have circulated since the fifty-nine-year-old Jordan, executive vice-president of the American Jewish Joint Distribution Committee, disappeared in Prague the night of August 16. His badly decomposed body was discovered in the river by a fisherman four days later, creating a major international mystery in which hard evidence remains exceedingly difficult to find.

But if proof is scarce, suspicions are not. Louis Broido, chairman of

The world will probably never know whether the Soviet secret police was actually involved in Jordan's death; but there is strong suspicion that Jordan, a top U.S. Jewish relief official, was a victim of the hate campaign in the aftermath of the Six-Day War. Significantly, old-line Communists, in justifying the 1968 Soviet invasion of Czechoslovakia, blamed Zionists for the liberalization program of the Dubcek government.

the Joint Distribution Committee—or "Joint," as it is widely known—
has said flatly that Jordan was murdered. In an interview in the Tel Aviv
newspaper *Maariv* October 13, he ruled out the possibility of accident,
suicide, or criminal attack.

"Someone from one of the Communist or Arab countries murdered
Jordan," Broido declared. "There are only three possibilities: the Soviet
Union, Czechoslovakia, or an Arab agent."

Jordan had gone with his wife Elizabeth on a vacation trip to the
Czech capital, a beautiful city in which even the depressing effect of
Communist rule has not obliterated the charm of old buildings and
bridges. Actually, he had planned to visit a number of Eastern European
countries, including the Soviet Union, but had curtailed his itinerary in
order to attend a conference in Israel on behalf of the Joint.

He then flew to Rome to pick up Mrs. Jordan, spent several days
in Rumania, and arrived at the Hotel Esplanade in Prague on Tuesday,
August 15. Wednesday night, Jordan told his wife that he was going
out to buy an American newspaper. Because it was a hot night, Jordan
was clad in a sport shirt and left his identification papers in his room.
Mrs. Jordan never saw him alive again.

Czech authorities tried to persuade Mrs. Jordan even before the
body was found that her husband had committed suicide. Subsequently,
officials of the Joint requested that two Swiss doctors be permitted to attend the autopsy, only to learn that Czech pathologists had proceeded
before their arrival and that several vital organs were missing from
Jordan's body.

Following a preliminary verdict of death by drowning, Czech authorities promised to continue the investigation. Some Americans close to the
case say, however, that the Czechs have shown a curious reluctance to
explore the possibilities of foul play. Meanwhile, other doctors retained
by the Joint are completing their own examination of tissue samples
which the Czech Government says are from the organs removed from
Jordan's body.

Friends of Jordan practically unanimously discard the possibility of
suicide. Jordan had worked with the Joint since 1941 in a wide range
of rescue, relief, and rehabilitation programs for refugees, by no means
all of them Jews.

He had been stationed in Hong Kong, had worked with Tibetan

refugees, and had gone to Vietnam on a U.S. Government civilian refugee mission. At the time of his death, he had been attempting to devise a plan for an Arab refugee settlement.

His friends say that he was an extraordinarily confident, ebullient, outgoing man who was continually making plans for the future. On the day of his disappearance, he had mailed several postcards telling others of his plans. He had intended to fly to Vienna from Prague and then go again to Israel before returning to New York.

Although U.S. Government officials familiar with the case are restrained in discussing possible motives for murder, they also tend to reject the notion of suicide or accidental death. The approaches to the Voltava River are well protected, they say, and it is unlikely that Jordan would have fallen into the river accidentally. Friends add that he did not know how to swim and for that reason would have been extra cautious. Jordan had visited Prague twice before and was generally familiar with the city, although his last visit was in 1948.

Other Jewish sources not connected with the Joint, and with independent channels of information, are far more explicit in attributing Jordan's death to sinister causes. They suggest that the Czech secret police may have seized him—possibly without the knowledge of high officials of the government—with the intention of brainwashing him and then having him "confess" to nefarious activities of the Joint in a new version of the Slansky trial.

In 1952, Rudolf Slansky, a former general secretary of the Czechoslovakian Communist Party and Vice-Premier in the cabinet, was executed after "confessing" that he had been an agent of the Western powers in an alleged international Zionist conspiracy.

During the trial, the prosecution singled out the Joint as a vehicle through which it said American Jews committed espionage and sabotage and conducted black market operations. Later the Soviet Government picked up the cry and charged that the Joint had helped organize the so-called "doctors' plot" against Stalin and other Soviet leaders.

When de-Stalinization began in 1956, Nikita Khrushchev formally acknowledged that the "doctors' plot" had been a monstrous fabrication. Eventually the Czech hierarchs dutifully followed suit and "rehabilitated" Slansky's memory, but the charges against the Joint were never retracted.

The Death of Charles H. Jordan

In recent months, these Jewish sources say, the Soviet Union has renewed its propaganda campaign against Zionism, possibly because Communist officials really believe it is a conspiracy or possibly because they are seeking to justify their backing of the Arabs against Israel.

An article entitled "What Is Zionism?" by Yuri Ivanov, appearing in a dozen Soviet newspapers in August, mentioned the Joint as an agency of "the international Zionist corporation" which serves as "a reliable driving-belt for the U.S.A. state and military apparatus." International Zionism, the article charged, has funds far exceeding those of the "Mafia 'Cosa Nostra.' "

As if to indicate central direction in Moscow, almost simultaneously the Polish Government addressed a letter to Jordan, received after his death, reportedly ordering the Joint to wind up all activities in Poland at the end of this year. This leaves Rumania as the only East European country in which the Joint still has an open official blessing (it was banned from Czechoslovakia in 1950).

For many years, the Czech secret police have had a reputation for doing Moscow's dirty work in areas from the Middle East to the Congo. Some Jewish sources believe that the Czech police may have co-operated with the Soviet KGB in a plan to seize Jordan as an agent of the Zionist "Mafia" and put him on trial after brainwashing him.

There was recent evidence of this kind of clandestine co-operation between Moscow and Prague. Only a year ago, a Soviet Aeroflot airliner was diverted from a Moscow-Paris flight to the Czech capital, where police seized Vladimir J. Kazan-Komarek, a Czech-American travel agent who had visited the Soviet Union.

The Czechs accused him of having worked for the Central Intelligence Agency in Czechoslovakia years before. Not until the State Department made the most strenuous representations was Kazan-Komarek released last February after being sentenced to eight years in prison.

Even without direction from Moscow, the Jewish sources continue, the Czech secret police could have had their own reasons for apprehending Jordan. There is evidence of a continuing quarrel between the Stalinists and "liberals" in the Czech hierarchy, as shown by the current crackdown on Communist writers adjudged nonconformist. The Stalinists may have hoped to use a show trial of Jordan as justification for the pro-Arab policy in the Middle East war which the government pursued in the face of what apparently was considerable public opposition.

What, then, happened to Jordan? There is every reason to believe that he was under surveillance in Prague. Passports are regularly registered with the police through the hotels and it is generally assumed that hotel rooms are "bugged." Jordan furthermore had an Israeli visa in his passport.

Those who believe that the secret police had a hand in his disappearance point out that if there had been violence, Jordan probably would have struggled and his body might have shown signs of it. But a police squad could have apprehended him, perhaps at gunpoint, without using much if any physical force. It is even conceivable that Jordan went along willingly in an effort to clear up what he thought was a minor technicality.

One theory is that the police placed a chloroform mask over his face in order to capture him without a struggle. Then, it is conjectured, they may have administered "truth" drugs in an effort to make him talk but found that because of allergies or other complications he had sunk into a coma from which he could not be revived.

At this point they may have decided to cast him into the river so that drowning would appear as the cause of death. Examination of the contents of Jordan's stomach, according to one American familiar with the record, showed that his death occurred within three or four hours after he had eaten, or the same night that he disappeared.

Presumably the presence of drugs in Jordan's body should have been revealed by the autopsy. But Dr. Henry Siegel, New York City Executive Deputy Chief Medical Examiner, who performed a re-autopsy after the body was returned to New York, says it is difficult to rule out all possibility of drugs unless the examiners know specifically what they are looking for. If the Czechs had used a drug unfamiliar to the outside doctors, the examination would not necessarily have disclosed it.

Of course, if the police were intent on mere murder, they would not have had to administer drugs. Jordan could simply have been overpowered and held under water in a tank somewhere, or in the river itself.

Suspicion that the police may have had a part in his death has been aroused by a letter from a leader of the Jewish community in Prague to a Swiss Jewish leader. It spoke of Jordan's "tragic death" and added that "suicide must be excluded." Significantly, he went on to say that "it is possible that murder was committed here, but our own doctors, as well as the Swiss professor, could not detect any traces of violence."

In view of the fact that the letter went through the regular mail, the guarded language is regarded as a between-the-lines hint that the writer believed the death actually was murder. The mention that no traces of violence were found could be a further hint that the secret police had taken pains to hide the circumstances of death.

Another highly placed source familiar with the case disputes the theory of police conspiracy as far-fetched. It is much more likely, he believes, that Jordan was assassinated—by Arabs, who are in Prague in large numbers, or by mere hoodlums.

In the course of his own inquiries, the source says, he obtained firm information that at the time Jordan was in the Czech capital, the government was giving secret courses to Arab students. Among other things, they were taught that Jewish voluntary agencies such as the Joint were vehicles for American and Israeli "aggression" against their countries.

Furthermore, according to a foreign student in Prague, the Arab students were told by an official of the 17th of November University that the Czech Government could not halt visits by representatives of Jewish voluntary agencies but that students were free to show their disapproval.

Thus, the source speculated, Arab students could have set out deliberately to liquidate Jordan—though how they could have accomplished this without the complicity of the police, who presumably had him under surveillance, is an unanswered question. Certainly an assault would have been difficult in a public place. Jordan was a large, powerful man who undoubtedly would have shouted and put up a fight.

Inquiry also has disclosed, according to the source who speculates about the Arab students, that two other Jordans were registered at the Hotel Esplanade at the time Charles Jordan was there. The source does not know the nationality or business of the others, but there is thus a possibility of mistaken identity.

The one point on which all who have studied the case agree is that the Czech explanations have been unsatisfactory. The police seemed determined to "prove" suicide or accident and uninterested in following up any indications of murder. They even suggested that Jordan had gone out to meet a black market agent after receiving a telephone call—which would have been difficult, since there was no telephone in his room.

Two separate sets of police—uniformed Prague police and plain-clothes men—interrogated Mrs. Jordan extensively. Even before the body was recovered, they asked her repeatedly whether she had quarreled with her husband before he left the hotel room.

This she vigorously denied. A hotel maid testified that she had heard loud talk, but even if this were true it could have been accounted for by the fact that Jordan was almost completely deaf in one ear.

At one point in the questioning, the police reportedly asked Mrs. Jordan whether she would be willing to go to Bratislava to identify the body if it should be found there. Bratislava, the capital of Slovakia, is on the Danube River about 200 miles from Prague. This questioning is interpreted by some as indicating that the police already knew that the body would be found in a river.

Mrs. Jordan, who by that time was staying in the American Embassy, replied that she was too frightened to go out of Prague for any reason. She finally left Prague August 23. In New York, she has declined to talk to the press.

Circumstances of the autopsy also were suspicious. Officials of the Joint asked that outside doctors be present and the Joint's health director in Geneva, Dr. Alexander Gonik, and the deputy director of the Legal Medical Institute of Zurich, Dr. Ernest Hardmeyer, flew to Prague. But by the time they arrived, Czech pathologists had already dissected the body and several vital organs had been removed, although Dr. Hardmeyer was given what were purported to be tissue samples of the organs.

After the re-autopsy in the United States by Dr. Siegel and Dr. Russell S. Fisher, the Maryland Chief Medical Examiner, it was concluded that there was no evidence of a fracture or penetrating wound but that "the advanced state of decomposition of the body could have obliterated evidence of superficial trauma such as bruises."

The American doctors say that their final report probably will not change the initial conclusion of death by drowning in undetermined circumstances. They also say they are certain from their tests that the tissue samples given them were actually from Jordan's body.

The Death of Charles H. Jordan

Medical personnel have been careful not to charge bad faith against the Czech authorities. It is normal practice in parts of Europe, they point out, to retain vital organs after an autopsy. Moreover, the Czech doctors' proceeding with the autopsy before the Joint representatives arrived could be blamed on sheer red tape, inasmuch as the Joint's request to delay the examination did not reach the government until the previous night.

Similarly, some sources acquainted with the case hesitate to single out anything unusual in the questioning of Mrs. Jordan. They contend that it is a police custom in many countries to explore the possibilities of suicide in instances of mysterious disappearance before taking up other theories.

It is, of course, conceivable that there is a reasonable explanation for Jordan's death. Czech authorities may have shown no more than usual furtiveness in dealing with a situation which they found embarrassing because the death occurred in their country. The Communists have a doctrinal disbelief in the possibility of sheer accident as a causal factor in human affairs.

But when every effort is made to extend the benefit of the doubt, the suspicions remain. They are increased by a long chain of circumstantial evidence which indicates that unless the Czech authorities are guilty of incredible inefficiency, they know more than they have told about what happened to Jordan.

The continued Stalinist grip on Czechoslovakia has left a long, sad record of arbitrary arrests, show trials, and persecutions since the Communist takeover in 1948. Because of this history, it is possible to assume in the absence of convincing evidence to the contrary that Charles Jordan was yet another victim whose fate was sealed behind what is still in many essential respects an Iron Curtain.

SIX

At the United Nations

The Need for a Jewish State

BY *Andrei A. Gromyko*

During the last war Jewish people underwent exceptional sorrow and suffering. Without any exaggeration this sorrow and suffering are indescribable. It is difficult to express them in dry statistics on the Jewish victims of the fascist aggressors. The Jews in territories where the

The Soviet line today is that Israel was created by Western "imperialists." However, in the late 1940's, it was the Soviet Union that took much credit for helping to establish a Zionist state (no doubt hoping that it would serve as a wedge in undermining British influence in the Middle East).

Gromyko's speech of May 14, 1947, before the General Assembly, in which he refers to Jewish family dissolution in Europe after World War II and pays tribute to Jewish suffering under the Nazis, contrasts sharply with current Soviet refusal to grant its Jewish citizens emigration rights for the sake of family reunion, and propaganda that links Israelis and Nazis.

Hitlerites held sway were subject to almost complete physical annihilation. The total number of members of the Jewish population who perished at the hands of the Nazi executioners is estimated at approximately six million. Only about a million and a half Jews in Western Europe survived the war.

But these figures, although they give an idea of the number of victims of the fascist aggressors among the Jewish people, give no idea of the difficulties in which large numbers of Jewish people found themselves after the war. Large numbers of the surviving Jews in Europe were deprived of their countries, their homes, and their means of existence. Hundreds of thousands of Jews are wandering about in various countries of Europe in search of means of existence and in search of shelter.

It may well be asked if the United Nations, in view of the difficult situation of hundreds of thousands of the surviving Jewish population, can fail to show an interest in the situation of these people, torn away from their countries and their homes. The United Nations cannot and must not regard this situation with indifference, since this would be incompatible with the high principles proclaimed in its charter, which provide for the defense of human rights irrespective of race, religion or sex. The time has come to help these people, not by words, but by deeds. It is essential to show concern for the urgent needs of a people which has undergone such great suffering as a result of the war brought about by Hitlerite Germany. This is the duty of the United Nations.

The fact that no Western European state has been able to ensure the defense of the elementary rights of the Jewish people, and to safeguard it against the violence of the Fascist executioners, explains the aspirations of the Jews to establish their own state. It would be unjust not to take this into consideration and to deny the right of the Jewish people to realize this aspiration. . . .

In analyzing the various plans for the future of Palestine, it is essential . . . to bear in mind the indisputable fact that the population of Palestine consists of two peoples, the Arabs and the Jews. Both have historical roots in Palestine. . . .

All this leads the Soviet delegation to the conclusion that the legitimate interests of both the Jewish and Arab populations can be duly safeguarded only through the establishment of an independent, dual, democratic, homogeneous Arab-Jewish State. . . .

If this plan proved impossible to implement, in view of the deterioration in the relations between Jews and Arabs . . . it would be necessary to consider the second plan which, like the first, has its supporters in Palestine, and which provides for the partition of Palestine into two independent autonomous states, one Jewish and one Arab.

The "Two Masters" Charge

BY *Morris B. Abram*

I deeply regret that my Soviet colleague has exceeded the normal standard of conduct here by twice making reference to my Jewish connection. I understand also that he has indulged in religious implications with
respect to another member who is Jewish in the deliberations of a
working party.

I have many private connections with foundations, colleges, and universities, one of them a Negro college, and numerous civil-rights organizations and bar groups in the United States. The Soviet delegate,
however, has now twice referred in caustic and sarcastic terms to my

At the 1967 meeting of the Human Rights Commission, held in Geneva, the Soviet
delegate, Yakov Ostrovsky, accused Morris B. Abram, the United States representative, of "obeying the orders of the Zionists and the Jews of America," and of
"serving two masters." Mr. Abram's reply was issued March 21, 1967.

connection with the American Jewish Committee. Of that affiliation, as well as others—Jewish and non-Jewish—I am proud. The AJC is the world's oldest human-rights organization, having been founded in 1906, to fight czarist anti-Semitism. And it struggles against all forms of man's inhumanity to man, and for all people regardless of race, color, or creed. The Soviet delegate knows this well, for he has several times used the American Jewish Committee's great human-relations library, which contains some of the world's best resources in this field. I myself have seen him in the AJC library at 165 East 56th Street.

The singling out of this one association of mine I have let pass three weeks ago, feeling that it might have been a human slip, but now it has occurred a second time, and this conduct is obviously deliberate and calculated. It is in keeping with the policy, which has become infamous in all the world, of claiming non-discrimination and tolerance while practicing discrimination and repression. It is in keeping with the policy behind the publication recently of the Kichko book, a crude *Der Stuermer* type of anti-Semitic tome, which evoked criticism of Communist parties all over the world when the book was issued by an organ of Soviet society.

It is a disgrace that in this place, the Human Rights Commission, and at this session at which we have passed the historic Draft Convention for the Elimination of all Forms of Religious Intolerance, that the Soviet delegate should raise this crude implication.

I am a man; but he would not refer to me as that. I am an American; he did not so identify me. I am honored to be the American Representative to this commission; he said nothing of this. I am a Jew and president of the American Jewish Committee. This, he chose to mention in an obviously angry and polemical way. The choice of this one association to which the Soviet delegate has now twice referred shows what all mankind knows—the deep prejudice which has been deplored by Communist parties in other states. I want it clearly understood that Communist parties in Poland, Rumania, and elsewhere fight anti-Semitism, and there is no necessary connection between communism and anti-Semitism. The manifestation of anti-Semitism is in the Soviet Union. The other Communist parties around the world were morally forced to condemn the Kichko book when it was published by the Soviet Union.

The crude attitude of the Soviet delegate is now unmasked. His pious adherence to high principle to the contrary notwithstanding, the Soviet delegate has displayed his bias by his barely concealed and coded message here. I regret that I was forced to make this statement with all my heart. With all my heart I wish it had not been necessary.

Soviet Jewry and the United Nations: The Politics of Non-Governmental Organizations

BY *Ronald I. Rubin*

The right of everyone to leave any country, including his own, and to return to his country is founded on natural law. For the Jew, the wanderer of history, this right rests upon another and more exigent law of nature—the law of survival. Contemporary reports of heightening anti-Semitism in the Soviet Union have pointed up the provision of the *Universal Declaration of Human Rights* which affirms this right for the individual citizen regardless of the country which he might inhabit. This provision, Article 13 (2), proclaims that "everyone has the right to leave any country, including his own, and to return to his country." The Fifteenth Session of the Subcommission on Prevention of Discrimination and Protection of Minorities, meeting at United Nations headquarters from January 14 to February 1, 1963, devoted a considerable portion of its agenda to a study submitted by an officially designated member on the background, conditions, and future of Article 13 (2). In view of the circumstances of Soviet Jewry, this study lent itself to the concern of five Jewish Non-Governmental Organizations enjoying consultative status with the Economic and Social Council of the United Nations.

The Jewish NGO's focused on the emigration issue within the context of the Soviet Union's foreign relations and the United Nations' experience in protecting human rights. The record of the 1963 session may well herald a new role for NGO's in assisting the world body to implement the human rights provisions of its Charter. It remains to be seen, however, to what extent these developments will affect Soviet foreign policy or improve the position of its Jewish citizens. Nevertheless, it is the thesis of this essay that the 1963 session of the Subcommission laid the foundation for NGO's to assume a more influential role in furthering human rights; marked a change in the international organization's policy toward a powerful member nation suppressing information on human rights; and dramatized the plight of Soviet Jewry through a process which might prove to be the basis for its eventual deliverance.

The provisions for human rights in the Charter of the United Nations rank among the great expectations of the ages. It requires no lengthy examination of the Charter to conclude that the measure of success of the international organization is its capacity "to reaffirm faith in fundamental human rights, in the dignity and worth of the human person, in equal rights of man and woman, and of nations large and small." In tracing the U.N. efforts to implement these provisions, however, there appears a gulf separating the assertion of a principle and its execution. The best that the U.N. could tell its public as late as 1962 concerning its declaration of human rights is that "it is a statement of what ought to be, not necessarily of what is. As a standard of achievement, it presents a challenge and a goal."

To be sure, the U.N. has scored solid achievements in the expansion of human rights since adopting the *Universal Declaration of Human Rights* in 1948. Furthermore, many official actions of member nations of the world body can be traced to the *Declaration*.

The human rights provisions of the Charter remain oftentimes unful-filled due to the inability of the world organization to intervene and redress the balance between individual liberty and state authority. The tendency of member nations to construe broadly the so-called domestic jurisdiction clause of the Charter (Article 2 [7]) when their immediate interests are involved militates against a harmonious reception to the human rights provisions. The universal enforcement of these provisions is especially prevented by the policy of such member nations as the U.S.S.R. to circumscribe the authority of the U.N. to "lawfully" inter-vene in state affairs. From the scrutinous evaluation of its "correct" share of the U.N. budget to its opposition toward the "colonialist" peace-keeping forces in the Congo and Middle East, the U.S.S.R. has set a precedent in interpreting the domestic jurisdiction article.

Accordingly, the allegiance of the U.S.S.R. to the human rights pro-visions of the Charter rests, in the main, on the potency of world public opinion. The narrow interpretation which the U.S.S.R. has traditionally accorded the Charter will not mellow unless it recognizes that universal opinion staunchly supports enforcing the rights contained in the *Univer-sal Declaration of Human Rights*.

In order to implement these rights the Commission on Human Rights established in March, 1947, a subordinate body, the Subcommission on Prevention of Discrimination and Protection of Minorities. The Commis-sion on Human Rights envisaged the Subcommission undertaking a series of studies ascertaining existing conditions throughout the world. The as-sumption of these studies was that by bringing together information on human rights, they will help foster a universal rights conscience. These studies were to serve as the bases for covenants on human rights. Such covenants were designed to establish specific international legal norms governing the relationship between the states as parties to the covenants and their respective citizens as well as the relationship between the con-tracting parties themselves *vis-à-vis* the international community.

In carrying out these studies, there is no guarantee that the govern-ments involved will necessarily supply a true and thorough description of the state of human rights. Thus, in reporting to the Subcommission in January, 1955, M. Charles Ammoun, the Subcommission's special rap-porteur on discrimination in education, noted:

. . . governments could hardly be asked to supply information on discrimination practiced by them in their educational systems, as they might well refuse to comply. The only feasible method was to collect as many factual data as possible on which to draw conclusions regarding discrimination.

The delicate nature of the issues examined by the Subcommission, therefore, warrants additional devices for obtaining accurate information on human rights. Particularly in investigating the right of everyone to leave any country, including his own, and to return to his country—a right to which issues of state sovereignty and religious discrimination are closely tied—the requirement for valid information is all the more cogent.

As a means for supplementing reports submitted by member nations, the U.N. authorized NGO's to provide information to the various organs of the international organization. (NGO's are private international associations advancing particular interests.)

The philosophy behind NGO participation in United Nations affairs is distinctly Western. It is based on the concept of free men, in free associations, participating in governmental activities. NGO's first distinguished themselves by their assistance in drawing up the *Universal Declaration of Human Rights*. Dr. Charles Malik, chairman of the Commission, observed, "If a covenant on human rights is going to emerge from our labors, it will be the agitation of these Non-Governmental Organizations which is going to move the governments to sign it."

Most recently, however, the effectiveness of NGO participation in U.N. deliberations on human rights has been a subject of contention. In appraising the record of the Subcommission prior to the Fifteenth Session and the actions of member nations to enforce its recommendations, there appears a sharp gap between adopting and implementing a resolution. In the absence of clear goals guiding its work, many items on the Subcommission's agenda seem beside the point. NGO disenchantment with the Subcommission is best understood in the context of studies it produced previous to 1963. These studies were *de jure*, formal, and apologetic. They were marked by abstractions and generalizations. They were neither specific nor critical in outlook.

Given this background of NGO activity and the record of the world organization in advancing human rights, this study turns to the right to emigrate as discussed in the Fifteenth Session of the Subcommission. Five NGO's representing Jewish organizations addressed themselves to this issue. They were the Consultative Council of Jewish Organizations; the Co-ordinating Board of Jewish Organizations; the Agudas Israel World Organization; the World Jewish Congress; the World Union for Progressive Judaism.

In order to appreciate the positions of these NGO's regarding the Subcommission's Fifteenth Session, it is instructive to trace their origins.

The Consultative Council of Jewish Organizations, founded in 1946, aims to further the advancement of human rights through international action by co-operating with the U.N., its specialized agencies, and other international and regional intergovernmental organizations. At the U.N., CCJO represents the following three Jewish bodies: Alliance Israelite Universelle; the Anglo-Jewish Association; the Canadian Friends of the Alliance. During the 1963 U.N. session, the American Jewish Committee also belonged to the CCJO. However, the American Jewish Committee has since left the CCJO and is represented today at the Commission on Human Rights by the International League for the Rights of Men.

CCJO has not pursued a militant policy at the U.N. on Soviet anti-Semitism. This battle, it argues, must be waged outside the world organization.

Agudas Israel World Organization, an Orthodox Jewish group, attempts to apply Torah directives to contemporary policy issues. Formed in 1912 in Katowice, Poland, Agudas Israel advises a course of action known as *shtadlonus* (quiet representations to governments as opposed to public protests or demonstrations) regarding Jewish security problems. In the judgment of Agudas Israel, invectives cast at the Soviet Union *vis-à-vis* the U.N. may endanger rather than benefit its beleaguered Jews.

The World Jewish Congress, organized in 1936, speaks for constituent groups in over fifty different nations. It is concerned with a broad range of issues (Zionism, anti-Semitism, interfaith relations) affecting Jewry. While the WJC has publicly taken issue with the Soviet Union's treatment of Jews, it has not engaged in bitter denunciations over this question. Indeed, Dr. Nahum Goldmann, WJC president, has argued that accusations against the Soviet Union in this connection were "too often being distorted" (*The New York Times*, June 11, 1965). Accordingly, the WJC has not used the U.N. platform for sharp attacks on Soviet anti-Semitism.

The World Union for Progressive Judaism, founded in 1926, is the international organization of Reform Jewish religious associations and congregations. In 1963, the WUPJ had official affiliations in twenty-five nations. WUPJ has generally limited the scope of its efforts to those sharing its liberal Jewish religious outlook. However, Rabbi Jacob K. Shankman, at the WUPJ's 1966 international conference, urged it to take a more outspoken stand regarding Soviet anti-Semitism. Earlier, the WUPJ had taken a more moderate position on using the U.N. to secure gains for Soviet Jewry.

The most militant of the five Jewish NGO's at the time of the 1963 session had been the Co-ordinating Board of Jewish Organizations. Established in 1946, the CBJO comprises the B'nai B'rith, the Board of Jewish Deputies of Great Britain, and the South African Board of Jewish Deputies. In fostering the principles of the *Universal Declaration of Human Rights*, especially relating to Jewish rights, the CBJO reasons that the U.N. is a vital public opinion forum. As such, it should be used to its fullest capacity.

The Subcommission on Prevention of Discrimination and Protection of Minorities remains the U.N. organ most frequently used by NGO's seeking to protect Jewish rights. In previous sessions, Jewish NGO's concerned themselves with the Subcommission's study of Discrimination in the Matter of Religious Rights and Practices as well as its survey of Manifestations of Anti-Semitism (Thirteenth Session, January 10–February 3, 1961). The Subcommission took up the latter issue as a result of an outbreak of swastika daubings on Jewish property the year before. How did the international organization's deliberations affect manifestations of anti-Semitism? Hardly, if at all. As concerns the results of the debate, one is hard put in tracing its impact on the cause of human rights. One Jewish NGO was uncertain whether to term the deliberations a "prologue or epilogue" on anti-Semitism. In the view of another NGO, one of the most striking results of the survey was that the influence of Jewish Non-Governmental Organizations rather than anti-Semitism suffered a set-back:

It was the Jewish Non-Governmental Organizations which unfortunately emerged scathed and compromised. Not that any member of the Subcommission doubted the right and duty of Jewish groups to be especially concerned with the question of anti-Semitism. They would have thought it unbecoming for these groups if it were otherwise. What many resented was what they regarded as their "parochialism," tactlessness, and lack of subtlety.

In any event, there is little which the Subcommission could do to eliminate anti-Semitic incidents, which transcend national boundaries, such as those which took place in the early 1960's. The chief function of the Subcommission is to prepare studies on the state of universal human rights as specified in the *Universal Declaration of Human Rights*. Jewish NGO's contributing to the work of the Subcommission argue, not for the rights of Jews as such, but for the rights of all mankind. In submitting information to the Subcommission, there is little advantage to be gained for the cause of human rights in accusing a specific government of following a policy of anti-Semitism. Thus the concern of Jewish NGO's with the Ingles report originated from their interest in assessing Article 13 (2) of the *Universal Declaration*, rather than from specific infringement of this right.

The Subcommission considered the Ingles report at the 381st to 397th meetings of its Fifteenth Session. The report, known as a *Study of Discrimination in Respect of the Right of Everyone to Leave Any Country, Including His Own, and to Return to His Country*, was submitted to the Subcommission by Mr. Jose D. Ingles, representative of the Philippines, to the session. Inasmuch as this essay is specifically concerned with the contributions of Jewish NGO's to the report, it is not necessary to summarize the Ingles study in its entirety. According to the report, one Jewish NGO, the Co-ordinating Board of Jewish Organizations, contributed "substantive data." In total, one *Category A* and nine *Category B* NGO's submitted data for the study. During the session, the Subcommission granted hearings to representatives from three Jewish NGO's.

Seven representatives from other NGO's also addressed the Subcommission. There were five Jewish NGO's present as observers, including the three whose representatives spoke before the Subcommission. The five Jewish NGO's were among the thirty-three which had observers present during the session.

Initially, the burden of the Ingles report was to point up the basic nature of the right enunciated in Article 13 (2). The report attempted to demonstrate that many other rights of the Universal Declaration relate to that right. It also sought to show the precedents established with respect to the exercise of this right within the framework of the world organization.

The wide interest of Jewish NGO's in the report relates to the pivotal importance of Article 13 (2) for the enjoyment of many other rights set forth in the *Universal Declaration.* Accordingly, the spokesman for the Jewish NGO making the most appreciable contribution to the study argued:

One of the fundamental rights is that of the right to leave a nation. Many of the other rights of the *Universal Declaration* are conditioned upon this right. This is the bedrock upon which the other rights rest. For if an individual is deprived of political or religious rights, the only way in which he can enjoy them is through leaving for another country.

The significance of the Ingles report concerning this study is that it directly cites instances whereupon nationals are prohibited from emigrating. Unlike previous Subcommission studies, the Ingles document incorporates statistics supporting its contention that a need exists for the adoption of provisions affirming Article 13 (2). That the Ingles report contains these references is due to the fact that NGO's, especially the Co-ordinating Board of Jewish Organizations, furnished information which would not have been otherwise available from the governments involved.

It is only in connection with the situation of Jews in the Soviet Union and, to a lesser extent, Jews in East European Communist nations that the Ingles report assumes political significance. According to Dr. Nathan Lerner, speaking for the World Jewish Congress, NGO's played a

. . . crucial role in the Ingles report. The importance of the report lies in the fact that he makes specific proposals referring to the protection of the right to emigrate. From the Jewish point of view the report is important because Jews were a wandering people.

The United States representative to the Subcommission, Mr. Morris B. Abram, maintained that the contributions of NGO's to the study were "indispensable" because governments discriminating in the matter of permitting their citizens to leave their nation are reluctant to bring such information to public attention. "The Ingles report marks a big advance for NGO's. It was one of the first if not the only time that their material was directly included in a Subcommission study." In the judgment of Dr. William Korey, representing the Co-ordinating Board of Jewish Organizations, the inclusion of information submitted by NGO's is attributable to the "courage" of Mr. Ingles, the special rapporteur. "The big issue was whether the special rapporteur had the authority to depart from tradition and include NGO information. This man has courage. He has set a valuable precedent." The inclusion of information provided by the Co-ordinating Board of Jewish Organizations was bound to stir controversy in the meetings of the Subcommission. Let us turn to the deliberations of the Fifteenth Session as they concerned the material submitted by NGO's on the status of Soviet Jewry.

The chief political significance of the Subcommission's Fifteenth Session relates to the inclusion of NGO information in the Ingles report. The representatives of the two Communist nations on the Subcommission, U.S.S.R. and Poland, questioned both the truthfulness and propriety of including information such as that provided by the Co-ordinating Board of Jewish Organizations in official studies. The United States representative upheld the inclusion of material in the Ingles report regarding religious discrimination and Article 13 (2) as submitted by Jewish NGO's. During the session, three representatives of Jewish NGO's appeared before the Subcommission. An observer from Israel also addressed the Subcommission and endorsed the provision of the Ingles report facilitating the reunion of families. Before long, the session turned into another of the frequent Cold War debates at the U.N. between the United States and the U.S.S.R. representatives.

The Soviet representative maintained that discrimination is widespread in colonial countries and that the Ingles report failed to devote sufficient attention to that condition. Mr. Boris S. Ivanov claimed that the special rapporteur ". . . dealt with various unrelated and artificially created problems and, in particular, with matters which were the exclusive concern of sovereign states." He accused Mr. Ingles of incorporating "tendentious material, colored by Cold War considerations, to document his study." Specifically, he had erred in including "slanderous" information provided by the Co-ordinating Board of Jewish Organizations.

Mr. Ivanov repeatedly attacked the inclusion of the Co-ordinating Board's information in the report. He termed it ". . . a United States organization rather than an international body, and its actions were motivated by political considerations . . . and by its provocative acts the Co-ordinating Board of Jewish Organizations could only do a disservice to that population." The United States representative, Mr. Abram, defended the inclusion of information provided by the Co-ordinating Board. In his view, the Co-ordinating Board was one of many NGO's meeting a responsibility which governments, on their own, leave unfulfilled:

Governments were not always right and statistics do not always reflect the true situation. . . . Most governments endeavored to justify their actions, but those actions should be subject to continuous scrutiny. The Non-Governmental Organizations were in a position to undertake such scrutiny.

He observed that in the latter part of the session, the Soviet representative "toned down his diatribes" against the Co-ordinating Board. Thus, Mr. Abram understood this change to indicate a recognition by the U.S.S.R. of the "proper role" of NGO's in Subcommission studies.

The appearance of the Israeli observer before the Subcommission served to compound further the disagreement between the U.S.S.R. and the United States with respect to the role of NGO's. In his statement, Dr. Meir Rosenne indirectly referred to the status of Jews in the U.S.S.R.:

This great Jewish community represents the last large residue of European

Jewry remaining from the eastward push of the Nazi barbarians. It contains literally hundreds of thousands of individuals who were battered, beaten, and torn apart from their kin in the unique Jewish tragedy of the war years. There is hardly a family in my country and in most other Jewish communities throughout the world that does not have, or did not have before the Holocaust, a member in that country.

The Soviet spokesman coupled his reply to the Israeli statement together with his criticism of "certain Jewish organizations who had made some utterly mendacious allegations about the Soviet Government." Mr. Ivanov also took issue with the inclusion of an Israeli monograph (Conference Room Paper No. 85) in the Commission's deliberations regarding Jews in the Soviet Union. He said it

. . represented a flagrant case of interference in the domestic affairs of the Soviet Union. It seemed that the Israel authorities considered the Jews in all countries as nationals of the State of Israel; thus Mr. Rosenne had been led to insinuate that the Jews living in the Soviet Union, numbering some 2 million approximately, should settle in Israel.

The aforesaid citations represent the highlights of the Subcommission's session concerning the right of the special rapporteur to include specific information in a study which conclusively places a member nation in an unfavorable light. The balance of the consideration accorded the Ingles report related primarily to the wording of draft principles and resolutions. The scope of this essay prevents an analysis of the debates, for the most part legalistic, preceding the adoption of the resolutions. The Soviet Union and Poland abstained from voting on most of the resolutions. As a result, most votes were of the nature of 9-0-1 or 8-0-2. The Subcommission approved the dissemination of the Ingles report. It asked that the International Travel and Tourism Conference convening in Rome in August–September, 1963, take into account the Ingles report. It also decided to retain the subject of the Ingles report on its agenda "in order that it may keep in touch with the efforts made to eradicate such discrimination and consider what measures, if any, should be recommended in the national and international fields."

The Commission on Human Rights—the Subcommission's parent body —meeting in Geneva in March, 1963, approved the circulation of the

Ingles document as an official United Nations study. It also passed a resolution of appreciation for Mr. Ingles despite objections from the Soviet Union. However, the Commission withheld discussion of the resolutions recommended by the Subcommission, and no conclusive action had yet been taken in this connection by 1966. But a precedent for public participation in the world body had been set: the Ingles report bears the official mark of U.N. approval—NGO material and all.

This essay has thus far traced the contribution of Jewish NGO's to the Subcommission's study of Article 13 (2) in the context of the struggle for human rights at the U.N. How do NGO's evaluate the Subcommission's treatment of the Ingles report? The opinions of Jewish NGO's interviewed in this study are representative of their differing estimates of the capacity of the international organization to implement the human rights articles of its Charter. They weigh the Ingles report from a perspective of their understanding of the role of NGO's in campaigning for Jewish rights through the medium of the world body.

In the range of opinion of the four representatives of Jewish NGO's interviewed, the least encouraging outlook was expressed by Mr. Moses Moskowitz, of the Consultative Council of Jewish Organizations. He argues that

. . . Jewish organizations are abusing their consultative privileges; that they are too much concerned with defending their own particular interests to show understanding of the interests of the United Nations, and that they are short on good manners . . . the powers that be do not always take the trouble of distinguishing between one organization and another.

In his judgment, Jewish NGO's are steadily losing their influence at the U.N. This results from the policy of some Jewish NGO's to gain publicity from the presentation of their "propaganda" to the international organization:

I am sure that if the Jewish organizations which are anxious for us to intervene in the United Nations had a clearer notion of the limitations and handicaps under which we are working, they would surely take a more conservative attitude. In the first place, we cannot be special pleaders and, at the same time, hope to exercise influence in the broader question of human rights which is of vital interest to all of us. But immediately more important is the fact that we are at a great disadvantage when we raise the issue of the Jewish community in the Soviet Union at the United Nations. We can never, under existing regulations, present our case in an intelligent and meaningful way. All we do is to provoke the Soviet representatives and provide them with the opportunity to denounce us and libel us.

According to Mr. Moskowitz, the public struggle against anti-Semitism in the Soviet Union must be necessarily carried on outside the world organization. The U.N. platform must be used only in the most serious emergencies, "or it becomes totally ineffective."

A more hopeful outlook on the role of NGO's and the rights of Soviet Jewry is expressed by The World Union for Progressive Judaism. The World Union considers the U.N. the most favorable institution to argue for Jewish rights. Nonetheless, it pursues a policy of caution in involving the world body in protecting Jews. Inasmuch as The World Union is a religious organization, it approaches the issue of Soviet anti-Semitism from a spiritual as well as political framework. It hails the *Universal Declaration of Human Rights* as a reaffirmation of ancient Hebraic ideals: "Every statement of human freedom stems from the universal and eternal truths first enunciated in our scriptures. We may be pardoned, therefore, for taking pride in the fact that mankind has taken the teachings which Judaism not only originated but faithfully and sacrificially struggled to foster through the millennia."

As for specific petitions to the United Nations concerning Soviet Jews, the executive director of The World Union notes: "It would be our position to support such emigration in every instance except where, for political or diplomatic reasons, such activity would knowingly impair the status of Soviet Jewry." The World Union qualified its activity in the world organization against the possibility of increased "discrimination" toward Soviet Jews. It acknowledges the difficulties the U.N. faces in attempting to enforce Article 13 (2) as it relates to these Jews:

We would foster every liberating move in behalf of Soviet Jews, but I do not think we would be vociferous if probable harm to these Jews would result. The forum of the U.N. seems the most likely source of eventual freedom of movement, and I feel personally that the anxiously desired improvements in the lot of Soviet Jewry will doubtless be associated with a general relaxation of controls by the authorities of the U.S.S.R., and not specifically for the benefit of Jews.

A third point of view is maintained by Dr. Nathan Lerner, of the World Jewish Congress. Unlike the conservative stance of the Consultative Council, cited above, Dr. Lerner holds that U.N. deliberations, such as those of the Fifteenth Session of the Subcommission, have an impact on the Soviet Union. He also minimizes the need for caution stressed by The World Union for Progressive Judaism. Dr. Lerner argues that "the Soviet Union is a member of the civilized world and a member of the United Nations. It has signed and ratified the *Declaration of Human Rights*. The Soviet Union is very sensitive to what is said at this international forum." The World Jewish Congress spokesman believes that the military power of the Soviet Union enables it to ignore statements of protest such as newspaper editorials appearing in publications of non-Communist nations. The only remaining means for petitioning the Soviet Union is through the world organization. These petitions, he maintains, will not result in an immediate reversal in the policy of the Soviet Union toward its Jews. He does not envisage a dramatic change in the position of Soviet Jewry. Nonetheless, the World Jewish Congress regards the Subcommission's discussion as a significant effort in the campaign for Jewish rights in the Soviet Union. It encourages the continuing participation of Jewish NGO's in this struggle.

The most glowing praise for the Ingles report and the contributions of NGO's to it is expressed by Dr. William Korey, of the Co-ordinating Board of Jewish Organizations. As previously noted, the Co-ordinating Board was the only Jewish NGO submitting "substantive data" to the Ingles report. The Co-ordinating Board was also the only NGO drawing the specific hostility of the Soviet Union's spokesman to the Subcommission for intensifying Cold War tension. Of the Jewish NGO's enjoying consultative status with the world body, the Co-ordinating Board's outlook is most anathema to that of the Consultative Council of Jewish Organizations. On an earlier occasion, Mr. Moskowitz, the Consultative Council's representative, took issue with the Co-ordinating Board's record:

Quite a number of the Subcommission's members shared their U.S.S.R. colleague's view concerning the Co-ordinating Board, for the simple reason that they had always resented the intrusion of what they regarded as Cold War polemics into the Subcommission's work. . . . Practically all the members of the Subcommission were agreed that the Co-ordinating Board had abused its privileges as a consultative organization. This was also the opinion of the Secretariat and of all Non-Governmental Organizations which cared to comment.

With regard to such criticism, Dr. Korey notes that "governments do not criticize one another in these studies. Only NGO's will supply critical information. To the extent that NGO sources are not included, these studies will remain in the realm of abstraction." Accordingly, the Co-ordinating Board expects criticism in the Subcommission from governments such as the Soviet Union which failed to supply the special rapporteur with information on Article 13 (2) and the rights of Jews. The repeated attacks by the Soviet Union have not resulted in the revocation of consultative status of the Co-ordinating Board by the United Nations Secretariat. Dr. Korey insists that his organization will continue submitting material to the Subcommission on Soviet Jewry and the implementation of Article 13 (2).

Dr. Korey praises the Ingles report as a

. . . very significant study. . . . For the first time such a study spelled out violations of the *Universal Declaration of Human Rights*. Even the United States spokesman was embarrassed when the report named that country as a violator of the Article for its behavior in the case of William Worthy, Jr. . . . The study helps give the Subcommission more stature and, as a result, will increase the binding force of the *Universal Declaration*.

We have thus far explored the viewpoints of four Jewish NGO's participating in the Subcommission's Fifteenth Session. The fifth NGO withheld comment on the significance of the session and the role of NGO's in it. In this regard, the Agudas Israel spokesman adheres to the policy of "quiet diplomacy" marking that organization's policy on Soviet Jewry. Agudas Israel argues that the "Jewish Establishment" is mistaken in stressing public protests on behalf of Soviet Jewry. Instead, caution and negotiations are the best instruments for lessening Soviet anti-Semitism.

While there is no definite proof that demonstrations have helped Soviet Jews, there is ample support for the notion that the Soviet Union is sensitive to foreign public opinion. Only after protests became widespread—and began to attract the attention of Communist parties in the West—did the Soviet Union scale down its attrition campaign against Jews.

Furthermore, the fate of Soviet Jews is not subject to negotiation, if only for the fact that it is an internal Soviet issue affecting Soviet citizens. Negotiations also assume mutual bargaining. What could Jewish "representatives" offer the Soviet Union? Nothing other than favorable opinion abroad; anti-Soviet demonstrations, accordingly, serve as a bargaining device even were negotiations to take place.

As for government-to-government talks on Soviet Jewry, the Department of State in its position paper, "The Jews in the Soviet Union" (distributed in 1967), states flatly: "We have found from past experience that government-to-government approaches to Soviet officials at all levels are totally ineffective. Our approaches in the past have been brushed aside by claims that there is no anti-Semitism in the U.S.S.R. and that, by raising the subject, we are attempting to interfere in the internal affairs of the Soviet Union for some 'Cold War' purpose." In concluding this appraisal, it would prove worthwhile to contrast the outlook of the NGO's with that of the United States expert, Mr. Morris B. Abram. Throughout the session, Mr. Abram countered the Soviet position on its opposition to including information supplied by the Co-ordinating Board and its denial of domestic anti-Semitism.

Mr. Abram maintains that the Co-ordinating Board performed an "effective" service for future NGO participation in Subcommission studies. The most noteworthy aspect of NGO involvement, in his opinion, was the inclusion of Co-ordinating Board material: "The Soviet expert was shocked when he learned that the special rapporteur decided to give credence to an NGO. The Soviet Union tried to get Mr. Ingles to retreat from including the NGO information. When the Soviet representative discovered that he would not retreat, he was simply shocked." The United States spokesman hopes that the Co-ordinating Board's example will influence other NGO's. "The NGO's must take advantage of the indispensable position they occupy in the attempt to advance human rights."

The purpose of this essay has been to demonstrate the role of Jewish Non-Governmental Organizations in the *Study of Discrimination in Respect of the Right of Everyone to Leave Any Country, Including His Own, and to Return to His Country.* The concern of Jewish NGO's with this study was based upon the issue of Jewish survival in the Soviet Union. Indeed, the refusal of the Soviet Union to permit Jews to emigrate, especially for the sake of family reunion, was the only feature of the Ingles report having immediate political ramifications.

This essay has sought to explore the role of Jewish NGO's in the framework of the U.N. experience in human rights and the conduct of Soviet foreign policy. Accordingly, it made reference to the transcript of the Subcommission as well as the individual testimony of NGO's and diplomats concerned. The most striking conclusion from this investigation of the Subcommission's study is the inclusion of information submitted by an NGO contradicting the position of a member nation. Subcommission approval of the study, despite the objections of the Soviet Union and Poland, no doubt sets a precedent for the role of the special rapporteur and the province of future studies. The incorporation of material furnished by the Co-ordinating Board of Jewish Organizations serves to embolden NGO's in submitting controversial data for the Subcommission's consideration. Yet what is the import of the Subcommission's action for some 2½ million Jews in the Soviet Union?

In approving the Ingles report, the Subcommission and, later, the Commission on Human Rights simply ratified a study of an article in the *Universal Declaration of Human Rights.* Following the completion of such a study, procedure is to enact either a declaration or convention on specific rights. The latter form of legislation has the force of international law behind it. In the political process of the world body it normally takes many sessions before either of the two conclusions are reached. Even when they are enacted, the U.N. has no direct executive authority to implement the human rights clauses in the Charter. In the last analysis, member nations abide by these provisions due to the force of world public opinion.

Accordingly, the Soviet Union will meet the wishes of Jews desiring to emigrate only when it faces impressively hostile foreign opinion, if at all. There is nothing conclusive in the Ingles report as it concerns the granting of the right to emigrate to Jews in the Soviet Union. The organization of public opinion protesting the denial of Article 13 (2) to those Jews must develop upon some foundation, however rudimentary. The Subcommission on Prevention of Discrimination and Protection of Minorities is such a cornerstone as regards the human rights provisions of the Charter. As the United States expert to the Subcommission, Mr. Abram, argues:

. . . The granting of every right is its assertion. We have to start somewhere. I'm sure that eventually there will be a convention on the subject. It may take many years before it is passed. And even if it is adopted, I am not sure that it will have any effect on the policy of the Soviet Union toward its Jews. Yet one can never be certain how the Soviet Union will react to a convention and public opinion.

Clearly, the most ineffective policy NGO's and world Jewry could pursue is a conspiracy of silence. For among the haunting memories of the Nazi disaster is the knowledge that world public opinion was neither vociferous nor united in crying out to save European Jewry. American Jewry has responded to the plight of Soviet Jewry by demonstrations, letter-writing campaigns, personal representations to the Secretary of State and the President, petitions to the Soviet Union, and special prayer programs.

As the U.N. grows in years it is likely to grow in stature. The individual citizen, from whatever country he may hail, increasingly shares the opinion which Dag Hammarskjold expressed in 1958:

. . . The view is often put forward that the United Nations should not only continue to function according to its existing arrangements but should increase its responsibilities. Indeed the views expressed have in general been to the effect that the Organization should do, not less, but more in world affairs. Those who advocate changes in the structure of the Organization do so with the avowed purpose of rendering it more effective.

Should such be the case, this study of the first efforts of the international organization to implement Article 13 (2) may prove helpful to future students of human rights at the U.N. and its influence upon the foreign relations of the Soviet Union. On the other hand, should the Soviet Union intensify Jewish oppression and ignore future appeals from the world body, this essay may also be of value in demonstrating how at a particular stage in the emergence of international organization, NGO's have affirmed that they are their brother's keeper.

SEVEN

Eyewitness Accounts

The Rejoicing of the Law

BY *Elie Wiesel*

Where did they all come from? Who sent them here? How did they know it was to be tonight, tonight on Arkhipova Street near the Great Synagogue? Who told them that tens of thousands of boys and girls would gather here to sing and dance and rejoice in the joy of the Torah? They who barely know each other and know even less of Judaism—how did they know that?

I spent hours among them, dazed and excited, agitated by an ancient dream. I forgot the depression that had been building up over the past weeks. I forgot everything except the present and the future. I have seldom felt so proud, so happy, so optimistic. The purest light is born in darkness. Here there is darkness; here there will be light. There must be —it has already begun to burn.

From group to group, from one discussion to the next, from song to song, I walked about, sharing with them a great celebration of victory. I wanted to laugh, to laugh as I have never done before. To hell with the fears of yesterday, to hell with the dread of tomorrow. We have already triumphed.

235

He who has not witnessed the Rejoicing of the Law in Moscow has never in his life witnessed joy. Had I come to Russia for that alone, it would have been enough.

It had snowed the week before. The day before, it rained. My friends in the diplomatic corps made no attempt to conceal their anxiety. Bad weather would ruin the holiday. Snow—that was all right. But we prayed to Him-who-causeth-the-wind-to-blow-and-the-rain-to-fall to postpone His blessing. For His sake, if not for ours, and for the sake of those who had waited all year long for this night, for this chance to prove that they are mindful of their origins, are mindful of Mount Sinai and their people.

The "festival of youth" has become something of a Russian tradition since it first began four or five years ago during the period of internal easement inaugurated by Nikita Khrushchev. At first the festivals were attended by a few hundred students; then the number grew into the thousands. Now they come in tens of thousands.

Objective observers like to claim that the gatherings have no relation to Jewish religious feeling. Young people come to the synagogue as they would to a club, in order to make new friends and learn new songs and dances. If they had someplace else to go, they wouldn't come to the synagogue.

I should say this explanation is not entirely correct. There is no lack of meeting places in Moscow; young people can get together either downtown, at the university, or at the Komsomol [1] clubs. If they come to the synagogue, it is because they want to be among Jews and to be at one in their rejoicing with their fellow Jews all over the world, in spite of everything, and precisely because of the attempts that have been made to isolate them from their heritage, and they come in defiance of all efforts to make Judaism an object worthy of their hatred.

If they were allowed to live as Jews in a different way, in a different time, or in a different place, it is true that they would probably not gather together at the synagogue on this holiday of light and joy. But they have no alternative, and if they seize the excuse to come to Arkhipova Street, it is a sign that they wish to live as Jews . . . at least once a

1. Soviet youth movement, attached to the Communist Party.—Trans.

year, for one full evening. Somehow that will make them capable of waiting until the next time.

But it must not rain. . . .

I, too, had made preparations for the night of Simhath Torah,[2] as if for a great test or some meeting with the unknown. I was tense and restless. The many stories I had heard about the celebrations last year and the year before only increased my apprehension. I feared a disappointment. What if they didn't come? Or came, but not in great numbers? Or in great numbers, but not as Jews?

In order not to miss this meeting of three generations, I had arranged to spend the last days of Sukkoth in Moscow. Unjustly, I had determined to rely neither on miracles nor on the Soviet airlines. I was afraid my plane might be delayed in Kiev or Leningrad, and I didn't want to arrive in Moscow at the last minute. I could not allow myself to miss this opportunity.

I might have seen the same thing in Leningrad . . . or so I was told. Thousands of students gather at the Leningrad Synagogue on the night of Simhath Torah. In Tbilisi, too, young people crowd the synagogue even on an ordinary Sabbath. In Kiev I tried to convince myself that precisely because the Jewish leaders were attempting to suppress Jewish feeling and to drive away the younger generation, it would be worth staying to see what happened. But I was drawn to Moscow. Moscow would be the center; there the climax would occur. What would take place in Moscow could not happen anywhere else, inside Russia or abroad; so I had heard from people who had been there the past three years.

I wanted to see young people, to measure the extent of their Jewishness and discover its means of expression. I rehearsed dozens of questions to ask them, scarcely realizing that when the moment came I would forget them all. While traveling through Russia I had spoken mostly with the elderly or middle-aged. Many of them had expressed anxiety about the younger generation, its increasing estrangement and assimila-

2. "Rejoicing of the Law"; last day of Sukkoth festival, celebrating the completion of weekly Pentateuch readings in the synagogue and the beginning of a new cycle.—Trans.

tion. They told me there was little hope for the perpetuation of Judaism in Russia. In America and Europe I had heard Russian representatives, Jewish and non-Jewish, who had taken the line of cold logic—there is no Jewish life in Russia simply because Jewish youth is not interested in it. It is for this reason alone that there are no *yeshivoth*,[3] no Jewish grade schools, no Jewish clubs, no writers and no readers and no future. Judaism is strictly for the old. This explanation is put forth by everyone who comes from Moscow to speak about the "Jewish problem" in Russia. Full blame is placed upon the younger generation.

But tonight we would discover the truth. Youth itself would take the witness stand. It was years since I had last prepared for the night of Simhath Torah with such anticipation, such a sense of awe and excitement. I knew something would happen, something vast, a revelation. I was taut and fragile as the string on a violin. One must not force things, my friends cautioned me; you expect too much, you will never be satisfied with anything less than perfection. Patience. As the sun began to set, its rays danced in a fantasy of color over the Kremlin's gilded domes. The sky was clear blue, and there were no clouds. The weather must hold. It must not rain.

It didn't. And it did not snow. There was a cold wind that cut to the bone. That's nothing, my friends said. Young people do not fear the cold. They'll come, if only to warm up.

Apparently the Soviet authorities also expected a large crowd, and they did their best to frighten it away. It had been made known that during the High Holy Days everyone entering the synagogue had been photographed. And now in front of the synagogue two gigantic floodlights had been installed, illuminating the entire street. The Jews were not to forget that someone was watching. The Jews would do well not to become too excited or to betray an overly Jewish character in their rejoicing.

They came nevertheless. Inside, the great hall of the synagogue was crammed with more than two thousand men and women. Many brought their children, for children, too, were to see that the Jews knew how to

3. Singular, *yeshiva:* rabbinic academy, institute for the training of rabbis.—Trans.

rejoice. The atmosphere was festive. Young girls stood among the men on the ground floor. The balcony was overflowing. People smiled at one another. Wherefore was this night different from all other nights? On all other nights we live in fear; tonight we are free men. Tonight one is permitted even to smile at strangers.

The old rabbi seemed calmer than he had on Yom Kippur. The hall buzzed with conversation. Eyes reflected hope and well-being. "Would you give your flag to my grandson?" an elderly man asked an Israeli child who held a pennant in his hand. The boy smiled and nodded. "Here you are." The Russian child took the Jewish flag and kissed it. An informer came up and demanded that the old man return the gift. He hesitated a second, took courage, then said no. His friends stood at his side. The informer bowed his head. Tonight he was alone.

When would the processions begin? They had long since finished the evening prayers. Why were they waiting? It seemed that they were just waiting; they had no special reason. They waited because it was pleasant to wait, because it was good to be in the midst of such a large and living crowd, in such a joyful place. If they didn't begin, they wouldn't have to end; they could treasure the perfection of the holiday. Expectation itself became part of the event. They drew it out, trying to expand the holiday past the limits of a single evening or a single day. If one could only remain here, united, until next year.

"Festivities are already under way outside," we were told by new arrivals.

The *gabbai* decided they had to begin. It was already late. One could not stay here all night, or even if one could, it would be dangerous. There was no knowing what people might do or say once they had been given a chance to release their feelings. There was no knowing what the repercussions would be from above.

They had to start. The *gabbai* banged on the table and shouted for silence. Useless. Thousands of whispers grew into an overwhelming roar. The *gabbai* continued shouting, but only those standing nearby, as we were, could hear him. The congregation had come to hear cries of a different sort, or perhaps not to hear anything, just to be present, to partake of the sacred joy of the holiday.

They began. Rabbi Yehuda-Leib Levin was honored with the first verse, "Thou has caused us to know . . ." He seemed to have recovered his youthful energy. His deep, sorrowful voice seemed more melodious. How many Jews in that hall fully understood his meaning when he sang, "For God is the Lord, there is no other beside Him"?

"The celebrating outside is incredible," we were told.

Inside, too, it was the same. The Israeli Ambassador, Mr. Katriel Katz, was given the honor of reciting a verse, "Thy priests shall be clothed in righteousness, and thy faithful ones rejoice." His voice, too, was lost in the roar of whispers, but his title was known, and the enthusiasm mounted. People stood on tiptoe to see the representative of the sovereign State of Israel. His presence made them straighten up; they seemed taller.

The scrolls of the Torah were taken from the Ark and the dignitaries of the community invited to lead the first procession. The night before, I had participated in this ceremony in a small side chamber where the *hasidim* pray. All the guests had been called for the first procession. Rabbi Levin had also been there, and we danced and danced until our strength gave out. We sang *hasidic* and Israeli songs in Yiddish and Hebrew. A tall, awkward, red-faced Jew had suddenly broken into the circle and caught the rabbi's arm. "Come, Rabbi, let us fulfill the commandment to dance! We must gladden our hearts for the Torah!" The two of them danced as we clapped our hands in time. The rabbi grew tired, but his partner goaded him on, more, more! They danced not for themselves but for the entire house of Israel. The tall one's happiness was mingled with rage. He could not sing, and he danced without rhythm in little jumps. His eyes shone with unworldly wrath, and I knew that his joy was real, flowing as it did out of an anger long contained. All year one is forbidden to be angry and forbidden to rejoice. Tonight one is permitted to rejoice. He was crying, too. Why, I do not know. Why does a man cry? Because things are good; because things are bad. Here the question is different; why does a man rejoice? Where does he get the strength to rejoice?

But that was last night, and they were *hasidim*. The people crowding into the synagogue tonight were simple Jews who had come to learn that it was possible to be a Jew and to find reasons for rejoicing . . . or to rejoice for no reason at all. Long-beards and workers, old and young, widows and lovely girls, students and bureaucrats. Among them there were many who had never prayed but who had come to watch the processions and to honor the Torah.

Processions? How could they lead a procession through this mob? The Jews formed an impenetrable living mass. No matter. Here everything was possible. It would take time, but no matter. They had the time, and patience too. Somehow the parade would pass. In the meantime they sang, louder and louder. They were all looking at us, the guests, as if to say, "Well, what's with you? Let's hear something from you." The entire Israeli diplomatic corps was present, together with their wives and children. We sang, "Gather our scattered ones from among the nations, and our dispersed from the corners of the world." Five times, ten times. A number of the diplomats belong to left-wing parties. In their youth they had scorned religion, and religious people in particular. Tonight they celebrated the holiday with *hasidic* enthusiasm and abandon. Differences of opinion and class were left behind. An American writer once told me, "As I stood among the Jews of Russia, I became a Jew." He was not alone; many who come here as Israelis also return home as Jews.

"Outside they are turning the world upside down."

Should we go out? There was still time. Here, too, the world was in uproar. Men who had not sung for a year were raising their voices in song. Men who had not seen a Torah all year long were embracing and kissing it with a love bequeathed to them from generations past. Old men lifted their grandchildren onto their shoulders, saying, "Look, and remember." The children looked in wonder and laughed, uncertain what was happening. No matter; they would understand later, and they would remember. Tzvikah, the vocalist in the Israeli corps, assembled his chorus and gave them the pitch, "David, King of Israel, lives and endures." There was not a Jew in the hall who was not prepared to give his life defending that assertion.

The dignitaries had made their way back to the pulpit. The first procession was over. The *gabbai* announced that all guests were to take part in the second, and the congregation responded with new bursts of song. From one corner came an Israeli tune, "*Heivenu Shalom Aleichem*—We have brought peace unto you"; from another, "*Hava Nagilah*—Come let us rejoice." A third group preferred a traditional song, "Blessed is our God who created us in His honor and separated us from the nations and

241

implanted in us eternal life." Instead of resisting one another, the various songs seemed to fuse into a single melodic affirmation. Those who had spent years in prison or in Siberia, those who had only recently become aware of their Jewishness, now proclaimed their unity: one people, one Torah. Each of them had stood once at the foot of Mount Sinai and heard the word, "*Anochi*—I am the Lord thy God." Each of them had received the promise of eternity.

We held the scrolls tightly to our chests and tried to make our way through the congregation. But instead of opening a path for us they pressed in closer, as if to block the way completely. They wanted us to stay among them. We were surrounded by a sea of faces, creased, joyful, unmasked. Hats of all kinds, skull caps of every color, handkerchiefs in place of head covering. A young girl clapped her hands, an old man lifted up his eyes as if in prayer, a laborer sighed joyfully. Old men and their children and their children's children—everyone wanted to touch the Torah, to touch us. Everyone had something to whisper in our ears, a blessing or a secret. I have never in my life received so many blessings, never in my life been surrounded by so much goodwill and love. One pressed my hand, a second patted my arm, a third held my clothing. They would not let us move forward. They seemed to be trying to stop the progress of time. Through us they became freer, came closer to the reality of their dreams. They looked upon us as redeeming and protective angels. The fact that we were different, unafraid, was sufficient to elevate us in their eyes to the stature of saints and wonder workers. When I was young, we used to surround the holy *rebbe* in this fashion, begging him to intercede for us before the heavenly tribunal. But here, they asked for nothing. On the contrary, they brought us their gifts, their love, their blessings. Hundreds of them. Be healthy! Be strong! Be courageous! May we see you in the years to come! May we all live until that day! May you prosper! And may you sing! Do you hear? Just sing! A few went further, giving vent to their inmost feelings, but always in a whisper: I have a brother in Israel, a sister in Jerusalem, an uncle in Haifa. Short notices: brother, sister, grandfather, uncle, grandson. No names. They simply wanted us to know that a part of them was there, in the land of Israel. Others used clichés that in any other context would have produced smiles of condescension or contempt: "The people of Israel lives"; "The eternity of Israel shall not prove false"; "The redeemer shall come to Zion soon in our days." A Jew with a laborer's cap falling over his brow pushed forward and announced that he had something to tell me but no one was to hear. He began to hum in my ear the words of "*Hatikvah*," [4] finished the first stanza, and disappeared, his face alight with victory. A woman pleaded with me, "Say something to my daughter. I brought her so she would see Jews who are not ashamed or afraid." The girl was very beautiful, dark and mysterious, with flashing eyes. She said something in Russian; I answered in Hebrew. Neither of us understood the other; yet somehow we did. Her mother was satisfied; she kissed my hand, murmuring, "Thank you, thank you. Will we ever see you again?" I didn't know what to say. I forgot everything I knew, except these two words: Thank you, thank you. Thank you for the gift of this moment, thank you for being alive, for enduring, for knowing how to rejoice and to hope and to dream. Thank you for being Jews like us. And a thousand and one thanks for finding the strength to thank a Jew like me for being a Jew.

Our procession lasted about an hour. Pale and drenched with sweat, we relinquished the Torah scrolls to the next group of marchers and returned to our seats in the visitors' section. I was out of breath and exhausted. I wanted to rest, close my eyes and wait for my strength to return. The third procession had begun. The singing reached me as if from a great distance or from behind a curtain, as in a daydream. I had never imagined that the weight and power of this experience would stun me as it did. If I had come for this alone, it would have been sufficient.

"They're going crazy out there. We must join them."

We went. The remaining processions we would celebrate outside. Luckily there was a side door; we did not have to pass through the congregation. They would never have let us go. Two or three "agents" got up to follow us. Let them. The Prince of the Torah protects those who come to rejoice in His name.

The street was unrecognizable. For a second I thought I had been transported to another world, somewhere in Israel or in Brooklyn. Angels and seraphim were serenading the night; King David played his harp. The city burst with gladness and joy. The evening had just begun.

Deliberately or not, they had been lying to us. With good intentions

4. Israel national anthem ("The Hope").—Trans.

or bad, they had misinformed us. They wanted us to despair of Jewish youth in Russia, had attempted to persuade us of its increasing alienation from Jewish life. For years they had spread such lies, supporting them with arguments whose logic was hard to refute. After all, we were talking about the third generation after the Revolution. Even if they wished to be Jewish, where would they begin? Even if they wanted to study Torah, who was there to help them? It is only natural that they have forgotten their past; tomorrow they will have nothing to forget. And we listened, were saddened, but concurred. Yes, there was something to that. What can one do? It was the inevitable result of historical materialism. You cannot demand the impossible.

But they surprised us. Soviet Jewish youth has remained Jewish to a degree beyond anything we could possibly have expected.

I do not know where all these young people came from. They didn't tell me, although I asked. Perhaps there is no one answer, but tens of thousands that are all the same. No matter—they came.

Who sent them? Who persuaded them to come running to spend a Jewish holiday in a Jewish atmosphere and in accordance with traditional Jewish custom? Who told them when and where and why? I was unable to discover. Perhaps they knew but preferred not to say in public. Fine. Let them preserve their secret. All that matters is that they have one and that they came.

Still, there is something strange about it. Tens of thousands of youngsters do not suddenly emerge from nowhere at a specified time and place. Someone had to organize and direct them; someone had to make the contacts, maintain the necessary spirit, and inform them of the date and time. Who made all the preparations? Who breathed the spark into a flame? I didn't ask; they wouldn't have answered. Perhaps it is better for me not to know.

They came in droves. From near and far, from downtown and the suburbs, from the university and from the factories, from school dormitories and from the Komsomol club. They came in groups; they came alone. But once here, they became a single body, voicing a song of praise to the Jewish people and its will to live.

How many were there? Ten thousand? Twenty thousand? More. About thirty thousand. The crush was worse than it had been inside the synagogue. They filled the whole street, spilling over into courtyards, dancing and singing, dancing and singing. They seemed to hover in mid-air, Chagall-like, floating above the mass of shadows and colors below, above time, climbing a Jacob's ladder that reached to the heavens, if not higher.

Tomorrow they would descend and scatter, disappear into the innermost parts of Moscow, not to be heard from for another year. But they would return and bring more with them. The line will never break; one who has come will always return.

I moved among them like a sleepwalker, stunned by what I saw and heard, half disbelieving my own senses. I had known they would come, but not in such numbers; I had known they would celebrate, but not that their celebration would be so genuine and so deeply Jewish.

They sang and danced, talked among themselves or with strangers. They were borne along on a crest that seemed incapable of breaking. Their faces reflected a special radiance, their eyes the age-old flame that burned in the house of their ancestors—to which they seemed finally to have returned.

I was swept along in the current, passing from one group to another, from one circle to the next, sharing their happiness and absorbing the sound of their voices.

It was after ten. The cold brought tears to one's eyes. But it was easy to warm up; one had only to join in the singing or start talking with someone.

A girl strummed her guitar and sang a Yiddish folk song, "Buy my cigarettes, take pity on a poor orphan." A few steps away, a boy played "*Heivenu Shalom Aleichem*" on the accordion. Further on, others were dancing the *hora*. Still another group was heatedly debating Judaism and Israel. "I am a Communist!" a young student shouted. I asked him what he was doing here. "I am also a Jew." Suddenly I wanted to go from one to the other, begging their forgiveness for our lack of faith. Our disappointment in Russian Jewish youth is a thing of our own creating. It is they who reassure us, they who teach us not to despair.

Hour after hour I wandered through that street, which had become a rallying point for pilgrims from every corner of the city. It seemed to have lengthened and widened, become a thing of joy and beauty. It seemed to have taken on a new soul and with it the sanctity of a heavenly dream.

A dark-haired and vivacious girl stood in the middle of a circle, leading a chorus of voices in a series of questions and answers.

"Who are we?"

"Jews!"

"What are we?"

"Jews!"

"What shall we remain?"

"Jews!"

They laughed as they chanted their responses. Someone translated the dialogue for me, urged me to join in the laughter and hand-clapping. It was a splendid joke. The Kremlin was ten minutes away, and the echoes of the Jewish celebration reached to the tomb of Stalin. "It's too crowded here!" a boy cried. "Next year we celebrate in Red Square!" His audience burst into applause.

"Who are we?" asked the dark-haired girl.

"Jews!"

A little later I went up to talk with her. Would she speak to a stranger? She would. Not afraid? No, not tonight. And other nights? Let's stick to tonight. She was a humanities major at the university. She spoke Yiddish, she said, with her grandfather, sometimes with her parents, and occasionally even with friends when they were alone. Was she religious? Far from it; never had been. Her parents had been born after the Revolution, and even they had received an anti-religious education. What did she know about the Jewish religion? That it was based on outdated values. And about the Jewish pepole? That it was made up of capitalists and swindlers. And the state of Israel? That it was aggressive, racist, and imperialist. Where had she learned all this? From textbooks, government pamphlets, and the press. I asked her why she insisted on remaining Jewish. She hesitated, searching for the proper word, then smiled. "What does it matter what they think of us . . . it's what we think that counts." And she added immediately, "I'll tell you why I'm a Jew. Because I like to sing."

The songs they sang were mostly products of the nineteenth century. The most popular was a Yiddish folk song, "Come let us go together, all of us together, and greet the bride and groom." But they had updated the lyrics, substituting for the last phrase, "Come let us greet the Jewish people," or "the people of Israel," or "the God of Israel and His Torah."

One group of students had formed a human pyramid. The young man at the apex was yelling defiantly, "Nothing can help them! We shall overcome them!" His audience roared back, "Hurrah! Hurrah!"

More cheers came from a nearby group that was celebrating the holiday in a manner decidedly Russian, tossing one of their number into the air. Five times, six, seven. Higher, higher. A girl pleaded with them to stop, but they paid no attention. Eight times, nine, ten. Nothing would happen. Nothing did. A carpet of outstretched hands was waiting to catch the hero upon his return from on high. "Hurrah! Hurrah!"

This is how Russian soldiers celebrated their victory over the Germans, and how the Jews celebrate their triumph over despair.

"What does anyone in America or Israel care if my passport is stamped 'Jewish'? It doesn't matter to me, and it doesn't matter to these young people here tonight. So stop protesting about things that don't bother us. We have long since ceased being ashamed of our Jewishness. We can't hide it anyway. Besides, by accepting it we've managed to turn obedience to the law into an act of free choice."

The man I was talking to had served as a captain in the Red Army and had been decorated in Berlin. Like his father before him, he was a sworn Communist. But like all the rest, he suffered on account of his Jewishness. Were he Russian he would have long ago been appointed a full professor at the university. He was still holding an instructorship in foreign languages. One day, he said, he decided that as long as they made him feel like a Jew, he might as well act accordingly. It was the only way to beat them at their own game. "Two years ago I came to the synagogue on the night of Simhath Torah. I wanted to see Jews, and I wanted to be with them. I didn't tell my wife, who isn't Jewish, or my sixteen-year-old son. Why should I burden him with problems? There was time enough for that. I came back last year for the second time. The youngsters were singing and dancing, almost like tonight. I found myself

247

suddenly in the middle of a group of youngsters, and my heart stopped . . . I was standing face to face with my son. He said he'd been coming for the past three years, but hadn't dared to tell me.

"Would you like to see him?" he asked me.

"Yes, very much."

"He's here, somewhere," he said, gesturing at the crowd as if to say, "Look closely, they are all my son."

I talked with dozens of people. Some of them questioned me incessantly about the Jews abroad; others tried to debate with me the issue of diplomatic relations between Israel and Germany; a few almost openly acknowledged that they suffered because they were Jews. But not one of them criticized the state or the Russian authorities. And they all claimed, "They will never succeed. Jewish youth in Russia will not disappoint us."

Anyone who was there that night can attest to the truth of this statement. Young Jews in Russia want to return to Judaism, but without knowing what it is. Without knowing why, they define themselves as Jews. And they believe in the eternity of the Jewish people, without the slightest notion of the meaning of its mission. That is their tragedy.

Ilya Ehrenburg wrote in his memoirs that he would call himself a Jew as long as a single anti-Semite remained on earth. There is no doubt that this way of thinking is an important factor in bringing young people together at the synagogue to rejoice in the Torah. Precisely because it is not easy to be a Jew in Russia, Jewish consciousness will continue to grow. "We are Jews for spite," one student said to me. There is some accuracy in this. For want of better teachers, it is the anti-Semites who are making them Jews.

I said to one of them, "You don't know Hebrew, you never learned Jewish history, you don't fulfill the commandments, and you don't believe in the God of Israel—in what way are you a Jew?"

He answered, "Apparently you live in a country where Jews can afford the luxury of asking questions. Things are different here. It's enough for a Jew to call himself a Jew. It's enough to fulfill one commandment or to celebrate one Jewish day a year. With us, being Jewish is not a matter of words, but of simple endurance, not of definition but of existence. If my son were to ask me one day what a Jew is, I would tell him that a Jew is one who knows when to ask questions and when to give answers . . . and when to do neither."

"Hurrah!" the voices thundered. "David, King of Israel, lives and endures. Hurrah!"

This evening gave me new hope and encouragement. We need not despair. The Jews in Kiev, Leningrad, and Tbilisi who had complained to me about the doubtful future of Russian Jewry were wrong. They were too pessimistic, and apparently did not know their own children or the hidden forces which prompt them, at least once a year, to affirm their sense of community. Everyone has judged this generation guilty of denying its God and of being ashamed of its Jewishness. They are said to despise all mention of Israel. But it is a lie. Their love for Israel exceeds that of young Jews anywhere else in the world.

If, on this night of dancing, gladness finally overcame fear, it was because of them. If song triumphed over silence, it was their triumph. And it was through them only that the dream of freedom and community became reality. I am still waiting to see tens of thousands of Jews singing and dancing in Times Square or the Place de l'Etoile as they danced here, in the heart of Moscow, on the night of Simhath Torah. They danced until midnight without rest, to let the city know that they are Jews.

Tishah B'ab in Moscow

BY *Ronald I. Rubin*

In July 1966, I toured the Soviet Union. As a political scientist, I went to see the country firsthand, to talk with its youth and perhaps acquire background for my classroom descriptions of communism. As an Orthodox Jew, I hoped to check on the authenticity of press reports of the past few years regarding Soviet anti-Semitism. Though my observations of political society in the U.S.S.R. may in general have been hurried and fragmentary, I feel that my conclusions on the observance of Judaism there are based on reliable evidence. During my two-week sojourn I spoke with Jews in three cities—Minsk, Leningrad, and Moscow. The most poignant experience of all was the Tishah b'ab I spent in Moscow.

For some 2,500 years Tishah b'ab has been Judaism's national day of mourning. It originally marked the destruction of the temple in Jerusalem—first by the Babylonians in 586 B.C., then (on precisely the same day of the year) by the Romans in A.D. 70. Now it has come to symbolize all the misfortunes and disasters suffered by the Jews throughout their history. It has all the characteristics of the *shibah,* the period of mourning for the dead. Prohibited on Tishah b'ab are eating, drinking, and laughter, even the traditional handshake of greeting in the synagogue.

Normally Tishah b'ab falls in July or August of the Western calendar year. This year it was observed on Tuesday, July 26. In Moscow I attended Tishah b'ab services at the Central Synagogue—one of three in the area. (The others are in the suburbs; together the three serve some 500,000 Jews, about 10 percent of the total population of the area.) Though the Central Synagogue stands less than a ten-minute walk from Red Square, Moscow's chief tourist attraction, the taxi drivers who took me there on my four visits all had difficulty in finding the site—8 Arkhipova Street. Since the drivers were friendly enough, I concluded that their inability to find the synagogue at once was due not to prejudice but to the fact that this part of the city is little known.

The synagogue is a fairly large, plain building with a yellow exterior, its white entrance columns reminiscent of Greek Renaissance architecture. It fronts directly on the street, which, like most Russian side streets, I found to be virtually devoid of automobile traffic. When I attended services in the chapel on July 24 I asked about the cracks and holes in the chapel ceiling. I was told that repairs were under way, and indeed a painting scaffold clung to the front of the building.

Tishah b'ab services began at 8:30 on Monday evening in the main sanctuary. Present were from 150 to 200 men. In the balcony seat sat a few women (since Orthodox Judaism recognizes only certain prayers as incumbent on women, they are generally excused from actual attendance at the synagogue, and when they do come they sit apart from the men).

Most of the men at the services that night were elderly, mainly, I would judge, in their sixties and seventies, though one told me he was ninety-six. Their clothes were threadbare, as indeed were those of the average man I had seen on the streets. The few young men present seemed less able to follow the service than their elders; apparently Hebrew was unfamiliar to them. Instead of the traditional skull cap, some of the young men wore square Tashkent hats—a type of headgear, imported from Tashkent, much in style in Moscow this year.

The synagogue was dimly lit, in accordance with the ritual of this day of mourning. On the platform in front of the sanctuary were several low, unadorned benches—the type of bench used by Jews during the period of mourning for the dead. Recognizable by his attire—black hat and coat—was bearded Judah Leib Levin, Chief Rabbi of Moscow.

For one accustomed to praying in Western synagogues, certain features distinguished the Moscow service. The most telling difference was the scarcity of prayer books. I watched old men stoop over attempting to make out the print in prayer books held in the hands of others. I saw others reading from books disfigured, kept intact by tape. A few had Israeli-made books, identifiable by their small size and distinctive covers.

Prayers for the Tishah b'ab service are not contained in the standard prayer book; recited are special Lamentations, including Jeremiah's bleakest prophecies. Even fewer worshipers had the Lamentations than had the regular prayer books. Yet the paper-covered Lamentations book I had with me had cost only 20 cents in the United States. Three or four men shared the book during the service; one bent from the pew behind to look over my shoulder. Another, an elderly man seated beside me, stroked the little volume fondly.

Another difference from the accustomed Western service lay in the fact that many of the men present—about one-third, I would estimate—did not join in the prayers at all. Why was this so? For some, it was obviously lack of prayer books; for others, lack of knowledge of Hebrew. One of the few young men present—a boy apparently in his late teens—knew only the Kaddish, the memorial prayer for the dead. The farther from the front, the fewer there were who followed the service, and toward the rear, worshipers engaged in whispered conversation.

Still another contrast I noted was the conscious setting apart of certain worshipers from the rest of the congregation. For instance, Israeli diplomats followed the prayers from an area at the front right side of the sanctuary, where the seats were placed perpendicular to the rest.[1] Was the seating arrangement perhaps designed to make personal contact difficult between Israeli and Russian Jews?

Nevertheless, actual recitation of the prayers resembled that in services I had attended elsewhere. The Job-like melody, the dimmed lights, the old men straining eyes and heart, the torn or missing prayer books created in my mind an image of mourning and death. When the ninety-minute service had ended I offered my prayer book to one of the old

1. Diplomatic relations between Israel and the Soviet Union were broken off after the Six-Day War.—Ed.

men who had shared it. Obviously afraid to accept it openly, he looked about to see if anyone was watching, then slipped it into his inside pocket.

Outside the synagogue a group of worshipers gathered around me, conversing in Yiddish and Hebrew. Ours was not a casual conversation; they sought earnestly for information about Jewish life in the United States and Israel. How many *yeshivas* (religious schools) are there in the two countries? Did I know the whereabouts of this or that relative in Brooklyn or the Bronx? Are young American Jews religious? Are the infants circumcised into the Covenant of Abraham? What about religious divisions within American Jewry? (A week or so earlier a group of Reform rabbis from the United States had visited the synagogue; apparently the Russian Jews have but a vague idea about divisions in the United States.)

There have been no public classes in Hebrew for many years, yet one man in his late sixties told me in fluent Hebrew that he eats meat only on Jewish holidays; the rest of the year he eats only dairy products, fruits, and vegetables because kosher meat is either unobtainable or impossibly expensive. Usually the only kosher meat available at any time, I was told, is poultry. Several people told me that of all the Jews in Moscow only the chief rabbi regularly eats kosher meat.

When I returned the next morning for the remainder of the Tishah b'ab service I found even fewer people present. As the prayers ended I left the synagogue thinking that here was surely the most meaningful place on earth to observe Tishah b'ab, to reflect on the despair and courage that have marked its commemoration by Jews for 2,500 years.

The Power of a Song

BY *Shelomo Ben-Israel*

I did not arrive in Riga until late afternoon. The Intourist girl at my hotel explained regretfully that it was too late in the day to arrange for a guide, and suggested a theater or concert that evening instead. She produced a schedule of the week's entertainment, recommending especially a recital by a prominent Armenian organist. But I spotted something much more exciting: *Geula Gill, presenting Songs of All Nations, and Jacob Arkin, Israeli pantomimist.* I asked the girl if she could get me a ticket.

"Impossible, I'm afraid," she replied. "It's all sold out."

I glanced at the schedule again for the address of the recital and decided to try my luck. Hailing a cab, I told the driver to take me to the Daugava Sports Center.

"You want to go to the concert?" he asked. "It doesn't start until eight. You'll be two hours early."

The severance of diplomatic relations with Israel during the Six-Day War resulted in the curtailment of even these limited Israeli concerts, serving to sharpen the feeling of isolation of Soviet Jews.

The Power of a Song

The taxi driver was Jewish. He told me that all Riga was up in the air over the arrival of the two Israeli performers.

"They only put up four posters in the whole city," he said. "What do you think of that—four posters in a city of more than half a million! But everyone in town knew about it anyway, and by the time the box office opened, there was a long line. Some people had been waiting since four in the morning. In two hours, the tickets for all three recitals were gone. I was lucky; I have a ticket for tomorrow night."

The reason "everyone knew about it" long before the posters appeared was that the Israeli Government radio station had announced the recital two weeks before tickets went on sale.

In other cities, too, all the concerts were sold out. Many Jews told me they could not believe the Israeli artists were really coming until they saw the posters with blue Stars of David and photos of the two performers. Often Jewish teen-agers cut out the photos as souvenirs.

The Daugava Sports Center auditorium seats about 1,200. When my taxi pulled up, nearly 100 people, most of them young men and women, were already waiting for the doors to open. Some had come without tickets, hoping to sneak into the hall or, through some lucky break, to buy a seat from someone else. Many youngsters had brought autograph books for the performers to sign.

The crowd was in a festive mood. It was the first time the Soviet Concert Bureau had arranged for performances by an Israeli troupe. This was the stamp of legitimacy.

"*Meshiach's tzeiten,*" a young man said to me. ("The Messiah has come.") He and his wife had brought their ten-year-old son with them and were determined to get into the auditorium, even if they had to pay three times the established price for a ticket.

By seven o'clock the crowd had swelled to several hundred. The auditorium doors were open, but no one seemed in a hurry to go in. Every bus and trolley that stopped at the center discharged its entire cargo of passengers. People flocked to the hall from every direction.

I was told that a single 2-ruble ticket was selling for as much as 15 rubles, and I saw one man sell his for 12. (A ruble is equal to approximately one American dollar.) The man who bought it had come with his wife; the two shared the concert, each viewing half of the program.

A crowd had gathered around me, the visitor from America. Most

255

spoke excellent Yiddish; some spoke Hebrew fluently. I was amazed at the number of sixteen-, seventeen-, and eighteen-year-olds who spoke Hebrew.

They had learned their *Ivrit* from the Israeli Government radio programs. The Soviet Government has stopped jamming foreign broadcasts of late, and Russian audiences can now hear *"Kol Israel"* and the "Voice of America" without "technical disturbances." (When I asked an Intourist employe in Tbilisi where he had learned his English, he replied without a moment's hesitation: "From the English classes on the 'Voice of America.' ")

The general mood outside the sports center was open and apparently free of tension, but the young Jews were nevertheless on their guard. I soon discovered why, for it was here that I encountered for the first time that dreaded creature referred to in whispers as the *klapper*.

In the midst of a lively conversation, the group of Jews I had been chatting with suddenly stopped talking. When the conversation resumed, the talk was about the weather. What had happened?

A man had approached our group, stopped nearby for several moments, and then had left, as suddenly as he had come. "A *klapper*," someone hissed in my ear, with a flick of the eyelid in the direction of the vanished stranger. *Klapper*, literally "knocker," is the Yiddish word that Jews in Riga and Vilna use for informers. (The Russian word for "knocker," *stükach*, is also slang for informer or stool-pigeon.) In Kiev and Odessa, such individuals are known as *zoger*, "tellers"—for people who tell tales.

"Are you sure?" I asked.

"About this one? A hundred per cent. Everybody knows him; he's an unsavory character. Of course, there are others you can only guess about. But even when you can't tell for certain, it's healthier to play safe. Look out, here comes another one."

I looked for the woman whose husband had gone inside for the first half of the concert with the 12-ruble ticket. They had spent a lot of money for one evening—actually half an evening apiece—of Israeli music. Was it worth that much to a couple who, both working, earned only 110 rubles a month?

"Are you kidding?" the woman replied. "I'd go without food for a week for the chance to listen to Israeli songs. My husband and I never miss a recital by Nehama Lifshitz.[1] But these are Israelis. Do you really think I'd pass that up to save a couple of rubles?"

I waited outside until the end of the concert, which ran very late. Finally I heard a crash of applause, and the radiant audience came pouring into the street, lingering there for a glimpse of the artists.

I was more determined than ever to see the next performance from the inside, and on the following evening I managed to attend the concert, with the help of Geula Gill, herself.

The last time I had heard her sing was at a "Third Seder" sponsored by Histadrut at the Waldorf-Astoria in New York. In Russia, she sang many of the same songs, accompanied by the same two guitarists. Yet it was not the same. At the Daugava Sports Center, I realized, as never before, the magic of song, the power of the spoken word, and the mysterious bond that unites the Jewish people.

The repertory was the same at all the concerts. In Riga the programs were printed in Russian and Latvian, and in Vilna in Russian and Lithuanian, and the Russian girl who accompanied the two Israelis on their tour announced the numbers in Russian.

Jacob Arkin, a very gifted pantomimist, took up the first half of the program. His themes were not especially Jewish: "An Eagle," "A Flag Bearer on a Windy Day," and so on. The audience responded warmly to each sketch, but when his last pantomime was announced—a tourist who comes to visit a *kibbutz* in Israel and learns to dance the *hora*—the audience went wild as soon as they heard the two Hebrew words.

The blonde announcer introduced Geula Gill as an "interpreter of the folk songs of many nations." Her first song was "*Hallelu*," which the program listed as a "song of joy." The next, "*Taam HaMan*" ("The Taste of Manna"), was introduced as a "Persian song"; and Aaron Zeitlin's famous "*Bim-Bom*," which begins: "*Zogt der Rebbe Reb Mottenyu: A Gut Morgen Dir, Gottenyu*" ("Said the Rabbi, Reb Mottenyu: A Good Morning to You, Dear God") was announced as "a hymn."

The audience pretended to ignore this make-believe. Let them call "*Bim-Bom*" a hymn, if that's what they wanted to do, as long as it was Yiddish. The artist continued with "*Malagueña*" in Spanish, and "*Vegis*"

1. Nehama Lifshitz is a Russian folk singer who, for the past several years, has been a popular interpreter of Yiddish songs.

in Swiss German, followed by a French song and an English-language version of "*The Song of the Hammer*," which was listed in the program by its Hebrew title, "*Shir HaPatish*." The audience responded with special warmth to the Yiddish folk song "*Tum Balalaika*," in which a girl explains to her suitor that "love can burn without ceasing . . . a heart can weep without tears."

Then the announcer introduced " '*Eli, Eli*'—the song of the Ghetto." I shall never forget the next five minutes.

The stage was completely dark, except for a single spotlight focused on Geula's face. The silence was absolute. Then the ancient cry of pain rent forth: "*Eli, Eli*, O God, my God, why hast Thou forsaken me? . . . Hear my prayer, my weeping, for Thou alone canst save me . . . *Shema Yisrael*—Hear, O Israel, the Lord our God is One . . ."

The barriers between artist and public fell away, and they were one. From my seat in the first row, I turned and saw, in the eerie half-light reflected from the stage, a sea of white faces all the way to the back of the darkened theater. Many eyes glistened with tears.

There was a long pause. The spotlight spread, flooding the stage. Then, pandemonium. Amidst wild applause and shouts of "More, more," the audience pelted Geula with flowers—single roses, small bouquets— and slips of paper bearing messages of gratitude, affection, and longing for deliverance. The announcer did not return; nor did the artist identify her encores. She simply sang, and all her heart was in her voice. As she broke into "*Artza Alinu*," the song of the pioneer in the Jewish homeland, the words were drowned out by the applause. Then young and old joined her in Goldfaden's "*Rozhinkes und Mandlen*," "*Shir Ha-Palmach*," the Israeli Army marching song, "*Heivenu Shalom Aleichem*," and other Hebrew songs.

Once again, the performance ran far beyond schedule, and it was after eleven when the audience, faces aflame and eyes glistening, streamed into the street. The crowds outside fell upon them with questions.

"Did you enjoy the concert?" I asked a middle-aged couple who had come with their twelve-year-old son.

"I can't find the words to tell you how I feel," the mother replied. "It was an experience I've never had before. But it meant even more to our boy. He needed something to give him a sense of pride in being a Jew."

Geula Gill reports that the wife of one of the most famous intellectuals in Soviet Russia had expressed the same feeling, in even stronger terms. After one concert, this woman came backstage to congratulate Geula.

"Sometimes I feel as worthless as a grain of sand," she said. "I've been depressed, insecure, and even a little ashamed of my Jewishness. But suddenly, tonight, thanks to you, I have the strength to hold my head high and be proud that I'm a Jew. . . ."

As I stood outside that concert hall, it seemed to me for a moment that instead of the sports center in Riga, I was at the court of a *hasidic rebbe,* watching the inspired disciples stream out of their leader's home after a *Melava Malka,* a Sabbath night of feasting, song, and dance.

Again the people milled about, waiting for the performers to come out. A few dozen policemen tried, amid shouts of protest and annoyance, to clear the area around the little Philharmonia bus which was to take the Israelis back to their hotel. Actually, the police had no desire to deprive these people of their pleasure; they were there primarily to protect Geula Gill from her overenthusiastic admirers. (In Moscow, she was almost crushed by the surging crowds.) A number of teen-agers did manage to reach her and get autographed pictures, and cheers and shouts came from every direction.

"Shalom . . . shalom!"

"Next year in Jerusalem!"

"*Lehitraot*—we'll be seeing you."

Several youngsters ran after the departing bus, wildly waving their arms, as the two Israelis waved back. Only after the bus had disappeared from sight did the crowd reluctantly disperse.

"I never saw anything like this," said a perspiring policeman, wiping his forehead. "That little girl must be some artist."

The Ships That Will Sail
to Jerusalem

BY *Ben Ami*

One day I visited Derbent, some two hundred miles north of Baku on the Caspian Sea. This Persian-style city lies on the slopes of the hills which rise from the sea and is dominated by a huge fortress built by the Persian conquerors in the Middle Ages. The houses are low and set close together, the streets narrow; and only in the center of the city are modern Soviet buildings found. Of the tens of thousands of people who live there, more than a third are Mountain Jews. The remainder are various Daghestan peoples, mostly Lezghians.

Among the three million Soviet Jews are some 250,000 Oriental Jews—inhabitants of Georgia, Bukhara, and the mountains along the shores of the Caspian Sea—inhabitants for some two thousand years of what is now the Soviet Union. Unlike their European Jewish counterparts, they are regarded as indigenous and have never experienced intense anti-Semitism. Even so—as indicated by the author's reference to the tattered Haggadah—they too have suffered from the ban on producing new prayer books and other devotional articles for Jews.

The Ships That Will Sail to Jerusalem

Some of the Derbent Jews are farmers with considerable experience in the growing of the famous Daghestan wine grapes. They are organized into four *kolkhozy* [collective settlements—Ed.], the lands of which adjoin the city's residential quarters. Most of the *kolkhoz* members are Jews who live in the city; the city is therefore a semi-agricultural settlement. These Mountain Jews are among the few Jews in the Soviet Union whose occupation is agriculture. Most of them live in exclusively Jewish streets. Because I came there on the eve of Passover, I could easily identify their homes, which had just been painted blue in honor of the festival.

I attended the festive evening service. Their synagogue is not as sumptuous as those in Georgia, but it is very well kept. It was crowded with celebrants, among whom were many children. I was given a seat near the venerable *hacham* ["sage"—Ed.], who received me with warmth and spoke to me in impeccable classic Hebrew. The services were conducted partly in biblical Hebrew and partly in Tati translation. After the prayers the *hacham* introduced me to one of the prominent families of his congregation and told me that I would be celebrating the Seder as a guest in the family's home.

The head of the family was a broad-shouldered, vigorous man of about sixty-five who had been one of the district's leading vine dressers and had recently retired. When he heard that he would be my host, he gave me a bear hug and took me almost bodily under his wing.

The large family had already begun to gather as I approached his house, which was sheltered, Persian style, behind a high fence.

The mother had prepared the house for the Seder. A table, reserved for the men, stood in the main room, and on the carpeted floor there were colored cushions for the women. At the head of the table sat my host, with me on his left and his brother, a man of over sixty, on his right. On both sides of the table sat brothers, sons, brothers-in-law, and relatives. The male children were seated at the far end. Women and girls of all ages sat on the floor, their heads covered with colored bands and scarves.

On the gleaming white tablecloth there were round, homemade *matzoth*, bottles of honey-colored, home-brewed wine, and a profusion of Oriental foods. I added my own share to the table, to the obvious and loud pleasure of the assembly: a bottle of Israeli wine and a package of matzoth "made in Jerusalem," which I had brought from home.

The head of the family began the service and read each verse of the Haggadah first in Hebrew, then in Tati. After reading and translating the first paragraph, he honored me with the reading of the second passage, and then his brother and two or three of the family elders who knew Hebrew, with other sections. The others listened to the Tati translation; they did not have Haggadoth. The three Haggadoth in the hands of the elders were torn and tattered from constant use.

And so we read the entire ancient Haggadah verse by verse, and the family heard in their own language the story of the exodus from Egypt, the downfall of Pharaoh, the wanderings in the desert, and the redemption in the Land of Israel.

When the reading ended, spicy and tasty oriental food was passed around in shining copper pots. Goblets filled with Israeli and Daghestani wine were raised. As hearts grew warmer, the people began to sing their own Passover songs. They were delighted when I joined in with Israeli Passover songs.

At the close of this wonderful and memorable evening, the elders began telling stories and legends of the life of the Mountain Jews. One of these stories made a vivid impression upon me. It related that the Mountain Jews had been exiled from Jerusalem to Caucasia many centuries ago. While the first exiles were lamenting the loss of the temple and their expulsion, their leaders promised them that the Messiah would come sometime in the future and they would return to Jerusalem. This return would take place in three stages. During the first, which would span many centuries, the Jews would live in the mountain villages. If they maintained their religious traditions, they would reach the second stage: they would come down from the mountains and congregate in the large cities of the Caspian Sea. During the third and last stage, ships from Jerusalem would come to the shores of the Caspian and bring the exiles back to their land. (In ancient legend, the Caspian Sea seemed to be the common ocean. The fact that it is a closed sea and that Jerusalem is not a port does not disturb these people in the least.)

Turning to me, the storyteller added: "The first stage has passed. We have lived for countless centuries among our gentile neighbors and have preserved our faith and traditions. The second stage has begun a few decades ago. Most of the Mountain Jews have come down from the mountains and now live on the seashore and in harbor towns. And now, we are waiting and looking forward to the third, and longed-for stage."

With shining eyes the celebrants raised their goblets to the "leaping" of the ships from Jerusalem to the Caspian Sea.

Visit to Babi Yar

BY *Michael Kaufman*

Due to scheduling difficulties—I am not sure they were at all accidental
—a visit to this city in the heart of the Ukraine was to have been cut
down to only six hours. Arriving at the Kiev airport at 12:00 noon, Intourist told me I would have to catch my next plane out at 6:00 in the
evening.

My Intourist guide met me in the airport lobby, and told me that my
car and driver were "not here yet, but would arrive in a few minutes."
At 12:10 I asked him where the car and driver were, and he told me they
would arrive momentarily. When at 12:30 I got the same reply, I began
to suspect that there was more to the delay of car and driver than mere
happenstance. My suspicions were confirmed as my guide kept up a running conversation with another Ukrainian, which conversation was lib-
erally sprinkled with the word "*Yevrei*"—Russian for "Jew"—repeated
from time to time, punctuated with glances in my direction and uproar-
ious laughter.

At 1:00 car and driver had still to arrive, but they were "coming in
just a minute." My guide pulled himself away from his very funny con-

versation with his buddy for a minute to ask whether I would not, after all, like to spend the rest of the afternoon at the airport, since there was so little I could do in the interim. I told him, no, thank you, and did not add that since it seemed so obvious that my Ukrainian hosts were not anxious for me to spend too much time in Kiev, I was determined to "accidentally" miss that six o'clock flight so I could spend another twenty-four hours in the city.

At 1:30, after another "just a minute until the car and driver arrive," I informed my guide that if they were not there by 2:00 P.M. I would head out on my own. At this he became somewhat excited, and asked how I was going to get around without him. I told him I would manage. Promptly at 2:00 I picked up my bags and walked out of the air terminal. I found a taxi, and with my college Russian informed the driver I wanted to go to Babi Yar. He told me to get in, and started the engine.

As I sat down, my guide came running: "Mr. Kaufman, Mr. Kaufman, why are you going?" "Because you're not taking me anywhere," I replied.

"But your car and driver arrived," he said. "Fine," I said, "where is the car?" "Here," he replied, pointing to a car which had been parked in front of the building since my arrival two hours before.

"Where is the driver?" I asked. "Here," he replied, pointing to the very Ukrainian with whom he had shared laughter at my expense during the past two hours.

Rather than provoke an incident, I controlled my temper and left the taxi and entered the car. When they asked where I wanted to go, I told them Babi Yar. "We don't know where that is," my guide replied. "How unfortunate," I said. "Let me get that taxi again, for the taxi driver knows very well where Babi Yar is." "No, no," my guide protested as I made to get out of the car, "we will find it." (P.S. They found Babi Yar without asking directions from anyone.)

I knew that Babi Yar was a large ravine at the outskirts of Kiev, and the scene of one of the most horrendous slaughters of human beings in modern times. In this ravine some 100,000 to 200,000 human beings— the exact number is unknown—almost all of them Jews, were gruesomely murdered, machine-gunned, and pushed alive from a ledge into the ravine below. Living men, women, and children—35,000 in one day, according to one account—were massacred by the Nazis with the active help of Ukrainian police and some of its populace. The fact that it was Jews who were killed at Babi Yar was suppressed by the Russians for twenty-five years, until, in the early 1960's, the young Soviet poet Yevgeny Yevtushenko gained international renown almost overnight with his moving poem "Babi Yar."

En route to the car, my guide asked me whether I "had heard anything about Babi Yar." "A little," I told him. I asked him whether he knew about it. He answered cautiously that he did, that he knew "some people" had been killed there by the Nazis during the war. "What kind of people?" I asked. "Russians and Ukrainians," was his prompt reply. "Any Jews?" I asked. He said he did not think so—and anyway, Jews are equal to all other people in the Soviet Union and they are included in the over-all category of Russians and Ukrainians. I looked surprised, and asked him: "Then Jews now have the word 'Russian' or 'Ukrainian' and no longer have the label "*Yevrei*' on their internal passports identifying them as Jews?" He looked embarrassed and ill at ease, hemmed and hawed a bit, and finally said: "We're changing that situation in the next few months and Jews will no longer be labeled as such."

(P.S. Needless to say, this situation has, of course, not been changed. Jews are still labeled as such on their internal passports, as are members of other nationalities, and yet they are still not entitled to any of the advantages that members of other nationalities have—schools, newspapers, magazines, books, and religious periodicals in their own language. There is no way in which Jews may learn what is going on among Jews in the U.S.S.R. and throughout the world. In the Ukraine, for example, in 1956, 97 per cent of Ukrainian schools gave instruction in non-Russian native languages. None of these languages, of course, was Yiddish, although it is the mother-tongue of hundreds of thousands of Ukrainian Jews.)

Under persistent questioning, my guide finally grudgingly admitted that he was aware that the vast majority of those who had been murdered in the mass carnage at Babi Yar were Jews. "However," he added, "there were also some Russians and Ukrainians as well."

Babi Yar, ravine of infamy, was under snow. Around it stood new apartment developments, serene in the almost unnaturally pastoral midwinter scene. My guide left the car with me to walk to the newly installed, small, "temporary" monument that had been put up in response to the international pressure generated by Yevtushenko's poem.

I do not recall the exact wording, but I do remember vividly the guide's face when he translated the words "Russian and Ukrainian victims of fascism" who were killed by the Nazis at that spot. I looked at him, his face turned red, and he hastened to add that a permanent monument was going up in several weeks' time. (As of this writing, the best information available indicates that nothing has been done about this.)

I asked the guide to return to the car as I wanted to pray. He seemed surprised—I do not know whether because the idea of an educated young man praying seemed so foreign to him, or because I wanted him to leave while I said some *t'filoth* [prayers—Ed.]. As he returned to the car, I stood knee-deep in the snow overlooking this peaceful ravine, and tried desperately to bring to mind the horrendous scene of twenty-five years before, of Nazi machine-gunners who shot and Ukrainian helpers who pushed living Jews from the ledge to the ravine below, burying the living under the bodies of the dead, then the whole earth-covered ground heaving for days afterward as those still alive underneath the thousands of bodies sought to rise.

I said *t'hilim* [psalms—Ed.] and a *'moley* [prayer for eternal rest for the dead—Ed.] for their souls and my mind was nearly shattered as I strove to fix their Jewish faces in my mind's eye—one-hundred-thousand-times-one—and all I could see were the faces of my dear ones, relatives and friends. For like those faces, I realized, were the faces of those who were butchered here. But for the life of me I could not conjure up the faces of their Nazi and Ukrainian murderers.

I was visibly crying on my return trip to the center of Kiev, and my guide knew better than to engage me in conversation during the first part of this trip from Babi Yar. We headed for the synagogue. This, after another bout with my driver and guide, both of whom protested they "did not know where it was." My threat to leave the car and to find it on my own bore fruit, and somehow they found their way to the synagogue.

En route to the synagogue we passed Bogdan Chmielnicki Square, featuring the imposing equestrian statue of Chmielnicki. While my guide stopped the car to tell me all about this great hero of the Ukraine, my thoughts turned to a different version of the life of Zinovi Bogdan

Chmielnicki from the one being told by my Ukrainian friend. I thought of the vicious, sadistic, mass-murdering forerunner of the Nazis and "modern" Ukrainian killers, who in 1648–49 led his Cossacks in the horrendous massacre of 300,000 Ukrainian Jews.

I looked from the face on the statue to the face of my guide, and then I turned to the driver, and instead of their faces I saw the face of Bogdan. I peered into the faces of the pedestrians hurrying by in the snow, and in each of their faces, men and women alike, I saw the features of Bogdan Chmielnicki—and suddenly the faces of the killers at Babi Yar became illumined in a ghastly light.

EIGHT

Response and Protest

Student Struggle for Soviet Jewry

BY *Ronald I. Rubin*

How long must we plead
For the bound to be freed
From the chains that oppress and degrade?
How long? How long? How long?
How long must we wait
While the hour grows late
And our brothers grow faint and afraid?
Too long! Too long! Too long!

The concern reflected in this topical ballad is the motivating force behind a small but growing movement of youth dedicated to a Herculean task—the rescue of Soviet Jewry from cultural and religious extinction.

Over the past two academic calendar years hardly a month has passed without some student protest about the deprivations of Soviet Jewry.

Rallies, vigils, marches, fasts, and prayer sessions have dotted campuses across the country. New York City in particular has been the scene of major activity. The largest demonstration on behalf of Soviet Jewry was held there April 8, 1966. Called the *Geulah* (Redemption) March, it drew the participation of some 15,000 students.

These demonstrations are not haphazardly arranged. They are timed to coincide with significant Jewish or Russian events so as to most effectively arouse public opinion. Thus, about 1,000 students silently marched on the Soviet Union's Mission to the United Nations on May Day, 1964. A Menorah March and Rally, drawing 1,000 students, was held during the Hanukkah festival in 1965, and on the eve of Passover 1966 a *Leyl Shemurim* vigil was organized in front of the United Nations.

Typical of the protest demonstrations was the Jericho March of April 4, 1965. A group of 3,000 students assembled one block east of the Soviet Mission to the United Nations, located at 135 East 67th Street. The group was arranged in two great columns. Seven rabbis and Jewish leaders bearing Torahs, followed by seven students carrying shofars, advanced between the columns to the accompaniment of a simple chant. Two rabbis thereupon recited psalms. The seven shofars were sounded seven times and then the march around the Soviet Mission began.

As the demonstrators paraded, they sang the Hebrew verse from Isaiah inscribed on the U.N. plaza: "Nation shall not lift up sword against nation, neither shall they learn war any more," symbolizing their hope that the Iron Curtain between the United States and the Soviet Union would disappear and that the barriers of distrust and suspicion would melt away.

Like protest movements involving other political and social causes, the student effort to rescue Soviet Jewry has given birth to songs. "There's a Fire Burning" is among them:

> There's a fire burning brightly in the sky
> And the roar of thunder crashing from on high,
> I see a nation there awakening
> Iron yokes will soon be breaking,
> And a nation long oppressed shall arise—
> A nation long oppressed shall arise . . .

Student Struggle for Soviet Jewry

A trumpet rings through the night,
The dawn appears—we see the light,
We wake the world, we make them see
That our people must be free.
Freedom's train is racing swiftly through the land
And the tide of love is pounding on the sand,
I can hear the whole world crying
For a nation that's been dying,
It will soon hold out its helping hand.

Many of the tactics used by students fighting for Soviet Jewry resemble those used by civil rights groups in the early 1960's. Both the student movement for Soviet Jewry and the student civil rights struggle share one crucial feature: the bypassing of established institutional means for problem-solving in favor of mass demonstrations mobilizing public support.

Wherein lies the uniqueness of the student appeal for Soviet Jewry? The Soviet Jewry protest campaign has captured the imagination of youth to whom the Nazi disaster represents not simply a historical fact but a pressing reminder of the need for Jewish brotherly concern. Fate prevented these students from being alive in the 1930's and early 1940's and they are determined that this horror, in any of its manifestations, not be repeated in their generation. As such, the effort to save Soviet Jewry represents a new focal point for Jewish identification—in addition to traditional religious and Zionist organizations.

The principal student group involved in the protests is the SSSJ—Student Struggle for Soviet Jewry. Their headquarters at 531 West 122nd Street are close by Columbia and the Jewish Theological Seminary. SSSJ has either organized or co-ordinated many of the national youth protests concerning Soviet Jewry in the past two and a half years. Decidedly community-oriented, SSSJ has sponsored numerous adult programs involving major Jewish organizations and provides guidance, films, speakers, tapes, records, and leadership training programs to adult and youth groups alike.

The students' office and activities function on a volunteer basis, with no salaries paid to any of its workers. Most of its donations consist of $1, $5, or $10 contributions. SSSJ has received a few thousand such donations and each supporter is considered a member. The SSSJ symbol, carried on pins and organizational literature, is the shofar. The shofar represents a threefold meaning: a call to the conscience of the world, a call to action, and the hope for the redemption of Soviet Jewry.

Serving on SSSJ's Advisory Council are some younger Yeshiva University faculty members. Among its honorary patrons are Congressman Leonard Farbstein, Senator Jacob K. Javits, and Professor Abraham J. Heschel.

The prime mover and national co-ordinator of SSSJ is Jacob Birnbaum, thirty-seven, a native Englishman. He is the grandson of Dr. Nathan Birnbaum, the nineteenth-century European Zionist leader and originator of the term "Zionism." Birnbaum has been living off his savings since the founding of SSSJ, refusing to accept any salary for his work.

SSSJ's policy of mass demonstrations has four basic aims:

1. To cause the Soviet Government concern about its image due to its treatment of Jews.
2. To convince the White House that the situation of Soviet Jewry is a matter of burning concern to a very large segment of American citizenry.
3. To give much needed encouragement to Soviet Jews.
4. To arouse among Jews a new spirit of concern for the welfare and destiny of the suffering segments of world Jewry.

What have these demonstrations accomplished? Is there a link between student protests and the survival of Soviet Jewry?

There are no ready answers to these questions. Nevertheless, there is ample support for the thesis that the Soviet Union is sensitive to foreign public opinion, especially if such opinion embraces recognized spokesmen for peace. The U.S.S.R. is bent on expanding Communist influence and, accordingly, responds to events preventing such advances. Continuous press criticism of its policy toward Jews, denunciations by Nobel Prize winners such as Dr. Martin Luther King, letters of disenchantment by Lord Bertrand Russell, and pleas of conscience by Christian clergymen all serve to embarrass the Soviet Union. Reports of persecutions of Jews, moreover, strain the Soviet Union's relations with nations facing minority problems themselves. Finally, many Communist parties and publications in the West which otherwise sympathize with the Soviet Union take issue with its efforts to suppress Judaism.

Demonstrations remind opinion makers in the free world of the predicament of Soviet Jewry. They remind the Soviet Union that a vocal and informed public will never rest while it aims at obliterating Judaism. They remind complacent Jews in the West of the doom befalling their brethren—and word of these demonstrations fortifies the courage of this remnant in the Soviet Union. In short, the pickets are the voice of silenced Soviet Jewry.

However, it is a very youthful voice crying out to redeem them. For the initiative in publicizing their plight at the grass-roots level is largely the product of student effort. The adults may pass resolutions at their organizational conferences, they may attend lectures on this distressing subject, even work behind the scenes or publish important literature. But they do not "take to the streets" on behalf of their brethren behind the Iron Curtain. Adults rarely picket with signs or chant the mournful melodies echoing Jewish oppression through the centuries.

What explains the willingness of these young people with the many distractions which beckon them to take up a cause which, in the end, may be nothing more than an exercise in futility and heartbreak? A law student has offered a reply:

What I do for myself I try to see in the light of what I can do for others. In every generation there have always been those who labored to assure Jewish continuity. I think I am part of a tragically small group which is struggling to ensure the survival of the Jewish people in the Soviet Union.

The State Department's Position

DEPARTMENT OF STATE
Washington, D.C. 20520

December 5, 1967

Honorable Clark MacGregor
House of Representatives
Washington, D.C. 20515

Dear Congressman MacGregor:

Secretary Rusk has asked me to reply to your letter of November 22, concerning the plight of Jews in the Soviet Union.

The Department has long deplored the plight of Jews and other minority groups within the Soviet Union. We cannot stress too strongly our disapproval of the pressures that the Soviet Government has brought to bear against these people in an effort to prevent the normal maintenance and development of their religious and cultural life.

The Department has, through statements in the United Nations and in statements by the Secretary and other high officials of the Department, made its own effort to bring Soviet persecution of all religions and the plight of the Soviet Jewish community to the attention of world public opinion. On

276

The State Department's Position

August 4, 1966, Secretary Rusk expressed his continuing concern over the plight of Jews in the Soviet Union. He urged that efforts be continued to direct public attention toward the problem, in the hope that through the pressure of world conscience an amelioration of conditions could evolve. The Secretary emphasized that efforts of Jewish leaders to focus public attention to the plight of Soviet Jewry should not be abandoned.

In recent years the Soviet Government appears to have become increasingly sensitive to the unfavorable publicity it has received in connection with the plight of the Soviet Jews and may have moderated some of its policies accordingly. It at least has taken a few limited steps designed to offset or reduce this unfavorable publicity. Most prominent among these steps was Kosygin's well-publicized statement of December, 1966, on emigration from the U.S.S.R., to the effect that anyone who wanted to leave the U.S.S.R. could do so. The controlled Soviet press has sharply cut down the number of published accounts of so-called "economic crimes and other articles having an anti-Jewish slant." The publication of Yiddish-language books and periodicals has been slightly expanded. The trickle of Jewish emigration has increased slightly. *Matzoh* have been more widely available during Passover in the last three years than they were in previous years.

It is too early to tell whether these steps represent a true reduction of Soviet pressure against the Jewish community, and whether Kosygin's pledge to allow further increases in Jewish emigration will be redeemed. There is evidence to indicate that the Soviet Government may have allowed its Jewish emigration policy to lapse somewhat following the Arab-Israeli conflict last summer.

The Department continues to believe that appeals by private organizations and individuals, especially when joined in by leaders of all religious faiths and made on an international basis, are the most helpful procedure. Such appeals, in our opinion, are more likely to bring about a change in Soviet policies than official representations or censure by foreign governments. In the past, Soviet leaders have invariably rejected as interference in Soviet internal affairs the most serious representations which high-ranking officials of our government have made to them. While official actions by the United States Government can be publicly dismissed by Soviet authorities as "Cold War initiatives," the expressions of concern by large numbers of private individuals are more difficult to ignore. For this reason the Department continues to encourage the efforts of private American citizens and organizations to bring the situation of the Soviet Jews to the attention of world opinion to help bring the weight of this opinion to bear on Soviet authorities.

I am enclosing a background brochure, as of possible interest, which provides more detailed information on the plight of Soviet Jewry and our government's policy. Please be assured that the Department is concerned about the restrictions on Soviet Jewry and will continue to exert its best efforts to help mitigate, by every appropriate means, the persecution of Jews and other religious minorities in the Soviet Union.

Sincerely yours,

William B. Macomber, Jr.
Assistant Secretary for
Congressional Relations

Australian Communists and
Soviet Jewry

BY *Isi Leibler*

In view of Australia's geographical isolation, the marginal role of Jews in the Party and the absence of a numerically strong intellectual element, the Australian Communist Party was never really confronted with the question of Soviet Jewry.

Even in 1956 following Khrushchev's exposure of Stalin, the Jewish "question," which was badly agitating the European and North American parties, barely caused a stir. In 1953, J. D. Blake, then a member of the CP Secretariat, who during the "doctors' plot" had attacked "some of our Jewish comrades" who "tended to act more like Zionists than Communists," publicly apologized to Jewish Communists and regretted having described Zionism as nothing but "bourgeois nationalism." Apart

As a result of the campaign waged against Soviet anti-Semitism by the Jewish community, Australia raised the issue at the United Nations. Thus far, only a handful of nations have used the world body as a forum in protesting Soviet anti-Semitism. It is to be hoped that more will follow suit in the future.

from this vague reference, the Communist press does not suggest that the issue was of great consequence.

Only one pro-Communist group took up the Jewish question—the Melbourne-based Jewish Progressive Center, which catered primarily to Yiddish-speaking Communists and sympathizers. It had established itself as one of the staunchest defenders of Stalin's Jewish policy and in 1953 had gone so far as to organize public campaigns to justify the "Prague Trials" and "doctors' plot."

After considerable internal controversy, the Jewish Progressive Center in September, 1956, belatedly wrote a letter to the "Soviet Society for Cultural Relations with Foreign Countries" criticizing Stalin's treatment of the Jews and soliciting further information regarding the existing state of Jewish culture in the Soviet Union.

The reply was most unsatisfactory. It denied that Stalin had committed injustices to Jews as such, attempted to demonstrate that Soviet Jews had full civic equality, and insisted that the Jews themselves wished to avoid the "humiliation of ghettoes . . . and segregation of Jewish culture." The "national tongue" of the Soviet Jew was "either Russian or the language of the Republic where they live."

Three months later the Jewish Progressive Center replied. They appealed to the Soviet Union to make cultural restitution for the "destructive cloud" that commenced "with the opening of the Beria epoch in the years 1936, 1937."

The argument that Soviet Jewry did not desire Jewish culture was strongly rejected:

A national culture does not disappear overnight, not even in one generation. Precisely because of our own experience, we are convinced that the problems arising from these changes must not be solved mechanically and by administrative measures. . . . To forcibly hasten the end of a people's culture, even a weakling one, is not just, not humane, and not permissible.

In reply to the assertion that Soviet Jews enjoyed civic equality, the Jewish Progressive Center retorted:

That is not all. We Jews in Australia enjoy full civic rights, just as Jews do in many other democratic countries. But we do not make a fuss about it. Jews here, too, are free to occupy positions in all spheres of the national economy and culture and government.

Australian Communists and Soviet Jewry

This outspoken letter was published by Communist Party newspapers in Poland, Israel, Canada, Argentina, and other countries. About May, 1958, *Outlook*, a Sydney-based bimonthly initiated by Communists all of whom subsequently defected or were expelled, included it as a section of a symposium entitled *Documents on the Position of the Jewish People in the U.S.S.R.* The publication also included extracts from the writings of Salsberg, Professor Levy, and other Communists. But it was not taken up by the Australian Communist press. One is tempted to conclude that, after "having done their duty," the Jewish Progressive Center did not press too hard to make the question a major issue within Australian Communist circles. This supposition is strengthened by the fact that, after having signed its name to such a dignified and humane letter, the Jewish Progressive Center then proceeded to harass Jewish newspapers from 1957 to 1964 with a stream of letters and statements clearly contradicting the content and spirit of its March, 1957, protest.

From 1957, for about five years, the Australian Party followed the standard line of overseas Communist parties with regard to the Soviet Jewish question. But, generally speaking, the issue simply did not exist. All that happened was an occasional Novosti Press Agency reprint in *Tribune* or *Guardian* giving the official Soviet viewpoint.

In 1962, the Australian Jewish community initiated a major campaign to focus public attention on the plight of Soviet Jewry. This ultimately brought about the first Australian Communist confrontation with the issue of Soviet Jewry.

Judah Waten, a Jewish Communist writer, emerged as the Communist Party expert and guide on the subject. Waten is no Paul Novick.[1] By the brutal neo-Stalinist methodology he employed, and the obvious relish with which he handled the question, it was clear that his earlier approach to the question of Soviet Jewry had in no way been "influenced" by the facts that had emerged in 1956.

A series of unsigned articles dealing with Soviet Jewry written by Waten began appearing in the pages of *Tribune* and *Guardian*. The whole question was merely a Santamaria, D.L.P., fascist, Liberal stunt:

At a meeting in the office of a well-known lawyer, representatives of *The*

1. Novick, a leading Communist apologist on the issue of Soviet anti-Semitism, is editor of the *Morning Freiheit*, the Yiddish-language Communist daily newspaper published in the United States.—Ed.

Bulletin, a Liberal M.P., a representative of the National Civic Council, and several D.L.P.-influenced members of the Victorian Jewish Board of Deputies mapped out the campaign against the Soviet Union using the most fraudulent anti-Soviet material.

Following the publication of an article outlining the plight of Soviet Jewry in *The Bulletin*, the Soviet Embassy in Canberra also moved into the fray. Parliamentarians were approached and briefed and vast quantities of Novosti Press releases and other handouts denying the existence of anti-Semitism in the U.S.S.R. widely distributed. The U.S.S.R. Press Attaché, Mr. V. Gamazeichshikov, wrote a long vitriolic letter to *The Bulletin* in which undiplomatic language predominated, and claimed: "Frankly speaking, Jews in the U.S.S.R. are enjoying even better conditions compared with other Soviet nationalities."

On October 18, 1962, the Minister for External Affairs announced that the Australian Government would raise the question of Soviet Jewry at the United Nations. This took place two weeks later.

Soviet authorities were apparently concerned by this, because in addition to an intensification of activity on the part of the Soviet Embassy, "Moscow Radio" broadcast a series of English-language programs specially written by Aaron Vergelis, designed to refute the "vicious lies" being spread by "ignorant Australians." In addition, Mr. Samuel Rozin, of Novosti Press Agency, took the unprecedented step of writing a long letter from "Pushkin Square, Moscow," to *The Bulletin*, in which, among other matters, Moscow's Chief Rabbi was "quoted" as having allegedly reprimanded the "ill-informed Australian gentlemen" who "tell untruths about our life."

The Communist Party also felt obliged to counter the impact made by the Australian Government's decision to raise the question at the United Nations. The greatest obstacle was dealing with the documentary evidence of Soviet anti-Semitism that was being presented by Jewish leaders—particularly anti-Semitic extracts from the Soviet press. At first, efforts were made to justify such articles as legitimate anti-religious propaganda. When this line of approach failed, Judah Waten stepped in and solved the problem by questioning the authenticity of the quotations and demanding to see reproductions of original articles.

When these were produced, Waten made the extraordinary assertion that the photostatic reproductions could not "be treated as evidence of anything." Waten also asserted that the blood libel article which had appeared in the *Daghestan Kommunist* was a fake despite the fact that in his letter to *The Bulletin*, Rozin, of the Novosti Press Agency, had conceded that the article was genuine.

Waten's cynicism was reflected when at about the same time he wrote an article for the Communist press in which he violently attacked Emanuel Litvinoff, the respected editor of *Jews in Eastern Europe*, as a Cold War warrior and forger. Waten accused Litvinoff of using documents whose "ultimate source is the United States where there are many experts in the production of Cold War 'technically excellent montage.'" This violent calumny has yet to be retracted by the Australian Communist press.

A little later the Party reproduced Herbert Aptheker's American Communist pamphlet denying the existence of Soviet anti-Semitism. It carried a brief foreword by Harry Stein suggesting that the Australian U.N. intervention "was part of a plot aimed at splitting the Labor Party" and had been engineered by a combination of "Santamaria's National Civic Council, News Weekly, the Packer press, the Liberal Party, and certain reactionary leaders in the Melbourne Jewish community." Stein also claimed that it was "an international disgrace" that a government which "refuses to bar vile anti-Semitic material from the post, [and] whose supporters bar Jews from golf and other clubs" should have the "audacity" to raise such a "fraudulent" issue on a United Nations level.

In March, 1964, the Jewish community again initiated a public campaign relating to Soviet Jewry, this time centered on the Kichko book. Public protest meetings were held and a pamphlet consisting of reproductions of some of the caricatures, together with extracts and commentary on the Kichko book, was widely distributed.

By 1964 Judah Waten was no longer contributing articles defending Soviet anti-Semitism to the Communist press. But, even so, compared to protests from other Western Communist parties prior to the CPSU Ideological Committee's condemnation, the Australian Party was very slow to act. The first to break the ice was Rex Mortimer, editor of the *Guardian*, who made an impromptu statement to the *Australian Jewish*

News on April 3, condemning the book. This was reproduced in the *Guardian*.

Two weeks later the Jewish Progressive Center released the text of a letter it had sent to the Soviet Ambassador. The letter strongly condemned the Kichko book, noted that other anti-Semitic articles had appeared previously in the Soviet press, and concluded from this that the Soviet Government was not taking adequate and prompt measures to prevent anti-Jewish publications from appearing. It urged the Soviet Government to remedy this in the future and take legal action against those responsible for the Kichko book. This letter was important mainly because it appeared to reflect a change of policy from the intransigent and dogmatic approach adopted since 1958 by the Jewish Progressive Center on matters relating to Soviet Jewry. The letter was not reproduced in the Australian Communist press. Instead, at about the same time, rather belatedly, as the Soviet Government had already criticized the book two weeks earlier, the *Tribune* associated itself with other Western Communist condemnations. The opening remarks were rather tortuous—citing the Soviet withdrawal of the book as proof that "contrary to Australia and other capitalist countries, anti-Semitism is against the law in the Soviet Union." The statement then warned:

Occasionally manifestations of anti-Semitism such as Kichko's book . . . have a certain historical logic, but remain a cause for deep concern. Protests help the Soviet leaders in their struggle aganst this evil. . . . Because of centuries of suffering in Christian Europe, the Jewish people attach to their faith an emotional significance transcending purely religious limits. Therefore people scientifically criticizing Judaism have a special responsibility to guard against forms of expression which can rekindle anti-Semitic ideas.

This statement was hardly breathtaking in its scope compared to those of other Communist parties, but for Australian Communists it was an important step in the right direction. Unfortunately it was taken no further, not even when a copy of the anti-Semitic Mayatsky book—condemned by leading overseas Communist parties—was brought to the attention of Communist leaders.

It was also significant that the theoretical journal of the Australian Communist Party saw fit to publish an outdated overseas Communist apologia on the question of Soviet Jewry precisely when the Kichko book was under fire. The *Guardian* issue reporting on the condemnation of the Kichko book also carried a fantastic article by "a committee of Jewish members of the Communist Party of Australia" which included the assertion that "the Soviet Union has never pursued an anti-Semitic policy . . ." It was clear that if Australian Jewish Communists were still going to deny Stalinist anti-Semitism, there would not be policy changes without a struggle.

In June, 1964, the pro-Chinese Communist Party (Marxist-Leninist) published a strong attack on the Soviet Union for practicing anti-Semitism. Coming precisely from those quarters which had previously strongly resisted the de-Stalinization of the Australian Communist Party, it was clearly a cynical tactical move.

However, the break-away Communist Party (ML) did have a general impact on the CPA, because by indulging freely in polemics with them, more "liberal" CPA elements began to come out into the open.

Australia's strategic position in the world Communist Sino-Soviet split probably helped the liberalizers considerably. Their position ultimately became associated in the minds of outside observers with ideas popularized by the leadership of the Italian Communist Party, viz., greater autonomy, replacement of outworn slogans, elimination of Stalinism, and genuine co-operation with progressive non-Communist elements. Their philosophy was said to be expressed in Togliatti's memorandum released by the Italian Communists a month after his death.

Togliatti's statement could well have far-reaching implications for the fate of Soviet Jewry, despite the fact that the Jewish question was not mentioned. However, some of the general principles enunciated were more than pertinent.

For example, Togliatti called for a "repudiation of revolutionary phrasemongering and opportunist practicalism"; he expressed his unwillingness to re-establish "a centralized international organization" which might again interfere with the "autonomy of the parties"; he appealed to Communists:

to show enough political daring to overcome dogmatism in all its forms, to advance and solve new problems in a new way, to adjust the methods of work to the rapidly changing political and social situation . . . We can and must act more boldly, discarding the out-moded formulae no longer conforming to present-day reality.

Togliatti appealed for better relations with religious groups like the Catholics and the discarding of "the old atheistic propaganda" no longer of any use. Commenting on this, Luigi Longo, the Italian Communist leader, stated:

We consider it a mistake to regard religion as a weapon used by the conservative classes. On the contrary, sincere religious sentiment can make a valuable contribution to the struggle.

Togliatti urged Communists to "act as champions of the freedom of intellectual life, freedom of artistic expression and scientific progress." He concluded by stating:

The problem meriting the greatest attention—this concerns both the Soviet Union and the other socialist countries—is, however, that of overcoming the regime of restricting and suppressing democratic and personal freedom which was introduced by Stalin. We do not see an identical picture in all socialist countries in this respect. The general impression is that of slowness and resistance in the matter of returning to the Leninist norm, that insured within the Party and outside it, a broad freedom for expression and debate in culture, art, and also in politics. We find this slowness and this resistance difficult to explain, especially in view of the present situation, when capitalist encirclement no longer exists and economic construction has had tremendous success.

Togliatti apparently struck a chord with some members of the Communist Party of Australia.

Rex Mortimer, editor of the *Guardian* and a member of the Central Committee of the CPA, made front-page headlines throughout the Australian and overseas Jewish press by an outspoken prepared statement on Soviet Jewry which he released late in November, 1964, a week or so after his return from a visit to the Soviet Union.

Mortimer said that he was "very concerned that problems relating to Soviet Jewry were still unresolved." While the matter was in the process of being considered within the framework of the CPA, he expressed his "regret that the Australian Communist Party on the surface was not more active in taking initiatives on this question." He added that "the

Australian Communist Party was unfortunately not always 'as quick off the mark' in such matters as it should be." He emphasized that:

the Communist Party of Australia has previously pointed out that constructive criticism of negative features of Soviet life assist rather than harm the cause of peace and socialism. The question of Soviet Jewry falls into this category!

Mortimer's outspoken comments were correctly interpreted here and abroad as a most significant statement from a leading Communist functionary. The influential *London Jewish Chronicle* used the statement as the basis for its main editorial leader.

Not surprisingly, Mortimer's remarks created a certain amount of friction within the Communist Party. In a manner that smacked of an indirect rebuke to Mortimer, the *Guardian* suggested that his published statements were extracts of wider discussions and might give "a false impression." But it also stressed that what Mortimer had stated was essentially "a restatement of the Communist Party's publicly expressed views."

It is also clear that some Jewish Communists did not welcome Mortimer's statement. They were alleged to have complained that Mortimer's unilateral action caused them to "lose face" in the Jewish community and should not have been made without prior consultations. Presumably to make up for this, Mortimer subsequently co-signed a letter with Bernard Taft, which was sent to the Jewish press, and was to some extent a restatement of the official Soviet position on the Jewish question. The letter was bitterly attacked in the same issue of the *Australian Jewish Herald* which editorially accused Jewish Communists of exerting pressure against "liberal" ideas, and attempting to stifle any possible breakthrough on the Soviet Jewry level.

Mortimer's stand represents a break with the "dogmatic" line hitherto adopted by the CPA. There is little doubt that it will be fiercely resisted as part and parcel of the over-all "liberal" approach in which the question of Soviet Jewry is a symbolic representation. It is therefore no accident that those groups opposing dogmatic bureaucratic trends and neo-Stalinism within the Soviet Union have also been vocal on the question of anti-Semitism. Seen in the perspective of major developments within the international Communist movement—the growth of polycentrism, Italian-style "liberalism," and the Sino-Soviet conflict—Soviet Jewry is basically only a marginal issue. But as a result of this new constellation, the Communist Party of Australia now occupies a particularly important role in the Pacific and Southeast Asian international Communist movement. Hence, if Mortimer's approach were to be adopted, the CPA could have a much greater influence on Soviet leaders with regard to the Jewish question than its numerical size and influence would suggest under normal circumstances.

Philadelphia Supports Soviet Jewry

FROM THE Jewish Community Relations Council
of Greater Philadelphia

In March, 1965, the organized Jewish community of Greater Philadelphia carried out two direct action programs on the issue of Soviet
anti-Semitism:

1. A program of sustained picketing of the Soviet Embassy in
Washington.

2. A public rally to protest Soviet anti-Semitism that was held at
Independence Square, Sunday, March 28, 1965.

A petition campaign had been initiated some months earlier as a concomitant to the picketing program and the Independence Square rally.

The three programs were, of course, related. Each meshed with and
complemented the others.

The Philadelphia protest against Soviet anti-Semitism was a model of community
coordination. It could well be emulated by concerned people in other sections of
the United States and the Western world. Clearly, the Soviet Union takes these
protests seriously. This summary was written by Jules Cohen, the late executive
director of the Jewish Community Relations Council of Greater Philadelphia.

The Picketing Program

Thanks to the Board of Rabbis of Greater Philadelphia, the JCRC program to picket the Soviet Embassy in Washington on a sustained basis, and the public rally to protest Soviet anti-Semitism, received great impetus in December, 1964. In connection with the Hannukah period, the Board of Rabbis called on synagogues to hold special meetings on the issue of Soviet anti-Semitism and to carry out a petition campaign. Concurrently, other JCRC member agencies and JCRC Neighborhood Divisions convened similar conferences on the subject during December, 1964, and January, 1965.

It is impossible to know the exact number of people reached through this intensive program, but it must have been many thousands. One meeting held in the northeast part of Philadelphia, sponsored by a number of synagogues and the JCRC Neighborhood Division, drew some 850 persons; another, in the Old York Road area, sponsored by a combination of synagogues, drew an audience of some 350 on a cold night in December. Notice also must be taken of the impact through organizational mailings of the citywide and neighborhood publicity, often with pictures, which attended all such meetings.

In the JCRC committee, it was decided to carry out the program of sustained picketing of the Soviet Embassy in Washington between February 16 and March 25, 1965. The picketing delegations were to go by chartered bus; after about an hour of picketing, an effort was to be made for delegations representative of the picketing group to meet with officials at the Soviet Embassy, with representatives of the U.S. State Department, and with Pennsylvania senators and congressman from the Greater Philadelphia area.

JCRC staff made arrangements for the buses, took care of the scheduling on particular days, combined groups from organizations which, for various good reasons, could not fill a bus of their own, took care of the arrangements for kosher box lunches so the group could keep together during the tight one-day schedules, and other than institutional banners and signs, provided the signs, with uniform slogans, that were carried by the pickets on all days.

At the Washington end, JCRC staff also took care of the necessary details. Provision for adequate police protection and supervision, parking space, setting up appointments with the Soviet Embassy, the State Department, securing caucus and committee rooms in the Senate and House office buildings for the group conferences with legislators, and the arrangements for members of the Senate and House of Representatives to meet with the delegations each day.

The first bus, with leaders from the JCRC and its member organizations, was scheduled to visit Washington on February 16. Because of the danger of escalating military action in Vietnam in the days before February 16, this first trip was postponed to the second scheduled date, Tuesday, March 2. This decision was reached in consultation with the National Community Relations Advisory Council, the American Jewish Conference on Soviet Jewry, Pennsylvania legislators, and the State Department.

Between March 2 and March 24, groups from some forty Greater Philadelphia organizations visited Washington on eight days. In all, approximately 1,000 individuals participated in this picketing program. On all but one day (when the attempt was not made), delegations met with Soviet Embassy officials. On all days, meetings were held with representatives of the State Department, with senators and congressmen.

A special word of appreciation is due the congressmen from Greater Philadelphia. They not only met with the delegations, but actually joined in the picketing. A similar word of thanks must be noted to congressmen from other parts of the Commonwealth of Pennsylvania, who, upon hearing about the project, took time out to visit with the delegations. For example, Congressman Thomas Morgan, chairman of the House Foreign Affairs Committee. Also, Senators Newburger of Oregon and Inouye of Hawaii.

The Jewish War Veterans from the Washington-Baltimore area helped considerably. They joined the picket lines, produced the flags and uniforms which made the program more impressive, as well as colorful. They added to the public impact.

The trip by the first group of March 2 received wide publicity, both in Philadelphia and Washington, in the newspapers, on radio and television. As expected, subsequent delegations received somewhat less publicity, but there was some, on most days, in both cities. The program was reported not only in the general press but also in neighborhood weeklies interested in the trips of particular delegations. This served to extend the impact of the program.

While most of the participants were Jews, at various times many non-Jewish, white and Negro organizations and leaders participated in the picketing program.

Teen-agers and youth groups were very much interested in the picketing program. Since they could not participate in March because they were at school, the Conservative and Reform, as well as the B'nai B'rith, youth picketed the Soviet Embassy in Washington on April 13 and 15, during the school spring vacation. Again, the JCRC took care of the arrangements. Conferences with the legislators could not be held because Congress was in recess for the Easter holiday.

The Conference in the Soviet Embassy—March 2, 1965

Arrangements had been made in advance for a meeting with officials from the Soviet Embassy at 12:30 P.M. Promptly at that time, two members of the Washington police department escorted the delegation to the doorway of the embassy. Rabbi Theodore H. Gordon, JCRC vice-president and rabbi of Main Line Reform Temple, Beth Elohim, was spokesman for the delegation. The other members were:

Rabbi Martin Berkowitz, president, Board of Rabbis of Greater Philadelphia
Jules Cohen, JCRC executive director
James Jones, chairman, Human Rights Commission, Philadelphia Council AFL-CIO
Stanton W. Kratzok, chairman, JCRC Committee on the Local Implications of Anti-Semitism Overseas
The Reverend Henry H. Nichols, immediate past president, Greater Philadelphia Council of Churches
Milton J. Shapp, president, Delaware Valley Council of the American Jewish Congress

Monroe R. Sheinberg, national director, Jewish War Veterans of the United States

The delegation was received most courteously. It was met and greeted by Mr. Golubnichi, secretary to Ambassador Dobrynin, with whom the appointment had been made. The delegation was taken to a sitting room on the second floor of the embassy where we were introduced to and met with Anatoli G. Myshkov, First Secretary of the embassy, and a Mr. Bogachev. Mr. Golubnichi did not stay for the conference.

After introductions, Rabbi Gordon opened the conference with a brief word of thanks for the appointment and a statement of our deep concern about the plight of Soviet Jewry. The rabbi had barely finished his opening statement when Mr. Myshkov responded with a lengthy statement of some fifteen or more minutes. Following is a summary of the position taken by Mr. Myshkov in his opening statement and throughout the conference:

He denied flatly there is any discrimination or oppression of any nationality or religious group in the Soviet Union. The U.S.S.R. constitution is not a piece of paper but a meaningful document. It guarantees religious freedom. This does not mean religion may not be criticized, but it does mean there can be no interference with freedom of religion. We, meaning not only the Philadelphia delegation, but American Jewry as a whole, are falling for propaganda. Instead, we should look to the statements by rabbis and other Jewish leaders in the Soviet Union. Mr. Myshkov read at some length and leaned heavily upon a press release quoting statements from three or four rabbis in the Soviet Union to the effect that the Jewish community in Russia is not suffering any disabilities. He also displayed and read from the magazine *Soviet Life*, recent issues of which carry large spreads about the Jewish community, rabbis, and leading Jews and Jewish families in the Soviet Union. He also read statistics on the number of Jews in the Soviet Union who have prominent positions in the arts, professions, business, etc., far beyond the proportion of Jews in the U.S.S.R., according to Mr. Myshkov.

Although the picketing took place more than a block from the Soviet Embassy, the Secretary knew almost to a man the number of pickets; he quoted some of the slogans, and seemed particularly annoyed at the forthcoming protest rally at Independence Square in Philadelphia. He contended the picketing is "offensive" and an "insult." He recalled this was the third meeting with delegations from Philadelphia (two were held when Philadelphia congregations and a youth group picketed in October, 1964) and he couldn't understand why we were not persuaded by the statements of Jewish leaders in Russia as against listening to the propagandists, as he put it.

Every member of the JCRC delegation participated in the discussion, raised specific questions about particular forms of discrimination, and drew the distinction between provisions of a government constitution and actual practices.

Responding to a question on the issue of the baking of *matzoth*, the Secretary again read from the release on the statement by the rabbis to the effect that for a time in 1964 there was a shortage of *matzoth* because of the drought and lack of wheat, but that this situation was corrected and that there were sufficient *matzoth* for the 1964 Passover holiday. He also reminded the group that *matzoth* would be available this year in a number of cities as reported in *The New York Times*. The delegation reacted by reminding Mr. Myshkov that only a few cities have been named and there are Jews in many other parts of the U.S.S.R. for whom provision should be made. Also, the reports indicate *matzoth* will be available only to members of synagogues. The point was made that the eating of *matzoth* during Passover is a tradition that has been observed for thousands of years by all Jews, including those who may not be members of synagogues.

With regard to the paucity of synagogues, the Secretary replied there are ninety-seven synagogues in the U.S.S.R., no more, no less. The Jews can have as many synagogues as they wish, but obviously Jews, especially in the younger generation, do not want more synagogues. To this the delegation responded by recalling the overcrowding of synagogues on High Holy Days with overflow crowds; the large turnout on *Simhath Torah* and the large numbers of Jews, including young people, who turn out in such large numbers for performances by Israeli groups and American singers who are Jews.

On the matter of *yeshivas*, Mr. Myshkov said, apparently young Jews do not wish to train for the rabbinate. He cited the case of one rabbi who has seven sons who are engineers, lawyers, and in other professions, with not one who wished to train for the rabbinate.

He denied Jews cannot emigrate from the U.S.S.R. He cited the figure of 9,000 as the number of those who emigrated in 1964. He did not say from where or under what circumstances. The delegation took exception, noting the pressure that can be exerted by officials to keep people from applying for visas or discouraging them from emigrating after applications are filed.

He was asked why the rabbinate in the U.S.S.R. is not permitted to have associations similar to the national rabbinic organizations in America or local Boards of Rabbis. He replied there was no need for the Russian rabbis to follow the same practices as those in the U.S.A. He was pressed as to whether the rabbis in the U.S.S.R. could have such associations if they wished. He reacted by saying he saw no reason why they couldn't.

When asked why rabbis are not permitted to leave the country to participate in international rabbinic meetings, as ministers and priests are permitted to do, he replied he did not know anything about this and promised to look into it.

Regarding the book *Judaism without Embellishment,* his reply was that the Soviet Government promptly condemned the book.[1] When asked why the government did not also condemn the author, he suggested it wasn't necessary; that condemnation of the book surely could not be construed as a commendation of the author.

He denied the majority of those convicted and executed because of economic crimes are Jews. He contended the American press singles out the Jewish names as part of its anti-Soviet policy and campaign.

The delegation inquired as to why the Communist parties of Italy, France, Belgium, and other countries and friends of the U.S.S.R. like Lord Bertrand Russell have publicly protested anti-Semitism in the U.S.S.R. In reply he referred to the answers to Lord Russell. He did not mention the magazine, but obviously he was referring to the exchange of correspondence printed in *Commentary.*

On the point Mr. Myshkov had made about the meaningfulness of the Soviet constitution, members of the delegation, included Reverend Nichols and Mr. Jones, both leaders in the Negro community, recalled the struggle in our own country to achieve full civil rights for Negroes

1. In the wake of the Six-Day War, Trofim Kichko, author of this book, re-emerged as a commentator on Jewish and Zionist evils. In 1968 he received a high award for his scholarly contributions in this area.—Ed.

despite provisions for equality in the U.S. constitution and a civil war. The point was stressed that while much remains to be done, it is clear that the U.S. Government follows a policy of achieving equality for all Americans, and it would be well if the U.S.S.R. would make clear to the world that it follows a similar policy.

A number of times Mr. Myshkov repeated the point that we (meaning the entire Jewish community everywhere) have started a wheel going downhill which apparently cannot and will not be stopped until it crashes at the bottom to the serious detriment of the relationship between Jews in the Soviet Union and Jews elsewhere and to a similar deterioration of relationships between the United States and the U.S.S.R.

At one point, the Secretary suggested that this campaign is being carried on by the Jewish organizations because they need programming. It was clear to this reporter he was referring to the statement alleged to have been made by Rabbi Max Nussbaum as reported in *The New York Times* some months ago.

When asked why the Soviet Government did not convey its facts to the world, if indeed they are true, the Secretary contended the American newspapers do not print the truth. He asked rhetorically if any American newspaper had printed the release from which he had read. He was critical particularly of the *New York Herald Tribune*, which he mentioned a number of times. He was told by members of the delegation that if the facts in Russia are as he stated them, the Soviet Government has ample know-how and channels for getting its story across.

The delegation made it clear it was not persuaded by the rosy picture Mr. Myshkov had painted. They referred to and left with him a copy of the study *Realities of Soviet Anti-Semitism*, recently published by the University of Pennsylvania Foreign Policy Research Institute. (It was subsequently returned as having been left "accidentally.")

The Secretary was also told that the picketing program by Greater Philadelphia and the March 28 Independence Square rally are but one part of a national program of the American Jewish Conference on Soviet Jewry. A number of the organizations, such as the National Community Relations Advisory Council, affiliated in the AJCSJ, were named.

The Secretary urged upon the delegation (which did take) quantities of the press release and issues of the slick magazine *Soviet Life*. Later they were distributed to those in the buses on the return trip. It is to be noted that the current April, 1965, issue has as its cover page the Passover table displaying prominently the plate with *matzoth* on it.

He offered to come to Philadelphia to speak to any group convened by the JCRC and to answer all questions.

Both sides in this confrontation stood firm. The discussion became heated at various times, but there was no acrimony. Courtesy, with coolness, was the keynote on both sides. The conference ended with the customary amenities.

The Secretary refused to accept a petition which the delegation tried to leave with him.

The March 28 Independence Square Rally To Protest Soviet Anti-Semitism

In the JCRC, it was decided the public rally to protest Soviet anti-Semitism should not be a project sponsored by or aimed at the Jewish community only. Instead, it was agreed the project should be sponsored by an intersectarian and biracial committee, geared to enlist the support of the entire Greater Philadelphia community. Subsequent events proved the wisdom of this decision.

It was also decided the public protest meeting should be in the form of an outdoor rally at Independence Square on a date just prior to the Passover holiday, 1965. The date selected was Sunday afternoon, March 28.

The Independence Square rally was sponsored by the Greater Philadelphia Committee to Protest Soviet Anti-Semitism, comprised of approximately 100 leading state and city public officials, religious and civil rights leaders, and heads of business, labor, and civic organizations. Included in the appendix to this report is the letterhead of the Greater Philadelphia Committee, which reflects the prestige and representative nature of the committee. Its honorary chairmen are the governor of the commonwealth, the mayor of the city of Philadelphia, and the two Pennsylvania senators. Among the chairmen are the top leaders of all segments of the Greater Philadelphia community.

The religious advisory group comprises the heads of the Greater Philadelphia religious community: Rabbi Martin Berkowitz, president of the Board of Rabbis of Greater Philadelphia; His Excellency, John J. Krol, Archbishop of the Roman Catholic Archdiocese; Bishop Robert L. DeWitt, head of the Episcopal Diocese of Pennsylvania; the Reverend Herbert Gearhart, president of the Greater Philadelphia Council of Churches; and the heads of the principal Protestant denominations.

In January, the *Philadelphia Inquirer* reported a study of Soviet anti-Semitism made by the Foreign Policy Research Bureau of the University of Pennsylvania, which found that anti-Semitism is practiced by the U.S.S.R. The *Inquirer* kindly permitted the JCRC to reprint this story. The reprints were circulated widely. They proved to be particularly effective with church groups and in other non-Jewish circles.

The JCRC prepared a number of excerpts from the excellent materials on the subject made available by the national Jewish agencies. These were mailed to JCRC member organizations, and to all synagogues for reprinting periodically in organizational publications as a series.

Public attention was drawn to the rally by a continuing flow of stories to the general press, neighborhood, Negro, and sectarian weeklies. Releases focused upon developments appropriate at the time—the creation of the committee, its religious advisors, the rally program, participants, etc. As in the case of the picketing program, it is physically impossible to include in this summary report, copies of all the newspaper, radio, and television reports. Suffice it to say the coverage was tremendous.

The rally was publicized on every Greater Philadelphia radio station with programming ranging from a four- or five-minute taped report about the picketing program or the rally to a full two hours on a late-evening and early-morning interview show which has a large Negro listening audience. On the most popular late-evening interview program, a full three quarters of an hour was spent by a representative of the Episcopal Diocese of Pennsylvania and the JCRC in a discussion of the rally, why it was being held, the plight of Soviet Jewry, and the results expected to be achieved by the rally.

The mayor of Philadelphia proclaimed Sunday, March 28, as a day to protest Soviet anti-Semitism. He presented the proclamation to a group of religious leaders representative of the Greater Philadelphia Committee at a ceremony on the Friday before the rally. The proclamation and the ceremony also received publicity.

Philadelphia Supports Soviet Jewry

The Pennsylvania State Senate and the House of Representatives each adopted a strong resolution condemning Soviet anti-Semitism, in the course of which reference was made to the March 28 Independence Square rally.

The Greater Philadelphia Committee held one meeting, which was addressed by Moshe Decter, executive director of Minorities Resarch, and by the Honorable Paul D'Ortona, president of the Philadelphia City Council and a committee chairman. This meeting was attended by some thirty to thirty-five key members of the Greater Philadelphia Committee. The photos of various religious and racial groupings of those in attendance were carried in the respective sectarian and Negro weeklies.

The Independence Square Rally Program

Fortunately, Sunday, March 28, turned out to be a warm and sunny day. The police department and the mass media reported an attendance of some 5,000. After the rally, JCRC staff counted the signatures that were secured to the petitions that had been circulated and adopted as the resolution of the meeting. Fifty-six hundred signatures were counted.[2]

The statements by the lieutenant-governor and the mayor of the city of Philadelphia were most appropriate and very well received by the audience. The mayor, originally scheduled to leave after making his welcoming remarks, stayed for the entire time, saying it was too impressive an occasion for him to leave.

The spokesmen for the Board of Rabbis of Greater Philadelphia, the Greater Philadelphia Council of Churches, and the Roman Catholic Archdiocese made similar deep impressions. The song by a group of twenty cantors from the Philadelphia Board of Cantors added a touching note to the ceremony.

The relevance of the dramatic events that had taken place in Selma, Alabama, in the days before the rally was made clear in the huge twenty-four-foot banner that was strung across the platform. The slogan

2. The principal speaker was the Honorable Philip M. Klutznick, a member of the United States Mission to the United Nations, and former president of B'nai B'rith.—Ed.

read: "Selma or Moscow: Human Liberty is Indivisible. End Soviet Anti-Semitism." Also, during the rally, there was a standing memorial to the martyrs who have died in the civil rights struggle, from Medgar Evers to Goodman, Schwerner, Chaney, James Jackson, Reverend Reeb, and Viola Liuzzo.

Some unusual human interest notes and important peripheral activities should be included in this summary. For example, the golden agers at the YMHA made many of the signs that were carried at the rally and the 200 badges that were worn by the teen-agers who circulated the petitions for signature by those in attendance.

Both at Temple University and at the University of Pennsylvania, advance rallies were held as a build-up for the Independence Square meeting. The United Synagogue Youth, which held a weekend conference in Atlantic City on March 27 and 28, came en masse to the rally, and, in co-operation with the B'nai B'rith Youth, Reform Youth, and other Jewish youth organizations such as Habonim, acted as ushers and secured signatures to the petitions. At least eight synagogues came in chartered buses, each holding some fifty persons. Entirely unsolicited, a Catholic group in southern New Jersey came to the rally in four buses for a total of some 200 participants. With approval, the group distributed and secured signatures to a card urging support for the Ribicoff resolution. The students at the Temple School of Pharmacy, as well as synagogue and Jewish youth groups, also made signs for the rally and in other ways helped to promote attendance.

The Petition Campaign

Copies of the petition were widely circulated and signatures secured as part of all the activities that were carried on in connection with the picketing program and the Independence Square rally.

At the moment, the JCRC has a total of some 16,800 signatures. Signed petitions continue to come in daily.

From the very beginning, it was planned that these petitions will be delivered to the Soviet Embassy, either in Washington or New York, and possibly to the U.S. State Department and the U.N. This announcement was enthusiastically received at the Independence Square rally. The delegation that will carry out this part of the program also will be interreligious and biracial.

Over-All Conclusions

This threefold program of picketing, the Independence Square rally, and the petition campaign required months of back-breaking work on the part of the JCRC and its member organizations. It was worth it because:

1. This was a saturation program as regards education in the Jewish and the general communities on an important Jewish community relations issue.

2. There can be no question but that these programs have made a great impact on the Soviets, the State Department, the legislators from Pennsylvania, and the total Greater Philadelphia community.

3. On the basis of letters received by the JCRC and innumerable personal and telephone conversations, it is quite clear that these programs have served to boost the morale of the Jewish community. Everyone who participated in the picketing program, attended the rally, or in other ways helped to bring about its successful fruition reports a sense of deep satisfaction, a feeling of having contributed significantly to the welfare of the Jewish people and the cause of human dignity.

4. The respect and esteem for the Jewish community in non-Jewish circles has been enhanced as a result of these programs. They served to increase the knowledge in the general community of the abiding commitment of the Jewish people to the principles of freedom and equality, not only for Jews in Greater Philadelphia, but for our fellow Jews and all people, everywhere.

Appendix

Eighteen Points:
The Rights of Soviet Jewry

American Jewish Conference on Soviet Jewry

The American Jewish Conference on Soviet Jewry is the co-ordinating body of twenty-five national American Jewish organizations. In 1964 the Conference issued an eighteen-point appeal to the Soviet Government protesting the denial to Soviet Jews of basic means for spiritual survival.

The American Jewish Conference on Soviet Jewry protests the denial to Soviet Jews of the basic institutions and facilities granted to other religions and nationality groups within the Soviet Union. Considerations of humanity and justice require the Soviet Government:

1. To declare its policy of eradicating anti-Semitism by a vigorous educational effort conducted by Government and Party.

2. To permit the free functioning of synagogues and private prayer meetings.

3. To remove hindrances to the observance of sacred rites such as religious burial and circumcision.

4. To make possible the production and distribution of phylacteries, prayer shawls, *mezuzoth*, religious calendars, and other religious articles.

5. To restore all rights and facilities for the production and distribution of *matzoth* and kosher food.

6. To make available facilities to publish Hebrew Bibles, prayer books, and other religious texts in the necessary quantities.

7. To permit the organization of a nationwide federation of synagogues.

8. To sanction the association of such a federation with organizations of co-religionists abroad.

9. To permit Jews to make religious pilgrimages to the holy places in Israel.

10. To make it possible to allow all qualified applicants to attend the Moscow Yeshiva, to provide facilities for the establishment of additional *yeshivas* as needed, and to enable rabbinical students to study at seminaries abroad.

11. To provide schools and other facilities for the study of Yiddish and Hebrew, and of Jewish history, literature, and culture.

12. To permit Jewish writers, artists, and other intellectuals to create their own institutions for the encouragement of Jewish cultural and artistic life.

13. To re-establish a Yiddish publishing house and to publish books in Yiddish by classical and contemporary Jewish writers.

14. To re-establish Yiddish state theaters in major centers of Jewish population and to publish Yiddish-language newspapers with national circulation.

15. To eliminate discrimination against Jews in all areas of Soviet public life.

16. To end all propaganda campaigns which use anti-Semitic stereotypes, implied or overt.

17. To halt the discriminatory application of maximum penalties, including the death sentence, against Jews for alleged economic crimes.

18. To make it possible on humanitarian grounds for Soviet Jews who are members of families separated as a result of the Nazi Holocaust to be reunited with their relatives abroad.

We appeal for a redress of these and other wrongs and sufferings, for the elimination of discrimination, and for the full restoration of Jewish rights in the U.S.S.R.

Jewish Institutions in the Soviet Union

While the following list is not complete, it includes the main surviving Jewish institutions in the Soviet Union as of 1968.

Azerbaijan Republic

Baku—Ashkenazic (East European) and Bukharan Synagogue, 171 Pervomayskaya Street, is used by Yiddish-speaking Jews who settled here in the nineteenth century, and by the Oriental Jews from Bukhara.

Byelorussian Republic

Minsk—Synagogue at 109 Tsnianskaya. There is a joint grave with tombstone bearing inscription in Yiddish. Half of Minsk's prewar Jewish population of 230,000 was murdered by the Nazis. Jewish population: 40,000.

Georgian Republic

Tbilisi (Tiflis)—Synagogue, at 45 Leselidze Street, is the principal gathering place of the Georgian Jews. Attached to the synagogue are a ritual bath and a study hall. Most of the worshipers are descendants of the historic community of Georgian Jews, founded here 2,500 years ago. They still speak Sephardic Hebrew, as well as Georgian, but do not understand the Yiddish of the East European Jews. Intourist guides include this synagogue in their tour of the city.

Kutaisi—Synagogue at 8 Shaumyan Street. Jewish population: 15,000.

Kazakh Republic

Alma-Ata—Synagogue, at 20 Tashkentskaya Street, is the only one in the capital of the Kazakhstan Republic. There are some 6,000 Jews in this city. There is another good-sized Jewish community in Karaganda, whose synagogue was reported closed in 1961.

Latvian Republic

Riga—Synagogue at 8 Peytavas Street, near the Municipal Opera House. There is also a Jewish Home for the Aged here. At nearby Kaiserwald there is a monument to Jews murdered by the Nazis, erected by Jewish youth. A ceremony in commemoration to the dead is held there every year. Jewish population: 10,000.

Appendix

Lithuanian Republic

Vilnius (Vilna)—Synagogue at 39 Kom'yaunimo Street. An amateur Yiddish theatrical group gives performances here. Jewish population: 17,000.

Moldavian Republic

Kishinev—Synagogue at 8 Yakimovsky Lane. This city was the scene of a notorious czarist pogrom in 1903 which first called world attention to the plight of the Jews in Russia.

Russian Republic

Birobidzhan—The Jewish Autonomous Region, in name only, has no Yiddish schools or theaters. Yiddish culture is represented by a triweekly paper, the *Birobidzhaner Shtern*, and a few street signs in Yiddish. The synagogue, at 9 Chapayev Street, is a wooden shack. Less than 10 per cent of Birobidzhan's population today is Jewish.

Leningrad—Choral Synagogue, at 2 Lermontovski Prospekt, is one of the largest in Europe. In addition to this synagogue, Leningrad has private prayer houses. There is a Jewish cemetery about five miles beyond the city's limits, which contains a monument to the 7,000 Jews who were killed during the siege of Leningrad.

Moscow—Central Synagogue at Arkhipova Street. Services are held daily, morning and evenings. There are two other smaller synagogues in the suburbs. One is at 70 Lermontov Street in the Tsherkizovo section, and the other is at 2/5 Vyacheslavsky Lane in the Marinaroscha neighborhood.

Tajik Republic

Dushambe (Stalinbad)—Synagogue, at 26 Dekhanskaya Street, is a complex of four synagogues built around an open courtyard. The largest is the principal synagogue of the Bukharan Jews, who originally came to this region from Persia in the sixth century, B.C.E. They still speak a Persian dialect. Jewish population: 15,000.

Ukrainian Republic

Berdichev—Synagogue at 8 Sverdlov Street. Jewish population: 7,000.

Chernovtsy (Cernauti: Czernowitz)—Synagogue at 53 L. Kobylitsky.

Kharkov—The synagogue here has been closed since 1947, but there is a small prayer house still in use. Karl Liebknecht Collective Farm outside this city is one of the remaining Jewish agricultural groups established in the 1920's. Martyrs' Memorial over the mass grave of 100,000 Jews murdered by the Nazis stands on the edge of the city.

Kiev—Synagogue at 29 Shchekavitskaya Street in the suburb of Podol. Babi Yar, about five miles outside the city, is the place where in 1941 the Nazi executioners shot 33,771 Jewish men, women, and children, and dumped their bodies in the abandoned lime-and-sand pit. Recently, a marker has been placed on the site, with an inscription promising the erection of a monument. There is nothing on the marker to indicate that the victims were Jews. Lubyanovka Jewish Cemetery is about a mile and a half from Babi Yar. Sholem Aleichem House, 5 Krasnoarmieskaya Street, where the Yiddish author lived for some years, is marked by a plaque. Jewish population: 150,000.

Odessa—Synagogue, at 5 Lesnaya Street, in the suburb of Peresyp, is in a community that still numbers 200,000. The Brodskaya Synagogue, another large house of worship, is closed. Mendele Mocher Seforim's grave is in the main Jewish cemetery.

Uzbek Republic

Bukhara—Synagogue, at 20 Tsentralnaya Street, is one block from the leading hotel on Lenin Street.

Samarkand—Synagogue, at 30 Dinavsky Lane, is part of the oldest Bukharan Jewish community founded by settlers from Persia before the Christian Era.

Tashkent—Bukharan Synagogue, 24 Sagban Street, is the largest Bukharan synagogue in Uzbekistan.

Suggested Reading

In addition to the material included in this volume, the following references are cited for further investigation into Soviet anti-Semitism:

Cyrus Adler, ed., *The Voice of America on Kishineff*, Philadelphia, The Jewish Publication Society of America, 1904. A collection of speeches, sermons, resolutions, and editorial articles relating to America's mass outpouring of indignation at the Russian Government's complicity in the atrocities committed against the Jews of Kishinev.

———, and Aaron M. Margalith, *With Firmness in the Right*, New York, The American Jewish Committee, 1946. Records precedents of American diplomatic intercession on behalf of persecuted Jews in Russia and other parts of the world from 1840 to 1945.

Patricia Blake, "The Old and the New in Soviet Literature," *Proceedings of the Academy of Political Science*, April, 1965. A short, lucid essay on the Soviet Government's failure to silence the liberal writers and intellectuals.

Bulletin on Soviet Jewish Affairs, Institute of Jewish Affairs, 13-16 Jacob's Well Mews, George Street, London W.1. A scholarly periodical sponsored by the World Jewish Congress.

John C. Clews, *Communist Propaganda Techniques*, New York, Frederick A. Praeger, 1964. An in-depth assessment of the Communist foreign propaganda system; provides helpful theoretical background in understanding Soviet denials of anti-Semitism.

Lucy S. Dawidowicz, ed., *The Golden Tradition: Jewish Life and Thought in Eastern Europe*, New York, Holt, Rinehart, and Winston, 1967. An anthology of the social, intellectual, religious, and Zionist currents in the *shtetl*.

Moshe Decter, ed., *Israel and the Jews in the Soviet Mirror*, New York, Conference on the Status of Soviet Jews, 1967. A booklet of political cartoons from the Soviet press viciously portraying Israel as the successor of Nazi Germany, and a bellicose, bloodthirsty, money-worshiping imperialist power. Published in the wake of the 1967 Six-Day War.

———, "The Lvov Case: Self-Portrait of Soviet Anti-Semitism," *Midstream*, June, 1963. Documents through Soviet press excerpts the diabolical steps in a campaign to shut a synagogue.

———, "Silence and Yearning: A Report and Analysis of the Status of Soviet Jewry," *Congress Bi-Weekly*, Special Issue, December 5, 1966. A thorough compilation of material on the subject, including a comparison study on the more favorable treatment of German and Armenian nationalities in the U.S.S.R.

Simon M. Dubnow, *History of the Jews in Russia and Poland: From the Earliest Times until the Present Day*, trans. from Russian by I. Friedlander, Philadelphia, The Jewish Publication Society of America, 1916–20, 3 vols. The definitive historical work.

Harold E. Fey, "Cultural Genocide in Russia," *The Christian Century*, July 21, 1965. A leading Christian intellectual who visited the U.S.S.R. stresses the unequal treatment of Jews, and the value of protests in aiding their lot.

William C. Fletcher and Anthony J. Stover, *Religion and the Search for New Ideals in the USSR*, New York, Frederick A. Praeger, 1967. A compilation of papers on various aspects of religion in the Soviet Union, including an article, "Jews and Judaism in the USSR," by Hans Lamm.

Maurice Friedberg, "Defending Soviet Jews: Placards or Memoranda?" *Midstream*, September, 1965. A justification of the effectiveness of protest action on behalf of Soviet Jews by a Sovietologist; attacks advocacy of "quiet diplomacy."

Zvi Gitelman, "Nationalities and Nationalism in the USSR: The Jews," *Problems of Communism*, Special Issue, September–October, 1967. An overview of the Jewish position in the context of Soviet ideology and politics.

B. Z. Goldberg, *The Jewish Problem in the Soviet Union*, New York, Crown, 1961. Account of journeys through the U.S.S.R. in 1934, 1946, and 1959. The author's wide personal acquaintance with Soviet Jews enhances the book's arguments.

Maurice Hindus, "Jew—Russia's Stepson," in *House without a Roof*, Garden City, New York, Doubleday and Co., 1961. A first-hand report of the plight of Soviet Jews; shows the cleavage between Jew and non-Jew in daily life.

Jews in Eastern Europe, ed., Emanuel Litvinoff, 31 Percy Street, London, W.1., European Jewish Publications Ltd. This periodical is the most exhaustive and continuous recording of information relating to Jews in the U.S.S.R. An indispensable journal for anyone concerned with this issue. (Subscription cost is $5 annually.)

William Korey, ed., "The Status of Jews in the Soviet Union," *Survey*, Special Report, B'nai B'rith International Council, August, 1964. A fully documented analysis, replete with statistics, on Soviet anti-Semitism.

———, "What Monument to Babi Yar?" *Saturday Review*, February 3, 1968. Poignantly depicts the massive tragedy of Babi Yar, the world's indifference to

Suggested Reading

the recent trial of Nazi killers, and the cynical refusal of Soviet authorities to erect a memorial acknowledging the Jewish aspect of the catastrophe.

Anatoly Kuznetsov, *Babi Yar*, New York, Dial Press, 1967. A chilling documentary novel on the extermination of Kiev's Jews. Until the publication of this work, Soviet authorities suppressed the fact that Jews constituted the vast majority of Babi Yar's victims.

Mendel Mann, *At the Gates of Moscow*, New York, St. Martin's Press, 1964. A World War II novel of a Red Army officer despised and vilified by the military because of his Jewishness.

Israel Miller, "Don't Forget Us—The Three Million Jews of Russia," *Ave Maria— National Catholic Weekly*, December 9, 1967. A thorough summary of the dis- abilities suffered by Jews in the U.S.S.R. Urges protests by the U.S. Government and "humanitarians in the free world."

The New Leader, September 14, 1959. A special issue devoted to Soviet Jewry.

Harrison E. Salisbury, "The Rise of Anti-Semitism," in *A New Russia?* New York, Harper and Row, 1962. A former correspondent of *The New York Times* in Moscow relates his observations on the mistreatment of Jews.

Joseph B. Schechtman, *Star in Eclipse——Russian Jewry Revisited*, New York, Thomas Yoseloff, 1961. A stimulating volume of the problems of Soviet Jews as seen by a knowledgeable historian after his 1959 visit.

Solomon M. Schwartz, *The Jews in the Soviet Union*, Syracuse, Syracuse University Press, 1951. A thoroughly documented scholarly analysis ranging from the 1917 Revolution to the years preceding Stalin's death.

"Soviet Anti-Semitism: An Exchange Between Bertrand Russell and Aron Vergelis," *Commentary*, January, 1965. A penetrating indictment of the Soviet Union's Jewish policy by the famous British socialist. Vergelis is editor of *Sovyetish Heymland*, the only extant Yiddish periodical in the U.S.S.R.

Judd L. Teller, *The Kremlin, the Jews and the Middle East*, New York, Thomas Yoseloff, 1957. Especially worthwhile is the chapter "Voice from Purgatory," an anguished report on the fate of Jews in the Stalin era.

——, *Ideology and History of Soviet Jewish Policy*, New York, Farband-Labor Zionist Order, April, 1964. Cogently relates the philosophy of Soviet communism to the Jewish predicament.

U.S. Congress, House Committee on Foreign Affairs, Subcommittee on Europe, *Hearings: Antireligious Activities in the Soviet Union and in Eastern Europe*, 89th Cong., 1st sess., 1965. Primarily devoted to anti-Semitism in the Soviet Union; contains testimony of congressmen and Jewish leaders.

Grigory Vinokour, *The Commissar*, New York, Twayne, 1965. A fictional account of real events in Stalinist Russia by a Soviet author in the United States. Partly autobiographical, the book features as its hero a Jewish commissar who is also a writer.

David W. Weiss, "The Plight of the Jews in the Soviet Union," *Dissent*, July– August, 1966. A visiting American scientist movingly portrays his encounters with Soviet Jews.

Appendix

Elie Wiesel, "Will Soviet Jewry Survive?" *Commentary*, February, 1967. A follow-up article on the author's earlier visit to the Soviet Union (see above, Part Five, "The Rejoicing of the Law," for Wiesel's first impression). The mood here is stubbornly optimistic.

Roy Wilkins, "A Negro Leader Pleads for Soviet Jewry," *National Jewish Monthly*, June, 1966. The executive of the National Association for the Advancement of Colored People condemns the U.S.S.R. for its outrageous Jewish policy.

Program Manuals

For Soviet Jewry—Guideline for Community Action, National Community Relations Advisory Council, 55 West 42nd Street, New York, N.Y. 10036. Contains Soviet Jewry fact sheets and programming aids.

Handbook for Community Action on Soviet Anti-Semitism, Council of Concern for Soviet Jewry, 14308 Triskett Road, Cleveland, Ohio 44111. A comprehensive collection of material on Soviet Jews.

Jews in Russia—Common Sense Today, The Center for Russian Jewry, 350 Fifth Avenue, New York, N.Y. 10001. A handsomely published booklet setting forth a program of suggested protest actions.

The Jews of Russia, Parts I and II, Hadassah Education Department, 65 East 52nd Street, New York, N.Y. 10022. Describes the cultural heritage of Soviet Jews.

Soviet Anti-Semitism, B'nai B'rith, Current Issues Series, 1640 Rhode Island Ave., Washington, D.C. 20036. Outlines an informative program on the situation of Jews in the U.S.S.R.

Student Struggle for Soviet Jewry Handbook, SSSJ, 531 West 122nd Street, New York, N.Y. 10027. Includes programming suggestions, reprints of articles, Soviet Jewish songs and poetry.

A NOTE ON THE CONTRIBUTORS

Morris B. Abram is president of Brandeis University.

Ben Ami is the pseudonym of a Soviet-born Israeli who has made several trips to the Soviet Union.

Abraham Brumberg is editor of *Problems of Communism*, a publication of the United States Information Agency.

Joseph Brumberg was a Yiddish journalist, now deceased.

Moshe Decter is director of Jewish Minorities Research in New York City.

Robert H. Estabrook is a reporter with the *Washington Post*.

Andrei A. Gromyko is Foreign Minister of the Soviet Union.

Shelomo Ben-Israel is foreign news editor and United Nations correspondent of the *Jewish Daily Forward* in New York City.

Michael Kaufman is secretary of the Union of Orthodox Jewish Congregations of America.

William Korey is director of the United Nations office of B'nai B'rith.

Isi Leibler is a member of the executive of the Victorian Jewish Board of Deputies, Australia.

Ronald I. Rubin teaches political science at the Borough of Manhattan Community College of the City University of New York.

Joseph B. Schechtman is a historian on the staff of the Zionist Organization of America.

Elie Wiesel has written several novels of the Holocaust, including *Night*.